Advance Praise for *God's Ghostwriters*

"At once eminently readable and rigorously researched, *God's Ghostwriters* cements Candida Moss as the most compelling voice in biblical scholarship. The role of enslaved people in the writing and dissemination of the gospels has been ignored for far too long. We all owe Moss a debt of gratitude for this monumental and eye-opening work."

—Reza Aslan, *New York Times* **bestselling author of** *Zealot: The Life and Times of Jesus of Nazareth*

"A fascinating and beautifully written book. The Bible is the word of God—but who, precisely, put that word on the page? Here, Candida Moss makes the invisible hands that wrote the Bible visible. She writes with a depth of scholarship and a lightness of touch that make this book both powerful and compelling."

—**Catherine Nixey, author of** *The Darkening Age: The Christian Destruction of the Classical World*

"From the first paragraphs of *God's Ghostwriters*, I was entranced. Everything that Candida Moss writes is worth reading, but she has outdone herself here by bringing enslaved people in the ancient world to life, in the process shining a new light on the roots of Christianity. The results are thought-provoking, intensely interesting, and immensely readable."

—**Eric Cline, George Washington University, bestselling author of** *1177 B.C.: The Year Civilization Collapsed*

"A scintillating and unforgettable read, *God's Ghostwriters* recovers the social world of those enslaved intellectual laborers who powered the literary accomplishments of the Roman Empire—and of the early Christian church. In the process, it transforms our understandings of authorship, personhood, and faith. I marvel at the book's scholarship, its imagination, and most of all its ethics of attentiveness and care. In these pages, the long-overlooked finally receive their due."

—**Dan-El Padilla Peralta, Princeton University, and author of *Divine Institutions: Religions and Community in the Middle Roman Republic* and *Undocumented: A Dominican Boy's Odyssey from a Homeless Shelter to the Ivy League***

"*God's Ghostwriters* is a work of historical, theological, and literary scholarship that will hold your attention like a well-crafted novel. I found myself saying, 'Fascinating!' and 'I never knew that' on page after page. Dr. Moss provides a fuller sense of the social and economic milieu out of which the New Testament arose, and in so doing, helps every reader, whatever their religious background, to get a clearer sense of what it might have felt like to be part of the Christian movement at its very early beginnings."

—**Brian D. McLaren, author of *Do I Stay Christian?: A Guide for the Doubters, the Disappointed, and the Disillusioned***

"Scholarship, at its best, goes beyond increasing knowledge; it reorients our understanding of familiar aspects of our lives. And for Americans, there is no book more familiar, and yet more uprooted from its historical milieu, than the Bible. After reading Moss's groundbreaking book, *God's Ghostwriters*, no reader—religious or otherwise—will be able to think about the

Christian Bible as an abstract religious text that is innocent of slavery. Moss's extraordinary, accessible book provides crucial insights about why European Christianity has been so susceptible to justifying racial domination and equips contemporary Christians to have a more honest and ethical engagement with the New Testament."

—**Robert P. Jones, president and founder of Public Religion Research Institute, and** *New York Times* **bestselling author of** ***The Hidden Roots of White Supremacy***

"A lucid, deeply convincing, and deceptively transgressive book with significant implications for how the Church does exegesis, how it tells the story of its own beginnings, and how it engages with its apostles and 'their' writings. Moss demonstrates how even the liturgical life of the church and its doctrine reflect something of the enslaving culture of its day. *God's Ghostwriters* is a deeply humanizing work that gives the unfree a rightful place in history."

—**Rev. Jarel Robinson-Brown, author of** ***Black, Gay, British, Christian, Queer***

"A searing recovery of the role of enslaved individuals in the production and dissemination of the New Testament, *God's Ghostwriters* is both historically grounded and morally compelling in its delineation of how not only metaphors but also structures of slavery undergird Christian theology. Moss's attention to ancient trafficking, the connection of slavery to disability, and the function of both psychological and physical torture makes her book all the more essential for understanding Christian origins."

—**Amy-Jill Levine, Vanderbilt University, and co-editor of** ***The Jewish Annotated New Testament***

"Brimming with learning and buzzing with contemporary urgency, this extraordinary book catches and amplifies the long-muted voices of the enslaved workers whose creative efforts made ancient literature possible. At once provocative and humane, it tells a radically different version of the story of early Christianity to the one most of us grew up with."

—Tim Whitmarsh, University of Cambridge, author of *Battling the Gods: Atheism in the Ancient World*

GOD'S
GHOSTWRITERS

ENSLAVED
CHRISTIANS *and the*
MAKING
of the BIBLE

CANDIDA MOSS

Little, Brown and Company
New York Boston London

Little, Brown and Company
Hachette Book Group
1290 Avenue of the Americas, NY 10104

littlebrown.com

First Edition: March 2024

Little, Brown and Company is a division of Hachette Book Group, Inc. The Little, Brown name and logo are trademarks of Hachette Book Group, Inc.

The publisher is not responsible for websites (or their content) that are not owned by the publisher.

The Hachette Speakers Bureau provides a wide range of authors for speaking events. To find out more, go to hachettespeakersbureau.com or email HachetteSpeakers@hbgusa.com.

ISBN 978-0-316-56467-0

LCCN is available at the Library of Congress

Printing 1, 2024

LSC-C

Printed in the United States of America

For Justin, magnifier of dreams

CONTENTS

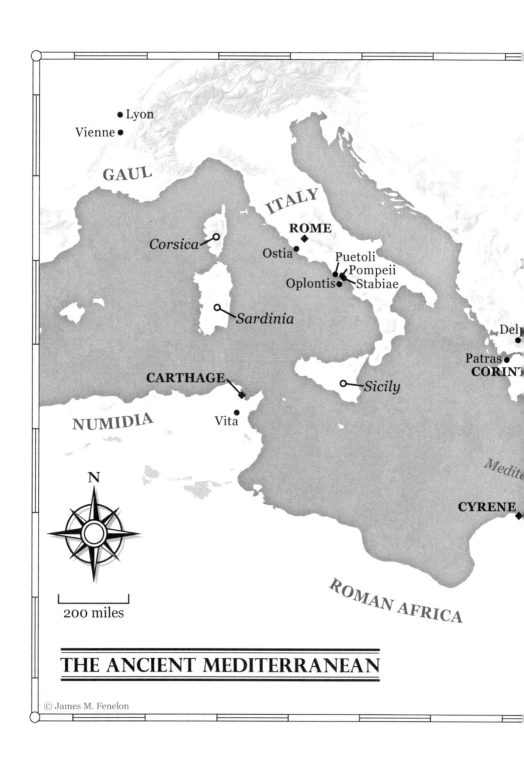

THE ANCIENT MEDITERRANEAN

© James M. Fenelon

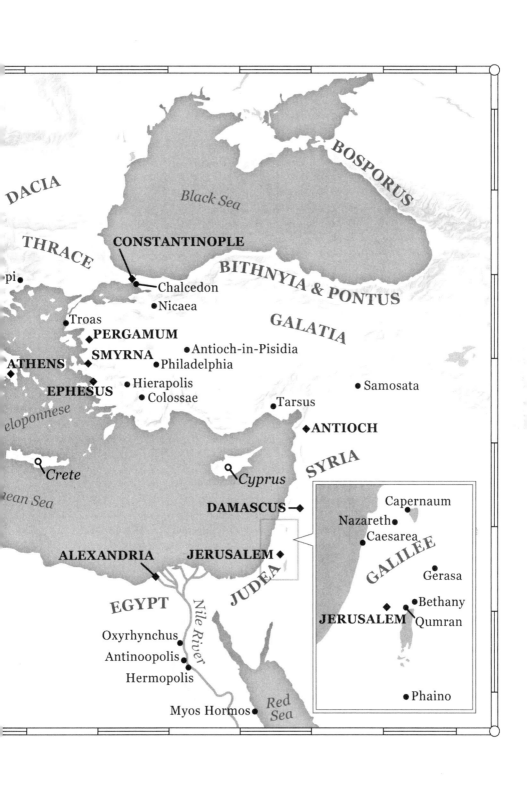

DACIA

THRACE

pi•

Black Sea

BOSPORUS

CONSTANTINOPLE

BITHNYIA & PONTUS

Chalcedon

•Nicaea

GALATIA

•Troas

PERGAMUM

•Antioch-in-Pisidia

SMYRNA

•Philadelphia

ATHENS

•Hierapolis

•Samosata

EPHESUS

•Colossae

eloponnese

•Tarsus

◆**ANTIOCH**

ean Sea

Crete

Cyprus

SYRIA

DAMASCUS→

ALEXANDRIA

JERUSALEM ◆

JUDEA

EGYPT

Nile River

Oxyrhynchus•

Antinoopolis•

Hermopolis•

Myos Hormos•

Red Sea

Capernaum

Nazareth•

Caesarea

GALILEE

Gerasa

•Bethany

◆

JERUSALEM Qumran

•Phaino

GOD'S
GHOSTWRITERS

AUTHOR'S NOTE

All history challenges the historian. What is said about the past always has implications for the present and frequently involves speaking for people who are long dead and have no ability to correct later narratives. Writing a history of enslaved literate workers and the ways in which they shaped the Bible and early Christian history, however, is an especially difficult task. The archives of history only preserve fragmentary glimpses of the lives of enslaved people who lived in the ancient Roman world. Often, what evidence we have is channeled through the perspectives of enslavers who claimed to speak for those they enslaved. Are the perspectives and experiences of enslaved workers there to be found, or have they been thoroughly overwritten by those who hold power? Any historian venturing into this terrain must remain vigilant: the enslaved contributions and interventions that we seek might, after all, have required the kind of agency that the conditions of enslavement made impossible.

Reconstructing the experiences of enslaved people, as recent scholarship on Atlantic slavery has revealed, requires both that historians use different tools and methods and that they adjust their expectations. This process involves reading into the gaps, engaging in what historian of Atlantic slavery Saidiya Hartman calls critical fabulation: a form of history-telling that is imaginative, and not untrue. The evidence is fragmented but is itself evidence.[1]

This method of history-telling involves imagination, refocus, and redress. The word *imagination* will undoubtedly give some readers pause, but it should not. All ancient history involves imagination: even for famous emperors, politicians, and philosophers, the evidence is scant and hyperbolic. We sift through the tissue of archaeological and literary material and piece together portraits that stem from ourselves as much as our evidence. More than one scholar, for example, has pictured the evangelists perched at their desks, working away at their tomes in libraries or studies, books lying open to either side of them as they scratch profound thoughts onto papyrus. This image underpins numerous scholarly hypotheses about how biblical texts relate to one another, but it has a fatal flaw: ancient writers do not seem to have used desks. We have imagined them and projected our furniture and writing habits into antiquity. All reconstructions of the ancient writing process are necessarily imaginative, and everyone who writes about the past should worry that they are writing about themselves.[2]

Many might wonder, quite rightly, if my imagination and the experiences that shaped it are well suited to this task. Am I—as a white Englishwoman living a life of privilege in the twenty-first-century United States—capable of the kinds of spectral listening without which there is no historical justice? To be sure, I do not know this world and I cannot imagine it. In my endeavors, therefore, I have drawn upon the words of others. I am grateful for the work of other writers, record-keepers, and scholars whose testimonies and studies of enslavement in other periods have been generative for my own research. I also draw upon the work of cognitive scientists and sociologists whose studies of intellection and labor help support some of the readings supplied here. It is impossible for me to credit every source in a book of this length and character, but this *is* a book about credit. Thus, I have created a website where additional sources, and references to secondary literature, can be found, and where the ancient basis for my more imaginative statements is documented in a fuller way than the constraints of this book allow. I am not a novelist; I would like my readers to be able to check my impulses.[3]

In using the experiences of others from different periods in time, any historian runs the risk of turning from ventriloquist to puppeteer. But if I do not try to turn the invisible contributors pictured as writing implements and hands in our sources back into people then these individuals and their legacy will inevitably remain abstract. I did not need to give names to the anonymous characters described in some chapters; I could have discussed the importance of certain principles in the abstract. But if I had done that, I would have obscured the power dynamics that turned the cogs of ancient society and the real people who felt their pressure. Abstractions can be useful, but they are also shorn of humanity.[4]

In thinking about how enslaved writers might have influenced and affected the contents of our Bibles, I will often—but not always—be thinking about these texts in light of enslaved experience. This should not lead us to conclude, however, either that the contributions of these collaborators were limited to the subject of slavery, or that every statement about enslavement stemmed from the enslaved writer. Nor should we assume that enslaved people are interested exclusively in slavery, or that when they are interested, their goal is always to dismantle the structures of oppression. Resistance is exhausting and dangerous. We should assume that the horrifying predicament of enslavement coerced people into replicating the structures of domination. Like everyone else, enslaved workers in the Roman world were multifaceted, complex human beings whose interests and experiences varied widely. They could speak about more than one thing. The task, then, is to look more broadly for what American historian Vincent Brown calls a politics of survival, interventions that transcended the question of resistance and pursued "a politics of belonging, mourning, accounting, and regeneration" for other enslaved people.[5]

Finally, some brief notes about language and its ideological underpinnings. Ancient Romans referred to people as "slaves" and "masters." It is a practice that many historians (including, in the past, myself) have thoughtlessly reproduced. As literary historian P. Gabrielle Foreman has noted, this language makes the conditions of slavery appear normal and natural, as if a person is, at their core, either "slavish" or "masterful." That framework is, of course, wrong, and so this book will use the language of *enslaved person* and *enslaver*. Though some have protested that this terminology is inelegant, such considerations should not outweigh ethics or simple facts. There are instances, however, when I will quote ancient sources that use this language, and I will replicate it to highlight its despotic character and goals. These are not endorsements of this perspective, but rather a way to emphasize the power of language in our lives. It is in learning language that we learn to communicate, to control, and to empathize.[6]

This kind of linguistic accommodation—as well as the many places in the book where I condemn ancient slavery—might be seen by some as symptomatic of the grave historical error known as "normative presentism." That is, some might argue that I am anachronistically projecting contemporary ethical norms (i.e., that enslaving other human beings is deplorable) onto the past rather than treating this ancient phenomenon on its own terms.

To such critics, I simply say this: While I agree in principle that the task of the historian is to analyze antiquity using terms and categories that ancient people themselves would have recognized, I am neither convinced that presentism is entirely avoidable, nor interested in perpetuating harm. Human trafficking continues to take place in our own day, contemporary societies still wrestle with the devastating effects of colonialization and the transatlantic slave trade, and a rising tide of white supremacists define themselves through appeals both to Roman history and the Bible. If, in making such statements, I break this rule, I am content. My goal is not to judge those who lived in the past, but rather to acknowledge that disinterested history is sometimes also morally negligent.[7]

As is often noted in books on the origins of Christianity, the first followers of Jesus were not Christians, but Jews. Followers of Jesus do not seem to have been called Christians until the end of the first century. Calling enslaved workers Christians is thus problematic for multiple reasons: it is difficult to know to what extent they had choices about their religious identity and, if they had, it is difficult to know if they would have identified as Christians.

Finally, when enslaved workers were freed in antiquity, they acquired a new status: that of a freedperson. The position of formerly enslaved people was precarious and often meant that they continued to be subject to violence and coercion. The blurry status of freedmen means that throughout this book I will sometimes use the language of servility to refer to work performed by enslaved and formerly enslaved people alike.

Blurriness is difficult to tolerate in history books, so I ask for the reader's generosity. I hope that others will take up whatever elements of this prove useful and discard those that are unhelpful. My work is neither the beginning of the conversation nor the period at the end of the sentence; rather, it is an ellipsis in between.

INTRODUCTION

S ometime in the middle of the first century CE, following a
decade of missionary activity in Turkey and Greece, the
apostle Paul set his sights on Rome, the beating heart of Roman
imperial power. Though he was filled with certainty about the
divine origins of his vocation, Paul had not had an easy time of
things. He had faced opposition from other leaders of the fledg-
ling Jesus movement, calculatedly brutal punishments meted
out by irate local authorities, a period of imprisonment, and
sleepless nights, but there was something about this particular
ambition that made Paul nervous. In Roman society, he would
possess none of the credentials or personal connections that had
greased his path in Corinth: he had never even been to Rome, or
mingled with people whose power oozed from their expensively
scented pores. The prospect of making it in the dazzling chaos
of the Empire's capital was intimidating. The competition would
be intense; other well-spoken, better-credentialed teachers and
philosophers were already jostling for airtime and patronage: he
would not have been the first philosophical teacher to fail to
leave his mark on the Eternal City.[1]

It was therefore with considerable trepidation that he
approached this new task of evangelizing in Rome. He could
not, as he had so many times before, just show up, set up shop as
a leatherworker near the public market, and start spreading his
message to passersby and business contacts. There were already

Jesus followers in Rome who were, presumably, quite content with their lives already. Paul was only known to them by reputation and, thus, the situation necessitated finesse.

His strategy was to begin with a letter, a carefully considered epistolary magnum opus that would introduce both Paul the man and Paul the theologian to the Roman congregations in advance of his visit. He was, to put it in the terms of ancient lawyers, "fishing for good will"; he was unacquainted with the Christ followers in Rome and so he needed to marshal every ounce of rhetorical skill to win them over. In pursuit of this goal, Paul

A nineteenth-century imagining of Paul dictating the Letter to the Romans to Tertius

addressed them warmly—as he did other communities—as "brothers and sisters," leveraged every social connection available to him, and took his time with the writing. The details of his argument were carefully worked out at length. He had to forestall every possible misunderstanding and objection.[2]

It was worth the effort. His Letter to the Romans is widely regarded as the most theologically sophisticated and influential book in the New Testament. There's no questioning its importance, and (unlike many books of the New Testament) no scholar has ever doubted that Paul himself wrote it. Yet this last point is remarkable precisely because it is so demonstrably imprecise. Paul did not *write* this letter—or, at the very least, he did not write it alone. Tucked into the conclusion of the letter is a simple but striking interruption: "I, Tertius, the writer of this letter, greet you in the Lord" (Rom. 16:22).

Who was Tertius? Almost every artistic depiction of Paul—from the carefully laid ancient mosaics of Ravenna to the color-saturated portraits of the Renaissance—shows Paul working alone, quill in hand, engrossed in the act of writing. In some images, he looks heavenward as if asking for or receiving divine inspiration. Paul rarely turns to another person. Yet here, in the letter itself, we find the name of another writer.

The most minimalist opinion on the subject is that Tertius was Paul's secretary (in Latin *amanuensis*). As Paul fervently paced the room, pausing to find just the right word or phrase to convey his ideas, Tertius sat dutifully recording every syllable. He was, in other words, one of the tens of thousands of erudite enslaved people who acted as stenographers, transcribed ideas, and edited the documentary output of the Roman world. With only a few exceptions, when tradition and scholarship identify Tertius they call him a "scribe," "professional," or "associate." Language like this creates the impression Tertius was an educated volunteer or friend, someone who willingly lent his skills to his spiritual mentor. It ignores the fact that the people who worked as ancient secretaries were not part of an ambitious and educated middle class: they were usually people whose freedom had been stolen. With a single name like Tertius, which simply means Third, the man who committed the Letter to the Romans to papyrus was almost certainly enslaved.[3]

While he's one of the few enslaved Jesus followers whose name is preserved in the New Testament, Tertius's is not the only set of enslaved hands to have played a formative role in the making of Christian scripture. For the past two thousand years, Christian tradition, scholarship, and pop culture have credited the authorship of the New Testament to a select group of men: Matthew, Mark, Luke, John, James, Peter, and Paul. But the truth is that the individuals behind these names, who were rewarded with sainthood for their work, did not write alone. In some meaningful ways, they did not write at all.

Hidden behind these names of sainted individuals are enslaved coauthors and collaborators, almost all of whom go uncredited. They are, you might say, the literate skills behind the haloed household names. The fact that they are not well-known today is no accident: in the ancient world, enslaved literary workers' legal status entailed and ensured invisibility. They were, according to the logic of slavery, extensions of the more powerful followers of Jesus or of those from whom they were rented or borrowed. And as such, their ideas and their labor belonged to their enslavers.

These enslaved collaborators may have been baptized Christ followers themselves, though we have no way to know whether that was by choice. According to the Acts of the Apostles, whole households were converted by the apostles at once. Those households would have included enslaved people, whose beliefs and feelings are not even considered, much less noted. If the male authority figure of a family (the *paterfamilias*) converted to

Christianity, then the whole household, which included enslaved workers, would also have been baptized. As people enslaved by devout Christians, their conversion and baptism were very literally assumed.

Choice, like consent, is problematic when applied to enslaved people, who lacked bodily autonomy or the ability to refuse their enslavers anything, whether it was to run an errand, to grant a request for sexual services, or to participate in religious practices. We do not know whether enslaved people were always or ever willing participants in baptism rituals, and we do not have access to their interior lives, but we do know they were viewed as Christians and attended religious gatherings and participated in Christian rituals. Even so, and despite the egalitarian message in Paul's writings, the language of "brothers and sisters in the Lord" so poignantly used by Paul and Tertius did not have staying power. Enslaved Christians were still enslaved. When followers of Jesus filed out of the homes or workshops where they met to read scripture, break bread, and sing hymns to Christ, they picked up their hierarchical roles at the door — if indeed they ever put them down.[4]

For some readers, it may be tempting to remove Tertius and his kind from contention for authorship altogether, and to dismiss them as mere conduits for the words of others. But if we look closely at the work of enslaved literati in the Roman world, we will see them for what they were: coauthors, meaning-makers, missionaries, and apostles in their own right.

Indeed, low-status literary workers made an enormous but unheralded contribution to the writing and formation of the New Testament and the spread of early Christianity. They wrote, carried, read, and interpreted sacred texts for the early church. It was enslaved or formerly enslaved hands that moved rapidly over the page, consigning the words of Paul and the stories of Jesus to papyrus. It was trusted unfree couriers who undertook lengthy journeys to foreign cities, spreading the gospel abroad to sometimes inhospitable audiences, and facilitated connections between the budding congregations of believers. It was the editorial eyes and cramping hands of secretaries and copyists that laboriously reproduced and corrected successive generations of Christian books. And it was servile readers, trained to read texts aloud, whose animated gestures and intonation brought the stories to life in Christian gatherings where most people were illiterate. Christian proclamation was not just the work and accomplishment of a dozen hand-picked freeborn disciples, but owes as much to the enslaved, often invisible workers whose names have been erased and whose status has been obscured.

Historians frequently state that Rome's reliance upon the enslaved laborers acquired through military expansion propelled its economy and society forward. This bitterest of observations should be accompanied by the acknowledgment that rather than receiving credit, enslaved workers (and often the fact of their enslaved status) have been obscured. Though their work has been erased and mischaracterized, enslaved people are as central to the history of ideas as they are to the history of labor. Any accountable Christian history involves telling a story in which our understanding of the origins of ideas, texts, doctrines, and traditions is interwoven with the stories of the enslaved workers who participated in these projects. Unfree workers should not be relegated to the footnotes of intellectual or religious history; they deserve a place alongside the apostles, emperors, and bishops who helped make the Roman Empire Christian.

Understanding the role that enslaved collaborators played in the making of the Bible is especially important in this moment, when a similar reckoning has focused on the document itself.

The Bible, as many scholars and activists have shown, encodes and reproduces the violent and bloody tyranny of slavery, and has generated a pro-slavery legacy that has irrevocably shaped human history for the worse. While people might cite specific passages—Jesus' outreach to women and the socially marginalized, or Paul's statement that there is "neither slave nor free" in Christ—as signs that the Jesus movement was more egalitarian than peer organizations, these hopeful moments are insufficient. They are surrounded and suffocated by parables featuring the casual murder of enslaved messengers, and by instructions to enslaved people to accept mistreatment at the hands of the powerful. The Bible speaks across time, but it has not aged well.[5]

Moreover, even though Roman enslavement was not grounded in the racist theories of biological difference that were developed in the colonial period and propelled Atlantic slavery, it spawned and nurtured later theories of enslavement that were. The pain of that history is felt to this day in structures of power, in cultural gatekeeping, and in the lives of those who continue to be marginalized, discriminated against, threatened, and killed. In another bitter irony, enslaved workers were intimately involved in composing, writing, interpreting, and spreading a message that bolstered the power and prestige of their enslavers.

This is not to cast blame, of course—or to suggest that all the enslaved people who contributed to this grim history did so straightforwardly. Enslaved scribes had subtle ways to subvert the despotic dynamics of texts that they worked on, and to craft their own networks of belonging. That does not change the fact that the most eloquent statements that attempted to dehumanize enslaved people might equally have been devised by enslaved editors and writers; it merely complicates it.

Gathering and creatively assembling the fragmented evidence for enslaved Christian writers, interpreters, missionaries, and leaders means wrestling with a hard and bloody truth: in order to understand the New Testament, we must grapple with the horrors that shaped the lives of enslaved people, and must look at the violence, pain, and oppression they experienced. That process, however disquieting, is illuminating, revelatory, and, more than anything, overdue.

Enslavement is one of the central framing devices for the relationship between human beings and God in the New Testament. For some readers, the use of that language is unbearable; it rips through their very core, evoking ancestral and present-day trauma. It is, as Jamaica Kincaid puts it, an "open wound" that tears anew with every breath. For others, it is remote metaphorical garb that can be congenially embraced, only because it is a temporary costume that can be discarded. For everyone, however, the experiences of these anonymous people must be centered, because without them the New Testament is unreadable, unknowable, unwritten, and unshared. No honest history can ignore them.[6]

It is not just enslaved work that made the Bible possible: it is enslaved personhood that gave it meaning and brought it to life. Though stories were shared by Jesus' followers in marketplaces, dining rooms, crossroads, and porticoes, it was the writing of letters and Gospels that allowed the Jesus story to move and grow. At every step in this process—from the inscription of texts, to their movement to other parts of the Mediterranean and beyond, to their copying, and their performance and interpretation in Christian gatherings—enslaved people were present, playing a variety of essential roles, in the rise of Christianity. In so doing, they have shaped the world we occupy today. It is time that they move from the margins of the page to its center.

PART I

+

INVISIBLE
HANDS

CHAPTER ONE

ESSENTIAL WORKERS

Children can be cruel, they say. It might be more accurate, however, to say not just that they can be cruel, but that they have a special talent for it. A lack of restraint is only a part of the story; they have an instinct for identifying weakness and a knack for targeting the soft spots in the still-developing egos of their peers. In this, ancient children were no different than modern ones; they could sniff out the faintest odor of insecurity. It is perhaps because of this talent that, sometime in the second century, a Christian schoolboy from Rome named Alexamenos found himself the object of playground taunts.

Alexamenos received his education on the upper floor of a modest two-story building which was tucked among the imposing imperial architecture that crowds the southwest slope of Rome's Palatine Hill. The Palatine was an exclusive neighborhood in the heart of the city, but even emperors needed space for service workers. The building began as part of the palace of the hedonistic emperor Caligula but, after his death, lived several other lives as a kind of flex space that catered to injured athletes, served as a meeting place for administrative officials, and may even have functioned as a prison. At some point in the second century, the upper story became a school. It was here that Alexamenos spent his mornings learning basic numeracy, reading, and writing.

For whatever reason, and we should not assume that it was his religious commitments, Alexamenos struggled to make friends. One classmate, a budding satirist, used his newly acquired writing skills to scratch an ugly graffito on the classroom wall. An image of a tunic-clad youth gazing up at a crucified figure—a donkey-headed man—is accompanied by the inscription "Alexamenos worships [his] god." The graffiti artist was no great talent, but he got his point across, nonetheless. The figure on the cross is almost certainly Jesus as, by the second century, non-Christians had taken to describing Jesus as asinine. Donkeys had a bad reputation in antiquity: they were seen as stubborn, lazy, and gluttonous. Give a donkey free rein and it will flop

Line rendering of Alexamenos Graffito. Alexamenos (left) looks at the donkey-headed man on the cross.

itself down in a corner, gorging itself on any food available. They were mistreated, reviled, and often associated with enslaved workers, with whom they traded chores. It was the kind of comic association that, once it latches on, can never quite be shaken off. For pagans, depicting Jesus as a donkey became a derisive visual shorthand for the absurdity and servility of Christianity, its members, and its founder.[1]

Alexamenos, the caricaturist, and his classmates were not freeborn schoolchildren; they were enslaved members of the imperial family. *Family* might seem a strange kind of word to use for coerced individuals, but the family (*familia*) was the social building block of the Roman Empire. The imperial family (or household) incorporated enslaved people and freedmen who were unlikely to have biological ties to the emperor (even if this was a possibility). The room where the students were shaped into copyists, bookkeepers, and secretaries was in truth more a workshop than a school. But like any place of learning, it gave its students brief moments to discuss athletics, create their own sharp hierarchies of status and popularity, and make cruel jokes as only children can.

The genius of the schoolroom bully was not his selection of the image, nor even its placement among the autobiographical graffiti celebrating the graduation of students from the school, but rather the cruelty of its application. Crucifixion was a punishment that, in the Roman world, was reserved for those forced onto the lowest rungs of society: the bandits killed alongside Jesus, for instance, would not have been executed (and might not have been forced to steal at all) if they had not been pushed to the fringes of society and brink of starvation. But crucifixion was especially, and perhaps originally, associated with enslaved people. Thus, for Alexamenos—as for all enslaved workers in Rome—the cross was both a symbol and a concrete possibility.

For Alexamenos and the children of the Palatine school-room this possibility was oppressively close. The images of crucifixion that decorated the bowls, lamps, and flasks they shuttled about the houses of their enslavers served as pointed reminders of their precarious position. Shadowlike, the threat of violence followed them throughout the day, only partly receding in the quiet darkness when everyone was asleep.

Though the fact of Jesus' crucifixion may have attracted enslaved people to the story, the first Christians did not reproduce the cross in their artwork. The paradoxical power of Jesus' death and resurrection couldn't quite eclipse the ghoulishness of its form. It was in bad taste. Eventually Christians would subvert its meaning, but at this moment in the early second century, only non-Christians embraced the aesthetic. And so it happened that an enslaved pagan gave us one of history's first images of the crucifixion: an irreverent, shaky-handed caricature of a donkey-headed god.

The graffito in that Roman schoolroom is our only glimpse into Alexamenos's life. We know that this young, enslaved Christian was learning to read and write. That he has a Greek name and is shown in a tunic could gesture to his age and enslaved status, or it might suggest that he was a foreigner brought to Rome from elsewhere in the empire. Though some Roman elites were suspicious of highly educated foreign-born workers, he would not have been the only one in his cohort; another student at the school, Marianus, identified himself as an African in an inscription. If Alexamenos was an outsider, then his appearance may have drawn negative attention from his classmates. If a relative of his had been one of the almost 100,000 Judeans enslaved after the fall of Jerusalem (70 CE) or among the anonymous number sold for a day's rations after the Bar Kokhba revolt (132–136 CE), then his circumcision might have made him the object of ridicule. Some enslaved Jews attempted to conceal their heritage by wearing prosthetic foreskins in public bath houses: in the past, as in the present, small differences drew unwanted attention.[2]

If Alexamenos — or far likelier, a parent — had been brought to Rome, then they almost certainly would have been trafficked through one of the "slave markets" that operated in the long shadows of the Temple of Castor or the Pantheon. Here captives were caught in an invasive tug-of-war between prospective owners and traders. Traffickers were known to be deceitful; one first-century manual cautioned readers to be on their guard against vendors who depilated the hair of older boys to make them appear younger, reddened pale cheeks, and concealed marks of disease. The buyer responded in kind with a battery of intrusive tests. The subject was stripped naked and publicly inspected: eyes were poked, limbs raised and lowered, orifices probed and fumigated, breasts and abdomens palpated.[3]

It is often said that Roman slavery was not about race. This is in part because race as we think about it today did not exist in antiquity; it is a construct that was primarily and strategically developed in the postcolonial period. Aesthetics and skin tone were invoked differently in antiquity than they have been in the more recent iterations of this deplorable institution, but this does not mean that race should be dismissed from the conversation about enslavement. Slavery was about otherness. Genetics, and thus physical appearance, are local, and as Rome ruthlessly harvested enslaved workers as spoils of far-flung wars, enslavement might incidentally take on phenotypical contours. The million or so Celts who washed through the slave system in the wake of Julius Caesar's conquest of Gaul (corresponding roughly to the contours of modern-day France) around the turn of the era were known for their visually distinctive red wavy locks. Similar influxes of forced migrants after the fall of Jerusalem and the defeat of Dacia (106 CE) brought more ethnically identifiable captives into the city.[4]

Greek and Roman literature does not use language that directly maps onto our definitions of "race"; rather, it obsesses over stereotypes about "peoples," "nations," and "ethnicities." These ancient constructs of ethnic identity focus on language, religious customs, diet, dress, kinship, homeland, burial traditions, and sometimes blood. The author of the pseudo-Hippocratic treatise *Airs, Waters, Places,* in what is considered an early expression of environmental racism, explicitly linked the "Asiatic" tendency toward cowardice and "slavish" monarchy to the perceived homogeneity of the gentle climate. "Greekness" was sometimes located in elite education (*paideia*), and the Romans were distilled into a sartorial scrap as the "toga-wearing people." The purported "slavishness" of Jews, an idea that circulated among the upper echelons of Roman society from the first century BCE, had a quasi-religious basis. Unfounded claims that they worshipped a donkey in their sanctuary and were "born to be slaves" spread among elites who used xenophobic cultural slander to naturalize their own good fortune.[5]

These constructs of "Greek," "Roman," "Barbarian," and "Jew" were not immutable facts, but were constantly reconfigured by the shifting plates of historical events. In the first century BCE, for example, the Romans enfranchised the entire Italian peninsula so that all its residents were now Roman citizens; in 212 CE, the emperor Caracalla extended the privilege to almost all freeborn residents of the Empire. So too ethnicity could be cemented by taxation: after 70, a tax on Jews—who were identified exclusively by circumcision—redirected former temple taxes to the rebuilding of the Temple of Jupiter Optimus Maximus in Rome. Diaspora Jews, who might never have visited Judea themselves, were inextricably linked both to a land they had never seen and the newly enslaved population of Jerusalem and its environs.[6]

The fact that ethnicity was in flux and did not depend upon precisely the same shaky biological theories about race that undergirded the Atlantic slave trade does not make it irrelevant to the broader history of enslavement. Ancient notions of ethnicity are very different from modern ones, but they are intimately connected. Later generations of Christians would capitalize on ancient color symbolism in their own periods, and caricatures of Africans in Roman sculpture fed into and served as prototypes for later artwork that we now correctly and baldly reject as racist.[7]

It's possible, then, that Alexamenos was doubly marked both as enslaved and as belonging to a specific *ethnos* or people. If so, being a foreigner with strange religious interests would only have amplified his liminal status in the classroom. More probable, however, was that Alexamenos was what Romans called a *verna*, or home-born slave. Chilling theories of "slave management" espoused the advantages of home-born workers to their enslavers. The home-born could, like all children, be shaped and controlled from infancy and used as a hostage to ensure the loyalty of their biological parents. If Alexamenos knew his mother and father, his relationship with them was at least partly disrupted by their lack of legal parental rights. The threat of familial separation was ever present. Nevertheless, and particularly as city dwellers and members of the large imperial household (*familia Caesaris*), it's possible that they had a bond that lived in glances, small gestures of support and protection, and brief moments of intimacy.[8]

Many enslaved children never had the opportunity to form even fragile bonds with their parents. Though children could work from young ages, those freeborn people who lived on the fringes of the Roman starvation economy and on the edge of ruin could not always afford to support additional offspring. Sometimes the only option was to abandon their children at locations—usually trash heaps—where someone might claim them. One turn-of-the-era teacher, C. Melissus, was raised in slavery after being abandoned as a child by his parents. Their parentage was often unknown, but these abandoned infants (*expositi*) were a significant part of the supply of enslaved workers. An early Christian writer, the author of the *Shepherd of Hermas*, from the late first or early second century, similarly identifies himself as such a foundling. Though piracy, kidnapping, and debt bondage also funneled people into enslavement, these are unlikely origins for our Alexamenos. Enslavers were pragmatists and usually only paid to educate those that they could control from infancy.[9]

Enslaved children could become accomplished copyists and even accountants at a prodigiously young age. By prepubescence, once basic literacy and numerical skills were acquired, they might move on to apprenticeships to learn specialized skills like

Second-century gristmill inscription from the Palatine Hill in Rome

accounting or shorthand. A mid-second-century funerary inscription from the Roman port of Ostia attests to the skills of Melior, a thirteen-year-old boy who served as a bookkeeper for a prominent local administrator. That so many deceased children, both boys and girls, were buried with writing tools—pens, inkwells, and numerical counters for performing calculation—suggests that Melior was exceptional but not unique.[10]

When Alexamenos's classmates graduated from school on the Palatine, many of them could look forward to similar careers in accountancy, taking dictation, copying bureaucratic documents, and so on, where more technical skills would be acquired on the job. The graffiti they left behind brimmed with hope as well as humor. One poignant example accompanies an image of a donkey turning a heavy millstone to grind grain. In the inscription, the author implies that his work in the schoolroom has liberated him from the backbreaking work that so easily could have been his lot in life. The image of the donkey, like the cross, served many purposes in the ancient world.[11]

In scholarship on slavery, literate workers like Alexamenos are often said to have been better off than their contemporaries in the fields. Not only were their living conditions preferable, but the costs of rearing and educating a child made literate workers more valuable and thus, the economic argument goes, less likely to be mistreated. There's some legal evidence to support this view, and certainly the child who made the Palatine mill inscription had absorbed its logic. At the same time, and because no despot was the cool-headed rational agent that economists imagine them to be, it would be overoptimistic to think that any enslaved worker was protected by their skills.

When Alexamenos left the schoolroom, he would have hurried home; not to rest, but to change hats. (Only proverbially, though, because the senate had ruled against enslaved uniforms years before. If enslaved workers knew their numbers, the argument went, they would rebel against their masters.) In a wealthy household, he may have spent his evenings working at table as a cupbearer, helping guests out of their sandals, and propping them up with a bucket in hand if they drank too much. If he were deemed beautiful, as some of his classmates were, he may have been a *delicatus*, an "exquisite" boy who was a sexual plaything for a predatory male householder. In this case we should picture him as expensively dressed and sporting long coiffured hair. We might hope, for his sake, that he was not; being in any way remarkable came with considerable risk. Beauty, intelligence, and competence attracted attention, and with it came the dark impulses that in other contexts would have been called vices: lust, envy, and anger. The *delicati* were not only sexually abused, they were occasionally forcibly castrated to preserve their youth and looks. Out of desperation, some enslaved workers used their meager *peculium*—an ephemeral "salary" that could evaporate at any time—to purchase ointments that promised to hasten puberty. They didn't work.[12]

Even if he was not navigating the drunk predators of the dining room, Alexamenos still would have been put to work. If you give workers too much time to rest and converse, enslavers worried, then their thoughts might take a revolutionary turn. And so labor never stopped. The various titles that we find etched in ancient inscriptions—chef, cupholder, groom, or secretary—didn't limit a person's workday so much as they serve as evidence of an elite Roman obsession with labels and categorization. By the age of seven, all enslaved children were in service: as personal attendants who teased hair into the latest styles, brushed decaying teeth, or swatted flies; domestic help who fetched and carried water; and surrogate siblings who babysat. In a pinch, an otherwise unoccupied clerk-in-training could always get to work cleaning or folding clothes. Though nighttime and darkness offered some relief, rest was never guaranteed. There was no salutary horn to end the workday or demarcate leisure time. The emperor Augustus, who suffered from occasional bouts of insomnia, was known to call enslaved workers to read to him when he could not sleep. Enslaved people were forced to be hypervigilant: at any moment, day or night, they were primed to spring into action.[13]

Though the physical labor was lighter in the home than in the fields or bakeries, even educated *delicati* had to reckon with omnipresent violence. Beatings were unremarkable, but sometimes escalated into worse forms of violence and acts of exceptional cruelty. The emperor Hadrian, for instance, once stabbed an enslaved person—likely a secretary—in the eye with a stylus. Some joked about how "crippled slaves" turned to teaching because they were useless for anything else; stories such as Hadrian's reveal the hazards of living in proximity to the unrestrained power of the enslaver.[14]

Beyond the intemperate outbursts of enslavers, many other occupational hazards accompanied literary work. Most ancient writing took place on the ground or on benches. The scribe sat with their writing materials balanced on their left knee while they hunched, lopsidedly, over their work. The position was ergonomically disastrous. Back pain, neck aches, tendonitis, arthritis, and relentless discomfort would have been common, forming an aching baseline for the waking moments of any enslaved scribe or student. Writing during the mornings would protect the eyes, but enslaved workers did not make their own schedules and were called upon to read and write by scant lamplight. In the fourth century, a friend of the rhetorician Libanius remarked that Libanius's enslaved scribe was pale from long hours of writing. Upon completing a copy of Lucan's *Pharsalia* in the fourteenth century, Martin of Trieste, the copyist, jested,

"I can't feel my hand, my head's in a whirl / I'd swap for my pen a beautiful girl." We can imagine that literate workers in the Roman world often felt the same way.[15]

Reading could be arduous too—not least because, in the ancient world, possessing this skill often required enslaved people to read aloud frequently for others. In a letter intended to show his kindness and benevolence, Pliny the Younger (61–113 CE) recounts how, after traveling in oppressive heat, Encolpius, his *lector*—that is, an enslaved person who read aloud to him—fell gravely ill and began coughing up blood. Encolpius's throat, wrote Pliny, had been irritated by the dust of the journey. Pliny's concern for his *lector* is both self-interested and arrogant; Encolpius reads Pliny's words back to him better than anyone does, and it will be hard for them both, a somewhat delusional Pliny imagines, if Encolpius is unable to do so in the future. Almost 40 percent of ancient Romans had tuberculosis and maybe Encolpius was one of them. Perhaps the dusty conditions of the journey exacerbated his condition. How long did he read past the point of comfort? He might have worried, as he struggled, that Pliny would find him useless, a dangerous situation for an enslaved person. It was frowned upon to simply kill one's sick or aging workers. So, rather than pay for medical care and food, some owners abandoned them on a boat-shaped island in the Tiber, the main river that ran through Rome. Luckily for Encolpius, he recovered—but if, during his illness, he had worried about his future, he had reason.[16]

The long days and short nights took a toll on Alexamenos, too, and his situation left internal scars as well. He spent much of his childhood learning the ins and outs of emotional labor; how to suppress hiccups, hunger, and emotions. Fear was relentless. One steward treated by the second-century physician Galen was made sick by the possibility that his enslaver would audit his financial records. After he was (falsely) reassured that this would not happen, the steward made a full recovery. Galen thought the enslaved financial manager was either dishonest or incompetent, but he easily accepted that the stress of enslaved precarity could make someone ill. Although we can't measure the effects of psychological violence on enslaved ancients, we must assume that its effects were felt.[17]

These pressures were amplified by uncertainty: Alexamenos knew that violence was not only about his behavior; he could be beaten for anything that went wrong whatsoever. Those who were victims of sexual abuse might also have been targeted by spurned wives, who resented competing for their husbands' affections. Intrafamilial politics and personal disputes were worked out in and on the bodies of enslaved workers, who might be punished simply for following directions.

The enslaver's preferred tool of control, however, was not the whip but fear. Beat your workers too often, the logic went, and you risked either inflicting permanent injury or teaching them to withstand pain. As physical endurance was a sign of manliness and courage, it was unsettling to know, as elite Romans surely did, that some enslaved workers were simply better at it than they were. Gladiators encapsulated the problem perfectly. Although mostly enslaved and socially stigmatized, they were also local heroes, admired for their courage and physical fortitude. These were not characteristics that those in positions of power wanted to cultivate in the workforce, either in their homes or en masse. So instead they chose to inculcate a deep, prevailing sense of dread.[18]

Alexamenos's anonymous classmate, the student who authored the gristmill inscription, was already aware of the backbreaking nature of hard physical labor. This despotic enculturation was its own perverse form of education, part of a system of "household management" — polished to a high shine through use — that sought to break its subjects' minds as well as their bodies.

The system depended upon a menu of carceral mechanisms that both imprisoned and also intensified the condition of unfree people. It involved threats of corporal or capital punishment, imprisonment, sexual assault, and the possibility of reassignment to more laborious work. Even superficially benevolent aspects (like material perks, the opportunity to marry or have offspring, and the promise of manumission) were a part of this system. By offering the narrow hope of a window of escape to freedom, manumission conditioned people to obey. That rebellion was infrequent is not a sign of the system's gentleness; it is evidence of its efficacy.[19]

The Alexamenos inscription, therefore, is not just about a child's religious allegiances; it is also about his social status and the precariousness of his existence. Crucifixion was how enslaved people died. It was how enslaving Romans controlled the unfree: it was personal to these children. From a young age, elite children were taught to use crucifixion as a threat. Classroom exercises instructed them about the grammatically correct ways to order and intimidate. Although in some wealthier homes, free and unfree children sat alongside one another and learned the same alphabet and numerical system, they were enrolled in different curricula. The elite child learned to dominate; the enslaved child learned to internalize the threats of domination. Even for those on the path to high-status literate work, both the mill and the cross felt oppressively close.[20]

Some Roman secretaries defied the odds, not only surviving but also thriving within the narrow confines of their position—and sometimes beyond it. Cicero's assistant Tiro—his proverbial voice and right-hand man—was well-known to generations of Roman elites. The literati of the Antonine period (138–193 CE) bid lavish sums on manuscripts that Tiro was said to have personally transcribed. This reception continues even today. Novelist Robert Harris made Tiro the narrator of his bestselling trilogy about the last days of Republican Rome. Other well-educated workers became philosophers, grammarians, even imperial advisers. Many urban literate workers managed to obtain manumission, and some of these freedpersons became wealthy businessmen in their own right. One such example is Marcus Antonius Pallas, secretary to Claudius and (briefly) Nero, who accumulated vast wealth, power, and recognition after obtaining his freedom. The Roman senate, which initially despised Pallas, came to admire him for his efficiency and will to power — which extended to a cold appraisal of the institution of slavery and those still trapped in it. After he suggested a measure that reduced the legal status of freeborn women who cohabited with enslaved men to the rank of an enslaved person, the senators were entirely won over. They accorded Pallas honors and a small fortune. (Pallas wisely declined the cash prize.)[21]

Even if enslaved people were manumitted and became freedpersons, they were still bound by obligations that not only commandeered their time and energy, but also placed them within arm's reach of a former enslaver with a point to prove. Many continued to live in the same house and were obliged, as a duty (*officium*), to provide sexual services on demand. Those whose skills and social networks allowed them to branch out on their own and accrue envy-inducing success were the object of derision and hatred. Freeborn writers joked that the scent of enslavement clung even to the children of those who had formerly been enslaved. The situation was precarious: literary and legal conversations about reenslaving "ungrateful" freedmen intermittently bubble to the surface of the evidence. In 95 CE, Epaphroditus, the wealthy onetime secretary of Nero, was executed by the emperor Domitian ostensibly for failing to prevent Nero from killing himself nearly thirty years earlier. The execution prompted outrage but also shows us that the manumitted never entirely shrugged off the mantle of slavery. The residue of servility made Epaphroditus vulnerable decades after his supposed transgression.[22]

The success of men like Pallas only intensified the jealousy and resentment of old monied aristocrats. The Principate, the period of imperial rule that emerged out of the ashes of the Republic and under the auspices of the emperor Augustus into the first century CE, was an unfamiliar form of power. Once the ruling class, senatorial elites now felt the crush. In their view, they were squeezed between, on one hand, the pincerlike pressures of a novel imperial form of government that forced them to behave like servants, and, on the other, the rise of a new monied class of freedmen and arrivistes from the imperial provinces. Even decades later, as he passed by Pallas's monument on the Via Tiburtina outside of Rome, the senator Pliny the Younger was moved to rage by the honors recorded at his tomb: "You will laugh, and then you will be outraged," he later wrote to his friend Montanus, by "the honors wasted on this filth, this trash,...[this] scumbag." Pallas's success continued to eat away at Pliny. Not content with spitting social slurs at the freedman's memory, he felt compelled to research the case. Finding evidence of the senate's decree—with its excessive praise of Pallas—he only grew more indignant. Freedmen had overrun the imperial chancery! What a dark comedy, wrote Pliny, that history had heaped such honors on mere freedmen.[23]

For men like Pliny the Younger, a nostalgic yearning for the past barely concealed their dissatisfaction at being born after their time. Although Pliny saw the emperor Trajan as restoring social order, the heyday of the senatorial class was slipping further into the Republican past. The resentment fueled by upwardly mobile freedmen could be displaced onto others closer to home. To those with power, the bodies of enslaved workers were the tablets on which they could scratch their frustrations: concerns about thwarted ambitions, petty slights, and waning influence. As in their literary endeavors, however, enslavers used other unfree workers as proxies—for no respectable elite man would work up a sweat administering corporal punishment himself. Thus, one enslaved person in a household could be obliged to pummel the body of another.

Each householder could enact his own personal reign of terror, and under such circumstances the unfree were forced to walk the fine line of competence that divided inadequacy and excellence: err on either side, and one risked drawing unwelcome and violent attention to oneself. For every Tiro or Pallas, there were dozens more who were overpowered by the turning cogs of casual violence and household drudgery. Manumission, which for this period could not legally take place until a man turned thirty, might come too late. Some enslaved workers were expelled to legal freedom only once their bodies had been broken, their hands had been permanently clenched by arthritis, and their eyesight had faded.[24]

There were few followers of Jesus, especially in the first century, who lived in the wealthy households of the superelite, as Tiro had, or formed part of the imperial family, like Alexamenos and Pallas did. But enslavement and the fear that accompanied it were only one of the axes of marginalization in the ancient world. On a global scale there were many different ambiguous situations of bondage that do not neatly fit into the division of enslaved and free. Certainly, those who lived in poverty—for example, day laborers like Jesus—existed in a state of precarity that included the fear of starvation or even selling themselves or their dependent relatives into slavery. The possibility of enslavement likewise threatened those who were freeborn but lived hand to mouth. Anyone who got into debt risked imprisonment and enslavement: they were a single bad harvest or workplace injury away from destitution. Thus, countless ancients felt enslavement snapping at their heels.[25]

Certainly, a high-status enslaved worker in a wealthy household would have had greater food and housing security than the freeborn poor. Similarly, they had opportunities for post-manumission enrichment that a fisherman or construction worker from the Galilee did not, even though the latter were freeborn. But if they suffered an accident that rendered them unable to work, both an enslaved secretary and a construction worker might find themselves in the same place: begging for scraps on the streets. For the enslaved literary workers who toiled on the margins of history, this was not the worst or most violent outcome.

If being an influential writer is just a question of volume, then Pliny the Elder, the prolific author of the encyclopedic *Natural History,* has a strong claim to cultural importance. A Roman politician and admiral, Pliny embodied the acquisitive and anthological spirit of the early Empire. His thirty-seven-volume miscellany covered everything from geography to horticulture, medicine, anthropology, and diet. He was a collector, and the knowledge assembled in his book was not just the result of learning, but also of exploitation. Much of his information came from the ever-present workers who attended him and from whom he extracted information. The workers—some of whom were enslaved as prisoners of war—who assisted him with his project were also often his sources. His home was a microcosm of Roman despotism: there, he excavated the memories of enslaved people in the same way that the Empire mined for salt.

Pliny's thirst for knowledge meant that a *lector* and shorthand writer (*notarius*) accompanied him everywhere, from the baths to the dining tables of friends to formal military excursions. The air around him was thick with words and the impressions of words: either those voiced by enslaved readers who have since fallen silent, or by his own dictation, which was translated through the secretary's mind and pen. These collaborators, indeed, were with Pliny the Elder until the bitter end. Famed for his courage as well as his intellectual curiosity, he met his demise on August 26, 79 CE, in Stabiae, a small port town on the Bay of Naples that lay in the shadow of Mount Vesuvius. His nephew, Pliny the Younger, tells us that the Elder Pliny had sailed undaunted towards the ashy eruptions. Until the very end he "described and noted down every movement, every shape of that evil thing, as it appeared before his eyes." Neither Pliny the Younger nor modern biographies of his uncle mention the young notary who accompanied him on this dangerous and foolhardy mission and performed the actual notation. We know of the youths who supported him as he awoke wheezing on his final day, but nothing of their fates. But come hell, high water, or volcanic eruptions, this was how ancient elite writing was done.[26]

If the reader and writer who accompanied Pliny died for his enslaver's oeuvre, it would have reflected the importance that ancient elites in this period placed on literacy and literate work. While much rests on our definition of literacy (does being able to sign one's own name count?), one recent estimate suggests that only about 10 percent of the population of the Roman Empire was able to read and write fluently. These literary elites included the most accomplished members of society: senators, aristocrats, governors, and the emperor himself. The written word was a sign of power; most people in the Roman world encountered the emperor only on coins and through his written statements, which, once issued, were etched onto bronze plates and prominently displayed in the fora of cities and towns around the Empire.

By the end of the first century CE, the ability to read and

write—or, perhaps more accurately, being seen to read and write—carried a certain social cachet. The second-century tabloid writer Suetonius noted that Augustus had a distinctive handwriting style that he insisted on teaching to his grandchildren. Upwardly mobile business owners and their wives portrayed themselves in funerary art with stylus and book roll in hand. Books, and beautiful books in particular, were a sign of status. Like a college ring or Mr. Ripley's borrowed Princeton blazer, books and writing implements were the accessories of privilege and class: they were credentialing objects and accessories.

Marble bust of a woman displaying her literacy with a scroll (Constantinople, fourth or fifth century CE)

Because so few people could read and write, and because literacy was highly prized and costly to acquire, it's tempting to imagine that the literate elite were identical with the social elite. This is what elite writers would like their audiences to believe. It's certainly true that the children of the affluent started their secondary education with a grammarian or private tutor in the home, moved on to study rhetoric to prepare them for careers involving public speaking, and finally ended up "majoring" in philosophy and mathematics in their late teens and twenties. Education was more comprehensive for boys, so if you were lucky and male then your (grand)father—the *paterfamilias*—might sponsor your education in Athens or Alexandria, the Harvard or Oxford of their day. But the scions of the affluent families were never alone, and, thus, alongside this elite education ran a parallel form of education for enslaved literary workers, glimpses of which are preserved on classroom walls such as those on the Palatine hillside. The young aristocrat who attended school was accompanied by a *paedagogos*, an enslaved nanny-cum-tutor who would assist the pupil with his work and instruct him in everything from reading and writing to deportment. Freeborn men were expected to present themselves in a particular way: it was a delicate balancing act that involved dress, body posture, vocal intonation, table manners, and even how one laughed. Even the most powerful were constantly scrutinized; a misstep could, quite literally, result in one being branded effeminate and unmanly, just as a mispronounced word or foreign turn of phrase would reveal the deficiencies in one's education or the troubling pliability of one's judgment and origins. Roman aristocrats enjoyed the most comfortable lifestyle in the Empire, but it still had its pressures.[27]

Ironically, the behavioral traits of an elite male were instilled by an enslaved or low-status pedagogue who had to "master" them at least as well as any enslaver. When the young man eventually went away to "university" to study philosophy, he was accompanied by a small entourage of enslaved workers, at least one of whom would accompany him to class and serve as his notetaker. What this meant, of course, is that enslaved workers may well have been the most educated men in the room. After all, their well-being rested on accomplishing these tasks well. The predicament drove them, by necessity, to virtuosity in the arts of mastery.

From the homes of the wealthiest families, including the sprawling imperial family, enslaved children like Alexamenos were dispatched to special "slave schools" to learn the basics of reading and writing. Others were invisible participants in elite education, joining the classes of the enslaver's children as they were homeschooled, and sweeping beneath the benches after the freeborn students had departed. Not all of the children who lived within earshot of elite education would go on to become literate workers. Indeed, not every child in the imperial schoolroom on the Palatine was being prepared for a career as a secretary. Enslaved children were often given names that referred to the kind of work they were expected to perform or a personality trait desirable to enslavers. (Epaphroditus, for example, means "charming.") If the Palatine schoolchildren's names were their destiny, then we can infer that some were prepared to wait at table, to be doorkeepers, to become dressers or wardrobe managers, or to become medics or medical assistants. For some people, educating all the enslaved members of one's household was a sign of prestige. According to his biographer, Atticus, a wealthy friend of Cicero, filled his household with highly educated enslaved workers: even the night watchmen could read and write.[28]

Those who showed promise in elementary education might be sent to learn the art of stenography, or shorthand, an efficient writing technology that became all the rage in the first century

Second-century funerary relief of a teacher with three students, one of whom (at far right) is just arriving

CE. Stenography was uncompromisingly difficult to learn as it involved memorizing a system of thousands of complicated symbols. In addition to a base set of 600 to 800 signs that represented words, there were the bonus meanings—four to eight additional words that were indicated by a dot or a bar added to the base. A discarded second-century contract from Oxyrhynchus, Egypt, suggests that it took two years to become fully proficient in the skill. Once perfected, however, shorthand enabled the secretary to record speeches, trial proceedings, letters, and original compositions with great speed.[29]

Unlike the modern systems of shorthand that took off in the courtrooms and secretarial colleges of the nineteenth and twentieth centuries, ancient shorthand wasn't standardized. A scribe in the household of Cicero's friend Atticus might have learned a different dialect than that acquired as part of a formal apprenticeship elsewhere in the city of Rome. Individuals would modify the system to their particular needs: a doctor's attendant needed more abbreviations for body parts than the notary of an architect or tax official. This lack of standardization is important because ancient shorthand was not pictographic; to the untrained eye, it resembles squiggles or chicken scratch. This made it a useful tool for espionage—both Julius Caesar and the

Jewish rebels who led the mid-second-century Bar Kokhba revolt used it to communicate—and a thorn in the side of modern scholars. To this day, many ancient and medieval shorthand texts remain indecipherable.[30]

The mythology of shorthand credits its invention to enslaved workers. Latin shorthand was variously associated either with Tiro, the favored secretary of Cicero, or a freedman of Maecenas, an adviser to the future emperor Augustus and a patron of the arts. In a passage as much about his own feelings of inadequacy as the superior shorthand skills of secretaries, the Stoic philosopher Seneca the Younger sneered that it was "invented by the lowest-quality slaves." Even though it was taught and learned by enslaved people, the power of the enslaving class is felt throughout the educational project. Students learning Greek shorthand were assisted by a *Commentary,* a collection of sentences that allowed them to memorize the additional meanings of a symbol. Some of these sentences are lists of body parts, geographical locations, or philosophical slogans, but many are reminders of slavery's power. Shorthand writers learned that "the powerful man leads, bears, beats," that shackles "hurt," that "runaway slaves" will be caught, and that the "happy slave" will be freed. Even here, in a cryptographic medium that most could not understand, stenographers cautioned one another about the limits of their position. Just as when women were educated to be good mothers and wives, so too enslaved writers were reminded of their place.[31]

As complicated as the system was, it still could not capture the precision of longhand writing. There were roughly five thousand shorthand symbols or signs. For comparison, Merriam-Webster's *Dictionary* claims that modern English contains between 750,000 and 1 million words. Although Greek is slightly more economical, only a small fraction of its words was represented in ancient shorthand. Stenography was ambiguous and thus involved improvisation and interpretation: the secretary condensed and translated the words of the speaker into a series of signs that they later expanded into longform. The imprecise and idiosyncratic nature of the system meant that the same person who compressed Paul's or any other early Christian's words would have later expanded them into a readable copy, editing and expanding as they went. Whatever ancient Romans might say about these workers, or whatever modern readers might think of secretarial work, these writers were not fungible. Their interpretative work gave shape to the thoughts and words of the speaker and made them an indispensable part of the compositional process.

Education was necessary for the enslaved workers who did so much of the literary, numerical, and administrative work in the ancient world. Secretaries did more than take dictation, translate shorthand into longhand, and edit and copy manuscripts; they also oversaw financial affairs and managed correspondence. Alongside the secretary, a whole cast of other literate workers did a variety of tasks: the *librarius* navigated and memorized classic works of literature (sometimes specializing in iconic authors or specific languages); the *notarius*, or notetaker, specialized in stenography; and the *lector* read aloud from physical texts. Finding a particular passage or quotation in an ancient book roll (ancient Greeks and Romans, like Jews, mostly used papyrus scrolls for literary texts) was a difficult task. Even classics professors today are overwhelmed by the tumble of letters they encounter when they open an ancient manuscript: there are rarely spaces between words, nor accents to indicate emphasis, nor grammatical markers like periods or commas. No one has uniformly marked important phrases and transition points: merely locating the section of the book you are interested in is difficult. You have to practice.

For those who did not have access to houseguests, biddable

children, or well-educated domestic workers, but who needed to write letters, make up a will, or lodge a formal legal complaint, it was possible to hire a scribe at the marketplace. The coalitions of bakers, silversmiths, woodsmen, and rag dealers who formed voluntary associations might lease the services of a scribe or literate temple worker to take minutes, draw up charters and membership lists, and attend to correspondence. Thus, even if one was not liberally educated oneself, if one had funds, one could "read" and "write."[32]

Writing is hard work, even in the modern world: hands cramp from the pressure of forcing charcoal and ink into neat letters; backs spasm from being hunched over a desk or tablet; neck muscles tense and relentlessly pinch at nerves; and eyes grow bleary from hours of uninterrupted focus. Over the course of a day, familiar words become unfriendly and blur together, errors are increasingly difficult to identify, and the smooth ligatures of the letters grow shaky. Anyone who has ever taken a hand-written exam in school will recall the choreography of hand-wringing that accompanies frenetic writing.

The same was even more true in the ancient world, where good light was scarce. People wrote on a variety of materials: broken pottery shards, known as ostraca, were good for sending messages to business contacts or friends across town or for practicing the alphabet or writing. Wax tablets, inscribed with a stylus (a sharp implement), offered the most forgiving surface for the writer and had the advantage of being erasable. The soft wax enabled the user to write at speed and the hard wooden frame offered support for writing on the go. Not all tablets were made of wax: other unfussy examples survive in plain unwaxed wood, for example. Parchment, which was made from animal skin and was rarely used in the first century CE, was physically unwieldy because the surface pulled against the pen, making writing more difficult. Papyrus sheets, made from pummeled reed and inscribed with sharpened reed pens, were used for manifold purposes from letter-writing to magical texts to philosophical treatises and early Christian gospels. The sheets could be folded and bound into a codex (the format we call a book) or pasted into a scroll.[33]

Detail of a second-century mosaic from Tunisia showing a capsa *(book bag) holding scrolls*

Alongside this array of writing surfaces, we find accessories: reed pens, bronze and bone styluses, spatulas for smoothing wax tablets, inkpots, rulers, knives for trimming papyrus, and pumice stones for smoothing the ragged edges of a text. And finally, of course, ink: sepia milked from cuttlefish, black ink manufactured from processed soot, and expensive bright colors made of gold or the bodies of the predatory sea snails that lived on the western shores of the Mediterranean. None of these costly accoutrements were necessary for the determined writer, though. The graffiti that blanketed ancient villas, storefronts, and streets are proof that anyone with a sharp rock, a little education, and some elbow grease could write.

Yet even in the more forgiving medium of papyrus and ink, writing was laborious. One houseguest in fourth-century Egypt, who found himself pressed into service by his hostess, grumbled that he had "worn himself out by writing the letter." (The letter in question is the same length as Paul's shortest offering, to Philemon.) This grumbler could write but clearly didn't enjoy it or do it very often. Imagine how he would have balked at the idea of taking down Paul's Letter to the Romans or an entire romance novel.[34]

The pain of writing was one reason to outsource the effort, but positioned between the reluctant and the poorly educated was a third group of individuals who used secretaries: those who had to. For Paul, imprisoned in a series of damp, cold prisons in Asia Minor, the darkness may not have been the only reason he used a scribe: he lived in a world without glasses.

Today, roughly a third of the global population have some form of visual impairment. In antiquity, where treatments for eye infections, river blindness, congenital cataracts, diabetes, and many other conditions did not exist, the number was likely comparable. Archaeological and literary sources refer to congenital vision loss, temporary conditions, age-related vision loss, and accidental eye loss in the workplace or on the battlefield. Archaeologists who excavated the ancient healing shrines in Greece or Turkey found dismembered clay limbs, heads, and torsos dedicated as offerings to the god Asclepius, and noted that there were twice as many eyes as any other body part. Their number offers tangible evidence of the desperation of sufferers and the widespread nature of eye complaints. Paul, who by his own account wrote in oversized "large letters" (Gal. 6:11), would not have been alone in experiencing some vision loss.[35]

In the absence of corrective lenses and pharmaceuticals, people—often children, whose vision was superior—did the work of accommodative devices. Cicero relates several stories of politicians and philosophers who continued to publish and study even after they had gone blind. Vision loss wasn't the only problem attended to in this way. Scientific studies have shown that many people today use lip reading to follow conversations without even being aware that they are doing it. The same may have been true in antiquity. In group settings where texts were read aloud, the use of enslaved readers, who stood in clear view of the assembled audience and used choreographed hand gestures and bodily movements in their performance, may have enabled those with hearing loss to follow the flow and argument of a piece.[36]

Peter and Paul, a fisherman and a tanner, worked with their hands. Over a lifetime, the repeated motions of ancient manufacturing could eat away at the joints and ligaments. Mobility impairments, like those caused by arthritis, could escalate to the point that the sufferer could no longer grip objects or move their thumbs with ease. Gout, the rich man's arthritis, is commonly associated with the feet, but also crept into the hands, inflaming the knuckles. According to Suetonius, the emperor Galba was so debilitated by gout that he was unable to unroll or even hold a scroll. The Numidian (modern-day Algerian) grammarian Fronto complained that after a lifetime of writing he was no longer able to write himself. The mid-tenth-century scribe Florentius, who claimed that writing destroyed one's vision, broke the back and ribs, and harmed the kidneys, may have exaggerated, but not by much.[37]

Roman authors who thought about deportment and health were aware that that the repetitive motions of bookwork had damaging effects on the body. As a result, they cautioned their elite students against doing too much of it and avoided the most cumbersome tasks. Without use, however, these skills atrophy: handwriting turns sloppy, translation grows stiff, and hard-earned calluses soften and shrink. Scientists call this phenomenon skill decay. It is the reason why those in high-risk professions—pilots, nurses, and those in the military—complete continuing education programs and why you would be better served asking a phlebotomist than a consulting physician to draw blood from your arm. Skill decay nibbles away at education as well, particularly mathematical and linguistic abilities: even mother tongues gather dust when they fall into disuse. Ancient elites who shirked literate work would have experienced the same problem. As a lack of practice made ancient bookwork more difficult, those with means were incentivized to do less of it.[38]

In ancient societies that looked down on any kind of bodily frailty, the utilization of servile workers to read and write not only extended a person's bodily abilities, but it also allowed them to conceal the extent of their impairments. Those who failed at this were ruthlessly mocked for their shortcomings. One nouveau riche by the name of Calvisius Sabinus, who struggled to recall the names of Trojan heroes, relied so completely on enslaved workers that he had some trained to memorize poetry for him. They would sit at the foot of his couch at social events and whisper quotations in his ear, only for Calvisius to butcher the poetic morsels in repetition. It's an extreme example, and is unkindly relayed by a judgmental Seneca in his

Letters, but it gives us a glimpse at the complicated and fraught interplay of wealth, impairment, and enslaved assistance. While it was entirely acceptable to use other people to read, write, do accounting, manage estates, and so forth, one was not supposed to rely upon one's inferiors for the elite intellectual work of thinking, judging, or composing. Though wealthy Romans often used an enslaved *nomenclator* to recall people's names and to memorize whole texts for performance, Calvisius's failed attempts at erudition crossed a line.[39]

This state of affairs means that enslaved literate workers are everywhere and nowhere in our sources. While ancient elites could and did read, most of their "reading" was done by equally well-educated but lower-status servile individuals. When an elite writer says that they consulted a text of Homer or Plato, they almost certainly had an enslaved person do it for them. The same was true of writing: when someone in Mediterranean antiquity says that they were "writing," we should not assume that they held a writing implement themselves. It is much more likely that someone else was taking dictation, perhaps at high speed and compressed into shorthand, which that invisible person would later expand, revise, and edit into the finished text. Just because an enslaved worker is not noted does not mean that they were not there.

CHAPTER TWO

PAUL AND HIS SECRETARIES

According to the Acts of the Apostles (written circa 80–150), the turning point in the life of Saul of Tarsus came as he made the dusty journey up from Jerusalem to Damascus in Syria. As he approached the end of his journey, in the midday heat of the ninth day, Saul was knocked off his feet (and metaphorical high horse) by a flashing light and vision of Jesus. Though only temporarily blinded, Saul was permanently changed by this experience. Before his vision, he was a well-educated Jewish man from the Greek-speaking university town of Tarsus. He was a passionate man who had studied to become a religious scholar (a Pharisee) and had, by his own account, aggressively sought to uproot the followers of Jesus. He might never have become Paul, the self-appointed apostle to the gentiles, had it not been for his traveling companions.

Having overheard at least part of the conversation between Saul and Jesus, unnamed attendants saved the now-blind Saul from heatstroke (and perhaps worse) by leading him by the hand into the city and taking him to the home of a man named Judas.

Three days later, a Christ follower named Ananias hesitantly appeared to pray and restore Saul's sight.

We never hear of the companions again; some modern commentators do not even notice them. But they were instrumental in Paul's—and, as a result, the Jesus movement's—survival. And a plausible guess is that they were enslaved attendants.

That Paul was Jewish did not make him an exception in regard to slaveholding: like other inhabitants of Afro-Asia, ancient Jews were known to exploit the skills and labor of enslaved people from many backgrounds in domestic, agricultural, and literate work. Just as Christians baptized enslaved members of their households and Romans insisted upon participation in pagan rituals, so too Jewish enslavers would circumcise and ritually immerse in water any non-Jewish enslaved people who were trafficked or born into their families. In Paul's case, he may have needed help with logistics, baggage, and navigation— assistance that enslaved people often provided. Thus, in this story, enslaved people may have been the earliest witnesses to the conversion of Paul, the apostle who advanced Jesus' message to the gentiles—a crucial moment in Christian history.[1]

The work of Paul's assistants in Acts is but one small illustration—if only a hypothetical one—of the ways in which the spread of Christianity, even by the heralded leaders of the movement, depended upon the actions of uncredited workers. Just as enslaved people in the ancient world enabled a culture of learning and literacy, so too did they form an integral part of a new type of culture that was spreading throughout the Roman Empire in the first century CE: the culture of the nascent Jesus movement. Enslaved workers mixed with the other marginalized and oppressed adherents of Christ, yet they also stood apart from them. They performed a particular sort of labor that, in a world that fetishized writing and literature, ensured that the message of Jesus and his apostles reached a wider audience than it could have found without these invisible helpers.

Religious histories of the work of the apostles tend to picture them traveling alone or in pairs, buoyed only by the support of divine providence and the guidance of the Holy Spirit. Even the historically contested Acts of the Apostles itself is more nuanced in telling how the growth of the Jesus movement depended on social networks, cultural guides, practical support, and funding. Travel is expensive and neither the disciples nor Paul had the resources to support themselves.

Modern scholars and contemporary Christians alike use the terminology of "missionaries" and "missionizing" to describe the diffuse activity of Jesus' first followers. The terms conjure images of distinctly religious activity: of bright-eyed, neatly dressed young Christians traveling near and far to evangelize. For many observers today, these practices are perfumed with an aroma of colonialism, and indeed modern accounts often play into this perception by portraying Jesus' first followers as evangelical tacticians, plotting a religious revolution modeled on military campaigns. But these readings of the Acts of the Apostles reflect the missionary epoch of the eighteenth and nineteenth centuries; they do not capture the world of the first followers.[2]

In antiquity, there was no word for a missionary, much less a notion of what one might be. In their own words, Paul and others described themselves as followers of "the Way." The Greek word *apostolos* evokes the servile connotations of "messengers" and the ambassadorial spirit of "emissaries." That the message carried by the apostle was "good news" (*euangelion*) amplifies comparisons with imperial messengers and the official communication network that webbed its way across the Roman Empire.

There is one sense, at least, in which these early followers of

Jesus mirror latter-day missionaries: they were constantly on the move. Like other messengers of the day, Jesus' apostles hitched rides on the Roman roads and bridges that allowed people with means to move. The language of journeys, pathways, and travel seeps into the New Testament and, as a consequence, into our own daily lives in the present. Whether people take the high road or follow the straight and narrow, their choices are metaphorically structured by the quality engineering of real Roman roads. Though the language of travel seeps into the present, the realities and rigors of ancient travel have not.

Travel in antiquity was arduous not only because it was physically difficult, but also because it turned the travelers themselves into strangers wherever they went. As Christ followers headed north and west from Palestine into Syria, Asia Minor, Greece, and Rome (and beyond), they stood out not so much for their alien teachings as for their foreign bodies, accents, hairstyles, and dress. It took a certain kind of charisma and confidence to spread new ideas in unfamiliar spaces.

The men selected by Jesus for the project of evangelizing to the Roman world were unlikely candidates for the job. According to early Christian writings, Jesus and his inner circle came from rural Galilee. Though not all their professions are specified, they can be broadly categorized as Aramaic-speaking fishermen and craftsmen, men who spent their lives outdoors and probably developed distinguishing features—muscled shoulders, a perennial hunch, callused hands, and sun-lined faces— as a result of their labors. Zebedee, the father of apostles James and John, did well enough to hire paid help, but not so well that his sons were exempt from the tedious work of mending fishing nets. Some of Jesus' other original followers were slightly better-off, but not by much. The apostle Matthew, who was (according to tradition) originally known as Levi, was a tax collector clinging to a much-maligned lower rung of Roman bureaucracy when

Jesus ran into him; perhaps he was the owner of a local tax-farming franchise, or perhaps he was a paid literate helper—which would have placed him in the same profession as Alexamenos. Judas, who according to one account was the group's treasurer, must have had some familiarity with numbers, but that might have made his parents butchers or woodworkers. All these men likely spoke some Greek, in addition to Aramaic, but none of Jesus' inner circle had formal training as orators. They had watched and presumably learned from Jesus, but they were outsiders.

It is unclear how widely the original disciples traveled: the Acts of the Apostles places them in close enough proximity to Jerusalem that they could gather there at relatively short notice for a council around 50 CE. But if, as tradition maintains, they ventured farther north, through Roman Syria and into the Greek-speaking cities of modern Turkey, the cultural terrain around them would have grown unfamiliar. For Paul, originally from Tarsus (in south-central Turkey), the regional metropolis of Antioch-on-the-Orontes might have felt like home, but everyone was a stranger somewhere. Being an outsider was less of a problem in ports, where foreigners outnumbered locals, or in cosmopolitan centers like Rome, where thick accents and unusual dress blended in among the polychrome tapestry of big-city sociality. But in smaller towns, on islands, and in the rural areas through which they walked, immigrants were more obvious and more vulnerable. In Asia Minor, even Roman citizens, who were ostensibly part of a powerful elite, banded together in clubs, known as voluntary associations, to improve their relationships with locals and ensure their safety.[3]

The disciples may have lacked experience and education, but, more importantly, they lacked financial means. Some of the original Twelve may have had small nest eggs, but none was able to offer more than hospitality to their teacher and fellow students.

As a result, they had to rely on others for financial and practical support. According to stories of the Gospels and Acts, they stayed in the homes of sympathizers and supporters. Just as enslaved people assisted in navigation, bartering, translation, and travel, here too, in the warm homes of Christ followers, we hear their soft footsteps. Upon their arrival, the disciples were likely met by attendants who washed their feet and prepared their meals. They would have been guided around unfamiliar surroundings by domestic helpers, who summoned the friends and business contacts that came to hear them. The sick, brought to the apostles for healing, were likely to have been carried by family members or enslaved workers. And when letters or messages were conveyed by any named members of the movement — whether by people associated with Paul's wealthy patron Chloe, by the unnamed competitors Paul refers to in his letters, or by members of the households of affluent freedperson converts like Aristobulus, Narcissus, Lydia, or any other supporter identified in the Bible in this way — it is safe to assume it was by servile workers in their employ.

When itinerant Christian preachers enjoyed the patronage of wealthier enslavers as they traveled, it meant not just sustenance, shelter, and access to social networks — it also entailed the "loaning" of the expertise and time of these hosts' enslaved workers. If some of these people became Christ followers and subsequently volunteered their services, those donations were as substantial and valuable to the success of Christianity as the monetary resources supplied by the more affluent.[4]

Beyond the fact that the economic capital of elites was procured through the work of enslaved and dependent workers, some servile actors held financial power themselves — as agents for their enslavers or as members of collectives, if not as individuals. They might, for instance, be empowered to dispose of financial assets on behalf of their enslavers, or to act with a degree of independence in religious matters. Others might work in groups, a potentially subversive form of social cooperation that was not limited to single households: a first-century inscription from Ephesus lists roughly a hundred fishermen and fish dealers who donated resources for the construction of a toll office near the harbor. These were not wealthy men; rather, they were professional cousins to Jesus' apostles. Among them was a group of enslaved workers who donated between 5 denarii (the modern equivalent of a manual laborer's workweek of pay) and goods worth 40 or 50 denarii. We also know of four freedwomen from separate households in Italy who pooled their resources to lease and run a kitchen close to the Temple of Venus in Cassina.[5]

Although unfree, some servile and other lower-status people still had the ability to act as financial benefactors to a religious movement. The example from Cassina might make us wonder about the social status and relationships among the group of women named as patrons of Jesus in the Gospel of Luke. Perhaps they too were freedwomen, who had shared confidences long before they had heard of the Nazarene.[6]

In the cosmopolitan cities of the Empire to which Jesus' delegates traveled, the apostles found themselves competing with other religious and medical experts. Whispers of these competitors echo through the stories: some are casting out demons in Jesus' name in Luke 9:49 and Acts 19:13, for instance. Jesus himself was apparently unconcerned about these rivals, but sharper divisions emerged in the decades after his death. To set himself apart from these wonder-workers and diviners, Paul positioned himself as something of an amateur (1 Cor. 11:6). While slick professionals peddled religious teachings for coin, he writes, Paul "worked night and day" so as not to be a burden

(1 Thess. 2:9). And thus Paul worked in servile spaces as an artisan to support himself.

His insistence on some measure of financial independence meant that when Paul entered a city, he was looking for employment as well as followers. Though the specifics are debated, he was trained, broadly speaking, in the leather industry. There were different ways that people found work in antiquity: through word of mouth, personal recommendations, professional and ethnic associations, or just by congregating in the marketplace or near professional hot spots. Perhaps Paul had letters of introduction from locally known members of his assemblies, or maybe he used the services of a local fixer, who helped migrant workers secure jobs (for a fee). Once he was employed, however, he would have found himself rubbing elbows with small, mixed groups of servile and freeborn workers.

The archaeology of workshops doesn't allow us to see the social hierarchies of such groups; perhaps as a newcomer, Paul was initially an outsider. If he was a citizen, perhaps he could have worn his status on his sleeve — or perhaps it would have elicited eye rolls from his new colleagues. Social ties did not evaporate at the end of the workday; most urban workers lived crammed alongside each other in the small apartments stacked above workshops in tenement buildings. Perhaps it's here or in the tenement courtyard, where people did their cooking and cleaning, that we should picture Paul holding his first assembly meetings.[7]

Although Paul did not enjoy manual labor and was happy to set it aside whenever he was able (1 Cor. 4:12), the time he spent in trade gave him access to neighborhood associations (*collegia*) of artisans through whom he could solicit more work and expand his social network. In these organizations, followers of Jesus may have found support, recruited members, and drawn inspiration for the organization of their own groups. These were not the gentleman's clubs of Victorian London or New York. They were for the sub-elites—artisans, merchant traders, freedmen, enslaved workers, foreigners, and sometimes women— who did not have access to the power structures and systems of government dominated by landowning aristocrats. Often these groups crystallized around shared customs, identities, and professions. Members paid dues that were used to purchase goodwill in the form of sponsorship of religious sacrifices, games, holidays, and the construction of buildings. The group's purse covered the costs of burials and the social gatherings that formed the heart of collegiate life. More than anything else, *collegia* were dining societies where, much like associations of Christians, members shared meals and table fellowship.[8]

For Paul, preexisting associations offered the opportunity for him to piggyback his evangelical work on existing social networks. In a world without a formal concept of a church, much less architectural spaces dedicated to worship, they also offered a template for the structuring of proto-Christian groups and potentially physical spaces in which to meet. Crucially, they also gave him access—whether through wealthier group members, patrons, or collective funds—to literate workers who could help inscribe and copy Paul's writings. Though Paul insists that he did not accept donations for himself, he was happy, throughout his career, to take advantage of the skills of servile workers like Tertius (the secretary of Romans), Epaphroditus (who assisted him during his imprisonment in Ephesus), and Onesimus (the courier and perhaps scribe of the Letter to Philemon). The skills of these servile workers were so critical to his work that he begged Philemon, a Jesus-following enslaver, to send Onesimus back to him.[9]

There were other social locations where members of what— to us—might look like vastly different professions found

themselves thrown together. The mid-March festival of Quinquatrus, held annually in Rome in honor of Minerva, included a
procession in which cobblers, weavers, fullers, dyers, teachers,
doctors, painters, and engravers marched around the city
together. Some of these professions interacted with one another
on a regular basis. The stores of cobblers abutted the bookseller's district; the Sandalarium district of Rome was known to
house teachers and doctors; dyers and painters traded supplies
as a matter of course; and a shared professional use for urine
gave doctors, fullers, and leatherworkers common materials and
shared interests. Especially if we categorize the apostles as medical specialists, a high proportion of first- and second-century
Christian "missionaries" were eligible to participate in the
festival.[10]

The artisanal and servile flavor of early Christianity was
noted by some of its sharpest critics. Celsus, a second-century
philosopher and critic of Christianity, whose work is relayed to
us through the third-century theologian Origen, described Christians as "workers in wool and leather, fullers, and persons of the
most uneducated and rustic character." His remarks might read
as classist screed were it not for the Christian writings that support them. In the first and second centuries, we know of Jesus
followers who were fabric dyers, cobblers, and craftsmen. Their
interests may be reflected in the language of dry cleaning, commerce, and construction that ripples through the Gospels and
other early Christian writings. By the second century, says Pliny
the Younger, Christian assemblies in northern Turkey included
people "of every age, every rank, and also of both sexes." But
even an affluent Christian intellectual, like the second-century
Justin Martyr, met his students in an unremarkable apartment
above the baths in Rome and counted enslaved students among
their number.[11]

There is a fierce and ideologically freighted debate among

scholars about the social status and wealth of early Christians. Yet even if most early followers of Jesus were comparatively low-status and impoverished, this does not mean that enslaved people were absent from these groups. Even in lower-status Roman contexts, job titles often obscured who did the actual work. The dockworkers charged with unloading ships outsourced the grunt work to enslaved people. So too did an illiterate first-century warehouse manager in the port of Ostia, who trusted his enslaved secretary Nardus to draw up legal contracts for property rentals. Members of Greek voluntary associations who could not afford to hire a secretary could gain access to literate enslaved workers owned or rented by the group.[12]

Focusing on poverty and financial precarity of early Christians can sometimes occlude our vision of enslaved workers. The "pauperizing" of early Christianity, as one scholar has put it, "works to minimize the economic benefits derived from slave exploitation." The presence and contributions of enslaved and low-status workers are assumed in every aspect of early Christian activity, but their work is especially important when it comes to the making of the New Testament.[13]

For some four decades after the death of Jesus, Paul, the original disciples, their companions, and their unnamed servile helpers toured the Mediterranean spreading the news about Jesus. Our only reliable literary evidence of their activities in this period is Paul's letters: most other canonical texts describing Jesus and the apostles stem from the last quarter of the first century. In the intervening period, a catastrophic series of events radically reshaped both how the followers of Jesus thought and wrote about their place in Jewish and cosmic history and how non-Jewish inhabitants of the Mediterranean thought about Judeans and Jews in general.

In 70 CE, after a bitterly hot summer and an eight-month siege, Jerusalem fell to the ambitious Roman general and future emperor Titus. Even when Alexamenos and his classmates were studying on the Palatine Hill many decades later, the memory of the First Jewish War was relatively fresh. A glut of enslaved workers had been brought to Rome from Jerusalem, Asia Minor, and beyond, the memories of the city's last stand scorched into them. In the aftermath of his victory, Titus paraded prisoners of war and looted treasures from the Temple through the streets of Rome. As part of a hefty publicity campaign intended to legiti-mize his rise to power, Titus's father, the emperor Vespasian, had a series of commemorative coins—the Judaea Capta ("Judea is defeated") coins—struck in bronze, silver, and gold to cele-brate Titus's victory. These coins were issued throughout the Empire for twenty-five years; as a result, everyone knew that the people of Judea had been defeated and enslaved.

Line drawing of a sestertius of the emperor Vespasian (71 CE) in the Judaea Capta series. The reverse of the coin (right) shows Judea personified as a woman crying under a palm tree. The inscription reads "Judea is defeated."

Among those who were trafficked as captives of Rome were followers of Jesus. According to Paul's letters, there was a vibrant community of Jesus followers in Jerusalem prior to the First

Jewish War. Early histories of Christianity barely mention them. Later Christian writers liked to imagine that their religious fore-fathers, following a directive from Jesus (Mark 13:14), had fled the city when they saw the signs of impending catastrophe. These later writers saw the destruction of Jerusalem as divine punishment for killing Jesus, and thus it was important to them that Jesus followers had not been present or caught in friendly fire.[14]

Whatever later theologically motivated historians wanted to believe, it is unlikely that Christ followers who lived in Jerusalem escaped the war and its aftermath. If they survived, they would have been caught in the vise-like military grip on Jerusalem, enslaved, and trafficked through the ports of Italy, Asia Minor, and Egypt. These newly enslaved Judeans would have brought their stories about Christ with them, just as those Jews who had been enslaved by Roman generals Pompey, Cassius, and Gaius in the century and a half that preceded this also took their religious customs with them. That followers of Jesus were already present in Rome, Antioch, Ephesus, and other urban centers does not diminish the importance of these new arrivals. As uncomfortable as it may be to think about, the spread of Christianity was assisted by Roman roads and Roman human trafficking.

Those forcibly migrated from Judea to other parts of the Empire were critical to the dissemination of the Christian message. Moreover, their existence foregrounds the centrality of enslavement to Christianity. If today a modern pilgrim wanted to re-tread Paul's final journey as a prisoner to Rome, they would dock at the Italian port of Pozzuoli (ancient Puteoli), near Naples, and make their way north on foot. As they journeyed, they might pass the tomb of Claudia Aster (Aster is a Latinized form of the Jewish name Esther), a "captive from Jerusalem" who died in southern Italy in the last quarter of the first century. Enslaved

Judeans make cameos in the writings of the late first- and second-century authors Josephus, Petronius, Suetonius, and Lucian; though these figures are often presented as fraudulent religious entrepreneurs, their real-life counterparts are more likely to have been the victims of despotic marketing.[15]

It was in the aftermath of this devastating moment in Jewish history that the lives of Jesus began to be written down. The writing of the Gospels, the first biographies of Jesus, is shrouded in mystery, but even from the beginning their anonymous format was associated with low-status writers. Most scholars agree that the first and foundational life of Jesus, the Gospel of Mark, was written in the aftermath of the fall of Jerusalem. In its initial form, however, it is unlikely to have been called the Gospel of Mark. Academic consensus maintains that the Gospels first circulated anonymously without titles or authors just as "the gospel," even if they might have been associated with various individual authors. The anonymous format was itself seen as low-status. In the Principate, authorless texts lacked social status and authority; just as is the case today, any statement without an author was inadmissible in a Roman court. Ideas about authorship are always in flux, but in the first century, a period when authorship came to be synonymous with elite singular authorship, unattributed texts like the Gospels were the literary equivalent of the invisible workers who coproduced so much elite literature. In the minds of elites, these works lacked status, origins, and authority over themselves, and as such they were especially susceptible to revision and alteration. Notwithstanding the disruptive power of anonymity, the story of Jesus spread in a format that elites called "unmastered" and was seen by them as "slavish."[16]

The unmastered character of the Gospel of Mark might help explain the ways that his stories were rewritten and reused. Mark is important not only because he wrote the earliest canonical Gospel, but also because his text became the primary source material for the authors of the other three Gospels—Matthew, Luke, and, though there is some debate about this, John. The later evangelists revised, supplemented, and edited Mark in ways that would horrify a modern author. Though rewriting stories was a part of ancient education, and something that elite people did to entertain themselves and prove their erudition, works that were associated with servile authors were particularly prone to this kind of literary treatment. Supplementing and reconfiguring the words of others was not just an enslaving pastime: it took place in all areas of life and at every level of society. Graffiti from the back alleys and brothels of Pompeii, places not usually frequented by elites, reveals a dynamic of collaboration and revision in which people modified one another's words and drawings. While some of this supplementation—like that of Alexamenos's schoolroom—is mean-spirited and hostile, other examples indicate supportive relationships and camaraderie. People from all backgrounds were accustomed to reshaping the words of others.

Even though the Gospels first circulated anonymously, early Christian tradition supplies an elaborate account of the genesis of the earliest Gospel in which Mark was the interpreter and scribe of Peter. It is at this point, in the beginning of the second century, that historians first find evidence about who Mark was—or at least who early Christians thought he was.

The first known person to connect Mark the man to Mark the Gospel was Papias, a second-century bishop from Hierapolis, a tourist town in Asia Minor that was best known in antiquity for its hot springs and the cult of the Syrian goddess Atargatis. In his five-volume collection of early Christian traditions, Papias wrote that "when Mark was the translator of Peter, he wrote down accurately everything that he recalled of the Lord's words and deeds—but not in order. . . . He was intent on just one purpose: to leave out nothing that he heard nor to include any falsehood among them."[17]

Papias imagines Mark as exactly the kind of intermediary that Peter needed as he traveled into areas where fewer people spoke fluent Aramaic. Mark was the sort of person who could convey nuance, haggle over prices, and pick up on different cultural norms and social cues. The Gospel of Mark is not what anyone would call difficult or elegant Greek, but it was written by someone with facility in Greek, knowledge of Aramaic, and at least a smattering of administrative Latin. Whoever wrote Mark was conversant with several languages and familiar (as many were) with the bureaucratic terrain; there's a ring of truth to Papias's statement that he was an interpreter.[18]

Byzantine imagining of Peter (left) dictating the Gospel to Mark (right)

A great deal of ancient translation work was performed by enslaved people whose linguistic skills made them assets, but whose social status meant that their identities and their work are generally omitted from our historical records. By positioning Mark in this way, Papias explains why it is that the text lacks order (it is the unrefined text of a secretary or clerk) while simultaneously using this lowly status to defend the integrity of the content. Mark's account can be trusted, in Papias's logic, because texts written down by servile workers are more likely to be accurate.[19]

What was true of Peter would have also been true of the other apostles and first followers of Jesus. By the age of forty, which was admittedly old age in the first century, almost everyone would have needed help with paperwork. Christian tradition maintains that the Gospels were written to preserve the memories of aging apostles. Ignatius of Antioch, whose letters have been central to Christian thinking about ecclesiastical authority, was apparently in his seventies when he was "writing"; and tradition holds that the evangelist and apostle John was close to a hundred. These are just a few of early Christianity's more mature authors. Even if someone felt pressed to argue that Christians did not routinely use secretaries, they should concede that prior to the invention of refractive lenses, people of advanced age were generally unable to write alone. This is as true of the apostles as anyone else.

If Mark was doing servile work, then why was the Gospel named after him? Why not title it the Gospel of Peter? There is a second-century (arguably heretical) apocryphal gospel attributed to Peter but that was not written until decades later. It is not as if the name had been taken. Matthew and John were apparently disciples of Jesus, so their identification as authors makes sense—but Mark's servile status, by contrast, makes the name of his eponymous Gospel a perennial mystery. Paradoxically, the fact that Mark might have been enslaved—or at least was performing work that many enslaved people did at the time—might also hold the key to solving this puzzle.

Even though enslaved people were not thought of as author material, they were seen as faithful secretaries, record-keepers, and copyists. As a result, copies of a famous work that were manufactured by an author's trusted secretary were highly valued. In the second century, the Roman miscellanist Aulus Gellius, a rough contemporary of Papias, bragged that he had obtained a copy of Cicero's speeches signed by Tiro himself. Antiquarian interest in these "originals" ran so high that some unscrupulous booksellers forged Tironian Ciceros in their workshops. This alleged proof of Tiro's involvement assured elite consumers that they had the best possible copies. By the same token, the involvement of Mark, a conduit for the eyewitness Peter, authenticated the manuscript and message. By the end of the second century, at least a dozen different versions of the Gospels were circulating, causing confusion and concern. Naming the Gospel after Mark signaled that it was a reliable version of events, not the offspring of some ancient parlor game or a piece of scrappy hack work. It was because enslaved workers were seen as mindless conveyers of an author's meaning that the listener could trust they were hearing the real Gospel.[20]

In identifying Mark as the translator of another apostle, Papias summoned the specter of servility; that he may have done so for rhetorical reasons does not make the possibility of Mark's enslavement any less real. If "Mark" was a secretary or if a secretary was involved in the composition of the Gospel, that person was likely to be or have been enslaved, like the many others who took dictation at the time.

But Papias was wrong about at least one thing: Mark did not merely convey what he had heard. Whoever wrote the Gospel turned a Galilean message into written Koine, the *lingua franca* of the eastern Mediterranean. Whoever wrote it was familiar with the stylistic conventions of their time, dabbled in the genre of ancient biography, satirized imperial propaganda with a sly wink, and deftly interwove biblical quotations and allusions into an accessible tale about an unlikely hero.

Just as Alexamenos and those like him were scrubbed from history, Mark's servility—his presumptive status as an enslaved or formerly enslaved worker—now lives beneath a hagiographical patina. Tradition has fattened up Mark's pedigree by supplying him with a priestly family and rich apostolic lineage. To most Christians today, Mark is not an enslaved translator; he is an evangelist, a martyr, and a saint.

The impulse to elevate the social status of those like Mark is not emancipatory; rather, it renders them invisible. Putting the historically questionable evidence of Papias aside, Mark's language skills—and other ancient evidence that the Gospel was composed in Rome after the destruction of the Temple in Jerusalem—hint that he was the kind of Judean who had been enslaved and trafficked.

This does not necessarily mean that the Mark after whom the Gospel is named took dictation from Peter himself or that he was an eyewitness to Jesus, but it does highlight some inescapable facts about the birth of the Jesus movement in the first century. In the first four decades after the death of their leader, the original disciples needed assistance translating their message for new audiences; that assistance would often have been provided mainly by servile workers. What's more, the mass enslavement of the inhabitants of Judea and forced migration to other parts of the Empire after the First Jewish War helped move the gospel message around the Mediterranean. And finally, the earliest Christian commentators pictured the Gospel of Mark as a collaborative project between an apostolic eyewitness and a servile literate worker. Whether or not that version is true, it shows that Christians themselves saw their writings as collaborations with servile workers. Given all this evidence, the possibility of enslaved coauthorship is one that should not be shuffled to the side or papered over.

Mark and Alexamenos are rare sightings but not anomalous examples. If only because writing was hard and required education and practice, most early Christian authors wrote collaboratively with secretaries and scribes. These ubiquitous invisible workers are important because they did more than simply take dictation. They were artists who massaged their raw material into conventionally acceptable forms. Whatever other motivations they may have had, elevating and clarifying the words of the "author" was part of their assignment. It was they who pushed the levers that brought the named author into view. Their experiences, their hopes, their social relationships, their political lives, and their fears are every bit as relevant to the New Testament and our interpretation of it as those of any named apostles and authors. It is no exaggeration to say that these canonical "writers" could not have produced their testaments without them.

Sometime in the winter of 54 or 55 CE, the apostle Paul—the onetime Pharisee whose vision of the risen Jesus transformed him into a Christ follower—found himself imprisoned in Ephesus, in Asia Minor. He had not yet set his sights on the city of Rome, or dictated the letter to its inhabitants that would immortalize his enslaved collaborator, Tertius. Paul was still on the fringes of the Roman Empire. But his evangelizing was already getting him into trouble.

We don't know the charges that led to Paul's imprisonment, but there were many aspects of his ministry that rubbed people the wrong way. His insistence on chastity for men as well as women—including bans on intercourse with sex workers—was sure to have irritated some. (More than one apocryphal story about the travels of the apostles shows them being arrested as the direct result of their calls for sexual abstinence.) Almost all meat was dedicated to one divine being or another, so perhaps his advice against eating food sacrificed to idols was a thorn in the side of local meat vendors. Maybe he made enemies of the local guild of tanners, or of the other religious specialists whose customers he attracted. Or perhaps he was just a nuisance, an outsider whose insistent tone, foreign accent, and strange ideas were enough of a disruption to justify imprisonment. Whether he was attempting to uproot Jesus followers or spreading the gospel, Paul's religious convictions always ran hot, so his presence in the bowels of a prison in a coastal city of Asia Minor is not entirely unexpected.

What we know is that such confinement was far from comfortable. Roman prisons, as recent archaeological research has shown, were largely subterranean. Most consisted of small underground chambers. Ephesus's weather rarely dips lower than forty degrees Fahrenheit in the winter, but the high humidity and blustery winds make it feel much colder. Paul's subterranean chamber would have been damp, moldy, and bitterly cold. Most of the time it would have been almost entirely dark, with the only natural light in the room entering through a small lunate opening close to the ceiling. If Paul stood up, he might have seen the feet and ankles of harried passersby through the makeshift window. Watching the world came with some risk, though. Those who were drunk after an afternoon at the taverns, or angry, or just looking for cheap entertainment were accustomed to using the openings as public urinals and heckling the prison's occupants. If he was lucky, they would hurl only abuse.

This aperture, however, was Paul's lifeline. Roman authorities weren't in the habit of supplying their prisoners with creature comforts like sanitary conditions, lighting, or nutritionally diverse meals, and so Paul—like any other prisoner—relied upon the kindness of others to survive. But he used the generosity of his acquaintances and converts for much more than mere survival.

Given his situation, it's surprising that Paul managed to write letters to his churches, but we know that he did. At least four of his epistles were written while he was imprisoned, and many scholars believe that some were composed during his period of confinement in Ephesus.

The long, slow hours in the dark were offset by Paul's rapidly escalating worries about the communities he had founded in Greece, Macedonia, Turkey, and the Balkans. For all the time

A nineteenth-century imagining of Paul (right) writing his letter in prison and handing it to Tychicus. Tychicus is mentioned as an assistant in Paul's letters (e.g., Eph. 6:21), but this is an archaeologically implausible scene. Roman prisons had lower ceilings and were less comfortable.

and attention he had lavished upon them, Paul's congregations had a tendency to go off the rails as soon as he departed. Updating them on his situation, encouraging them to remain steadfast, and addressing the conflict and confusion that had arisen in his absence were pressing concerns.

Even if it had been his usual practice (and it wasn't), it would not have been possible for Paul to have written the letters alone in his cell, because there wasn't enough light for him to write and proofread his compositions. And even if Paul had wanted to attempt to write by himself in the dark, most prison windows weren't large enough to accommodate a wax tablet. A secretary might have greased the palm of jailors to gain access, as the wealthier inmates did and later historians like to imagine, but this was expensive and, even with a small lamp, it was difficult to see. Anyway, writing under such circumstances endangered the text as well as the scribe. A cautionary tale involved the philosopher Plotinus, whose vision failed him with advancing age. He was one of the few who attempted to write down his thoughts by hand rather than through dictation, and the results were somewhat disastrous. Porphyry, his biographer and self-appointed literary executor, admits that the texts were almost unreadable; indeed, the errors caused so much confusion that they undermined his reputation and textual legacy. Even if Paul's hands were unshackled and his vision keen, writing by hand was a risky proposition.[21]

We might imagine that someone — perhaps the secretary of one of Paul's wealthier followers, or perhaps a street-corner scribe hired for the day — squatted next to the window with stylus in hand and wax tablet balanced on his thigh, ready to take dictation. In years to come, the effects of this asymmetrical posture would haunt the scribe's joints, but if he were young enough, it was tolerable. Writing in the open air wasn't unusual. Many elementary schools met outdoors: the uneven stones didn't always make for comfortable seats, but the light was good; there was often access to broken pottery shards, which served as scrap paper for writing exercises; and if a student was lucky, they might snag a spot under a tree or on the shaded porch of a civic building. The reception hall of a large villa or the garden of a bath complex might be preferable, but any outdoor light was better than the dark and narrow rooms found in the hamlets in the countryside. Perhaps a nosy passerby might notice him sitting alone and try to catch a glimpse of his work, but he was largely left alone.[22]

Ostracon (pottery shard) containing lines from Homer's Iliad *in Coptic. This was possibly used for a schoolroom exercise.*

Paul had plenty of time to prepare—in his head—what he would say, but even so, he might have stumbled as he half-shouted his words through the narrow opening to the street. The heavy walls absorbed the sound of his voice and the scribe had to strain to hear the lines of prose. Many professional writers saved time and kept pace by anticipating what the author wanted to say, sometimes with deleterious effects: stonemasons who moved ahead of the instructions they were given either had to retrace their steps and produce ugly corrections, or leave errors in the inscriptions they carved. For secretaries, the situation was more easily remedied; by applying pressure to the wax tablet, they could erase any mistakes.

When the scribe was finished taking dictation, he read the letter back to Paul, but there may not have been an opportunity for the prisoner to review the final draft for errors or ambiguities. The secretary, therefore, had considerable influence over the text—and over the message that Paul transmitted to his fellow Christ followers.

Many scribes were used to improving the style of their customers: making people sound educated was part of the job. The Egyptian market-square vendors who wrote letters dictated to them by illiterate women, for instance, were accustomed to gussying up the style and language. Perhaps from this vantage point, Paul's anonymous scribe thought that an imprisoned leatherworker needed similar assistance. Nothing about his present situation indicated that he was making the best decisions, after all.[23]

A small example of this kind of rhetorical elevation might live on in Philippians 4:15, a prison letter usually dated to around 60–62 CE. Here Paul addresses the people of Philippi using the version of their name derived from the Latin (*Philippesioi*) rather than versions from the Greek (*Philippeis* or *Philippenoi*). Perhaps Paul had picked up some Latin in his travels, or his secretary thought it politic to address the mixed inhabitants of the small Roman colony in a way that recognized their founding by Mark Antony and Augustus.

Even when Paul was not imprisoned, he collaborated with secretaries. Towards the end of his Letter to the Galatians, Paul remarks on his handwriting and invites them to "see what large letters I make when I am writing with my own hand" (6:11). The implication is that the preceding section—what amounts to almost the entirety of the letter—had been written by someone else, in a smaller script. Paul makes a similar statement in 1 Corinthians 16:21, suggesting that this was his standard practice. This should not surprise us. This is, after all, how most people in the first-century world "wrote."

In the modern world, taking dictation is often (and somewhat erroneously) seen as mechanistic. Though ancient elites would agree with the view that secretarial work is mindless, in practice their methods of writing were quite different. Literate workers who helped with composition were ubiquitous. Depending on one's position in society, education level, and physical abilities, scribes were a luxury, a convenience, or a necessity. Most important of all, however, was the very active role these workers played in shaping the texts on which they collaborated. They were responsible for a whole host of tasks, from producing letters for their enslavers, to editing drafts, supplying corrections, and taking dictation. Yet even dictation, the most mechanical of secretarial tasks, was never mindless. Like every other literary task, it depended on the skills, style, and ingenuity of the enslaved worker.

Paul's letters show that collaborative authorship was as much a feature of early Christian writing as it was of Greek and Roman practice. Paul almost certainly coauthored all his correspondence with anonymous scribes as well as his named companions. But Paul was far from unique, and correspondence is one of the rare genres in which people name and reference their secretaries. Most early Christian texts were dictated because it was familiar, labor-saving, and in many cases necessary.

One dramatic example comes from the prolific third-century Christian philosopher and teacher Origen, who produced more than three thousand book rolls of theology, pastoral advice, biblical commentary, and philosophy. By anyone's standards, this is a staggeringly vast literary output. When scholars explain Origen's unparalleled productivity, they often gesture to an eye-catching detail in his biography: that he castrated himself at the age of seventeen, under the influence of a passage in the Gospel of Matthew that suggests people should "make ourselves eunuchs for the kingdom of heaven" (19:12). The story is almost certainly apocryphal—it's one of many salacious and scatological stories spread by gossipy Christians attempting to discredit their rivals—but it is repeated in university classrooms across the world. I have done it myself with a telling glance that says, "Only a man with no sex life could write so extensively."[24]

What is rarely mentioned, however, is that Origen's patron and sponsor, a wealthy convert called Ambrose, had put a team of enslaved men and women at Origen's disposal. Origen's most innovative work—the *Hexapla*—was a six-columned Old Testament that compared the various versions of the text in Hebrew, in Greek transliteration, and in various Greek translations. The process of assembling the text involved finding the relevant passages in at least six different book rolls, ascertaining which were parallel to one another, and copying them into a single manuscript. Origen was as worthy of the title "genius" as anyone, but his Hebrew could have used some work. Without a team of enslaved readers and secretaries who were fluent in Hebrew and Greek, as well as familiar with the content of the manuscripts, it's doubtful that such a thing would have been possible. Their language skills were critical in the *Hexapla*'s composition and, as a result, in the way early Christian theologians interpreted the Old Testament.[25]

Although Paul's patrons were apparently less affluent than Ambrose, it is likely that they, too, sponsored the writing of his letters. Tertius is traditionally associated with the deacon and community leader Phoebe, a wealthy member of the group of

Christ followers in Corinth. Epaphroditus, who helped raise funds for and supported Paul during his imprisonment in Ephesus, was obligated to at least one member of the congregation in Philippi. Onesimus was enslaved (or at least jointly enslaved) to a Jesus follower named Philemon. And perhaps even Timothy, who appears as a coauthor of several letters, was also enslaved. The identity of the scribe of Galatians is unknown, but Paul's letters suggest that he did not have the means to rent or purchase a literate enslaved worker himself. The secretaries who took dictation from him were either loaned to or hired for him by the wealthier members of his circle. These patrons or clusters of patrons who pooled their resources provided him with access to more elite modes of literary production. These secretaries gave him fluency in languages that he was only (but commendably) conversant in. They allowed him to extend his reach and his capabilities. And they shaped Paul's end product in ways that call that very possessive — Paul's — into question.

It is impossible to prove that Paul's secretaries came up with the turns of phrase, rhetorical flourishes, or intellectual arguments for which the Pauline epistles are known, but there are hints that they might have. Paul was known to cut a more impressive figure in his writings than in person: In 2 Corinthians, he tells us that his opponents described his letters as "powerful and rhetorically weighty," but his oratorical skills as "contemptible" (10:10). Perhaps he was just a bad public speaker, or perhaps the well-trained secretaries he used as scribes helped elevate his writing.

Many modern Christians worry that the practice of dictation might have adulterated or otherwise "corrupted" the original message. As corruption has been a watchword in discussions about the transmission of manuscripts, and most of us played the game of telephone (or some variant) as children, the concern is understandable. But dictation and its effects do not need to be understood in terms of alteration and error.[26]

One interpretatively important example from Romans 5:1 makes this case. As it is translated in the New Revised Standard Version, the passage reads, "Therefore, since we are justified by faith, we *have* peace with God through our Lord Jesus Christ" (italics added). The Greek manuscripts from which the standard critical editions of the New Testament are produced offer two primary options for the verb: *echōmen* (the subjunctive: "let us have") and *echomen* (the indicative: "we have"). The difference is in a single vowel. The former reading—which was popular in antiquity and is better attested in the manuscript tradition—exhorts addressees to make peace with one another. The latter is a statement of fact that expresses the condition that followers of Jesus already enjoy. What is not obvious to modern readers is that these words sounded the same in the first century. Whichever reading was the "original" written text, it would have been a decision on the part of Paul's secretary—a decision between two similar-sounding options. The uncertainty in the ancient manuscripts reflects the auditory ambiguity of the two. Tertius, Paul's secretary, did not change something or make a mistake as much as he made a decision. That decision shaped the text and its interpretation over the course of nearly two millennia. Collaboration does not have to be about corruption; it can be about cooperation.

Collaboration with enslaved workers is invisible to us not only because dependence upon one social's inferiors was embarrassing, but also because some ancient theories of the household pictured enslaved people as extensions of the body of the enslaver. Descriptions of enslaved workers portray them as tools, body parts, or prosthetic devices through which the freeborn "master" could extend himself. Cicero famously notes that without Tiro his work is silent and Martial absorbs his stenographer into his body as his "hand." These are not outlying examples. In the context of writing, the secretary or clerk was described as the hand of the enslaving author, or simply just a hand, as if all hands were interchangeable. Language like this folds the contributions and agency of the secretary into the figure of the enslaver. The underlying argument is reductive and dehumanizing: certain people are not people; they are mindless objects or body parts. As body parts, they did not threaten the judgment of the elite person or their status as thinker and author.[27]

The fiction, of course, is that hands are all the same and that the species of work located in the hands are mindless. The reality is more complicated: all work is mindful and all work is embodied. Athletes, surgeons, artists, artisans, and musicians are known for their neuromuscular virtuosity and dexterous fingers, but they do not possess identical skills even within the same profession. So too ancient secretarial ghostwriting involved kinesthetic skills and penmanship, an ability to wrangle unwieldy expressions into grammatical compliance, and an adeptness at imitating both established models of stylistic elegance and the quirks and compositional tells of the *dictator*. Even if ancient shorthand did not involve the active work of translation, it is inarguable that learning, dexterity, and intimacy underpin the notionally "mindless" work of taking dictation. Yet in the ancient model, all decisions and skills are credited to the enslaver, who becomes for us the author. The cost of this literary accounting scheme is both the erasure of unfree collaborators and the mischaracterization of their individual skills—as well as the legacy they left.

The roof of a temple in modern-day Pietrabbondante, Italy, is an odd place to look for writing, but unexpected places are appropriate locations to seek out invisible actors. Sometime during the first century BCE, two women took a break from the monotony of shaping and laying out roof tiles to press their sandal-clad feet into the soft clay of a freshly made terra-cotta slab. Having carefully placed their feet in line with one another, they added an inscription. Above the footprints, someone wrote in Oscan, the language of the local Samnite population, "Detfri, slave of Herennius Sattius, signed with her foot"; and under them, in Latin, her friend inscribed, "Amica, slave of Herennius, left her mark when we were making tiles." The roof tile had not even been fired when they marked it, but this remnant of friendship found its way onto the temple roof, where the inscription was hidden from view.

It's an irresistible artifact that defies academic generalizations about literacy, gender, and affluence. These two enslaved

Line drawing of a terra-cotta tile with footprints inscribed by Detfri (above) and Amica (below). The shoe prints are the same size, suggesting that perhaps the women exchanged footwear in order to make the inscription symmetrical.

women, who were, broadly speaking, engaged in construction work, could not only write, they also could compose full sentences. Despite their ostensible differences—Amica is a Latin name and Detfri's origins are unknown—a friendship worthy of commemoration had blossomed. Bilingual inscriptions can be found all over the Roman Empire, but why were enslaved women who could read and write and, in Amica's case, speak multiple languages making roof tiles? And were they disciplined for defacing the tile, or did the act of quasi-vandalism go unnoticed? Perhaps Amica (which just means "friend") and Detfri (the meaning of which is unknown) were pseudonyms or pet names, assumed here to avoid detection? Were the women still there when the site was razed by the Roman general Sulla a few years later?[28]

Perhaps this is an example of resistance, an insistent claim to presence that defied hierarchies of erasure, or perhaps it is just a moment of fun poking through the mantle of control. The tile is a glimpse at sociality, literacy, and agency. And herein lies its greater significance. It is widely recognized that enslaved people acted as agents of enslavers and had autonomy to draw up contracts, to strike bargains, to extend loans, and even to purchase other human beings. But when it comes to the writing of what we call high literature and to the development of ideas and concepts, we are reluctant to see evidence of their influence.

What the practices of writing in the Roman period reveal are the opportunities for enslaved interventions, contributions, and subversions. The utilization of readers and scribes often entailed a shift of media and physical locations. Those who took dictation on wax tablets—in longhand or shorthand—would later transcribe the material onto papyrus, out of sight of the speaker. The movement from tablet to page, room to room, person to person, and sometimes language to language opens up space for enslaved agency.

Shorthand was unintelligible to elites, yet fundamental to the production of knowledge in the ancient world. The illegibility and ambiguities of shorthand erased what might be said to be the "record" of the elite author's words. It created the space for expression, resistance, improvement, and correction. Certain aspects of the configuration, structure, and language of a text and particular elements of its contents would have been immovably set, but shorthand required that the scribe use his or her own judgment in contracting and subsequently expanding the text. What sociologist James Scott called the "hidden transcript" is, in this case, not hidden but cryptographic. If, once expanded, these fragments of agency were questioned or corrected, it would be difficult to consult the record of what had been originally said. The ambiguous nature of the system provided a certain amount of cover and afforded the scribe the possibility of a kind of stenographic escape. Even without destruction or erasure, the record of what was said was illegible to most. And even if the author had reviewed the legible version himself, the process of translating spoken words first into symbols and then into written words created the possibility for the insertion of what ancient historian Dan-el Padilla Peralta describes as "floating fragments" of enslaved subjectivity and resistance into the text.[29]

The practicalities of ancient writing destabilize the imagined power dynamics between author and secretary, for elite Romans, early Christians, and modern readers alike. Tertius and other enslaved workers were legal subordinates, but their work required that they exercise their own judgment in transcribing and editing texts attributed to others. To put this in Pauline terms: the eye surely cannot say to the hand that it has no need of it. This is not to say that the writings of Paul, the evangelists, Ignatius of Antioch, or Origen are less "reliable" or "authentic" than

Christians currently believe them to be, but rather that they are the products of multiple collaborators — only one of whom is currently credited for their work.

Some have asked why enslaved writers would have bothered to make authorial contributions at all. Although the question is well-intentioned and stems from a recognition of the strictures of ancient slavery, it is, frankly, classist. Why wouldn't they? A tax roll from Fayum includes an obscure joke based on a verse from the poet Callimachus in its margins. The scribe (who was not enslaved but was no elite writer or poet either) seems to have slipped the reference into the money register for no reason other than their own entertainment. The enslaved tile makers from Pietrabbondante might have risked a beating to find a moment of joy.[30]

Other corrections might have been thoughtful. Several years ago, I stumbled, quite accidentally, across a papyrus fragment, now housed in Berlin, that contains a historian's first draft of an account of the siege of Rhodes. The second-century CE fragment is from Egypt and can be identified as an autograph by the aggressive deletions that interrupt the writer's flow and the inky corrections that spill into the margins. To look at it, the fragment is impulsively messy, and you can feel the composer rooting around for words and details. One of the small insertions, levered between two lines atop an ugly erasure, alters a list of the battle's spoils so that the word "catapults" is replaced by "catapult engineers." This seemingly small emendation brings the draft into line with other known versions of the story, but it also centers captive people. Who made the change? I wondered if the correction had its genesis in someone other than the unknown author. Perhaps an enslaved secretary noticed the mistake and wanted to foreground enslaved prisoners of war? I wondered if they were annoyed by the obfuscation. Did they see the engineers as kindred spirits and take satisfaction or even delight in reintroducing them into the story? I cannot say, but these are among the range of plausible explanations.[31]

Second-century Greek manuscript describing the siege of Rhodes. The manuscript contains corrections made both in the process of writing (left column, second line) and later while editing (between-the-line alterations, see left column, fourth line).

In the works that made it into the New Testament, these moments of agency may not have left observable marks, but they affected the shaping of Christian ideas. Take, for example, the famous passage in 1 Thessalonians 5, in which Paul and his collaborator wrote that the Day of the Lord would come "like a thief in the night" and recommended that the Jesus follower should soberly "stay awake" while others sleep. This section about the Parousia (return of Jesus) is a metaphorical play on light and dark, day and night, sobriety and drunkenness, but it also resonates with real-world elite concerns about nocturnal home invasion. Those who could afford it deployed enslaved workers as night watchmen to guard against intruders. While their enslavers slept, these people spent long nights keeping watch. Paul's recommendation that his audience "stay awake" suggests that Christ followers should adopt the practices of enslaved workers (1 Thess. 5:2–6). In presenting the obligations of following Jesus in this way, Paul and his collaborator set traditional social roles on their head. While the passage would have spoken to anyone, regardless of their legal status, it encodes the idea that real fidelity to Jesus involves a certain "slavishness."

The same idea of sleep-deprived watchfulness coupled with invocations to "stay awake" reappears in Gospel parables about Judgment Day. In Luke 12, the enslaved people who spend the night alert, anticipating the return of their enslaver, are symbolic representations of faithful Christians. Nocturnal vigilance became the preeminent model for awaiting the return of Jesus and forms the basis of modern Christian beliefs about the rapture, but it has its roots in enslaving culture. And, arguably, the idea comes from an enslaved scribe who themselves may have spent some exhausting nights awake.[32]

Other elements may have been playful. Paul's Letter to the Galatians is best known for his sharp tone and passionate rejection of circumcision for gentile converts, but it is also full of language that refers to scribal work. Though this flies beneath the radar in English translations, there are numerous bookish double-entendres in the letter. The apostles James, Peter, and John, for example, are identified as *styloi* (Gal. 2:9). The term is usually translated as "pillars," but it might also refer to a stylus, the implement with which words were transcribed onto a tablet by a scribe. "Pillar" might be the primary meaning here, but

A sleepy enslaved boy with a lantern waits for his enslaver (first or second century CE*).*

there is a secondary, coded reference available to literate collaborators. One of these allusions to book technology may have functioned as a private joke for the secretary. On two occasions, Galatians refers to people being enslaved to *stoicheia* (4:3, 9). In many English Bibles the word is (accurately) translated as "elemental spirits of the world" and, broadly speaking, refers to the material world. But the term can also mean letters of the alphabet, or syllables. No other Pauline letter uses bookish language as extensively. In fact, the pervasive bookish language used in Galatians is a complete outlier in the Pauline corpus. Perhaps, then, it stems from the person who recorded it. Paul's anonymous secretary, who would have been familiar with the fact that enslaved workers were hired by the line and enslaved to the alphabet, found a way to capture Paul's meaning while also inserting themselves into the letter. Perhaps they let slip a wry smile as they inscribed the words.[33]

Reflecting on the generation of culture, the Dutch historian and social theorist Johan Huizinga famously wrote that "play cannot be denied," and perhaps these moments of autonomy cannot either. Cognitive psychologists argue that people cannot help but crave agency. In every time period for which scholars can trace the interventions made by (freeborn) lower-status collaborators, it is clear that these people did make important changes to the texts they worked on. Surely the ancient secretaries who recorded line after line of the books of the New Testament were not immune to these impulses and habits. Even though it is impossible to pull apart their individual contributions or speak with complete certainty, the fact of their impact remains.[34]

No set of books is as discussed and dissected as the New Testament. Scholars and religious leaders alike pore over the language of the evangelists. Doctrinal battles are fought over the meaning of Paul's prepositions, with constant recourse to our understanding of what these authors intended. These debates cross from the pulpit to the public domain in modern cultural debates about what the Bible meant in the past and means in the present. If the more elite authors of the New Testament worked collaboratively, as it is now clear that they did, then the contributions of their coauthors are essential to our understanding of the life and message of Jesus. How did their insights, perspectives, and experiences shape the story that changed the world?

CHAPTER THREE

REREADING THE
STORY OF JESUS

In one well-known Gospel story, Jesus was at (probably) Peter's home in Capernaum when word got out that he was there. Locals swarmed around him, filling the house where he was staying, and tumbling out into the courtyard outside. It was difficult to keep them out, for the house was part of a domestic complex and the only thing separating the interior rooms from the courtyard was a straw mat or curtain; even the lock on the wooden door that sealed the main entrance to the complex lacked the kind of sturdiness of doors archaeologists have found elsewhere in the region.

As Jesus spoke with this group, four men arrived carrying a portable bed. The man on the litter is identified only as a *paralytikos* or, in English translations, a paralytic. Seeing the crowd around the doorway, the four attempted a different approach. Having hoisted themselves and their charge onto the roof, they began to tunnel their way through it, raining a hail of dried clay and sweat on the occupants below. They removed the web of supporting reeds to create an opening between the wooden beams and lowered the paralyzed man down into the room. Archaeologists remark on the shoddy craftsmanship of the homes in Capernaum, but rudimentary construction is no excuse for vandalism. Nevertheless, Jesus seems to have overlooked it. Noting that the four's work had "saved them," he forgave the sins of the paralytic. After a brief but tense exchange with the assembled scribes, Jesus plays his trump card and instructs the paralyzed man to "take up his bed and walk."[1]

The story is filled with architectural and narrative gaps: the open doorway, the unplanned skylight in the roof, the unnoted destruction of someone's home, and the absence of names. Most noteworthy of all are the identities of the four who carried the paralytic. They are not even identified as *people*: Greek allows their identities to evaporate out of the sentence. Generations of interpreters have sought to plug these lacunae, using materials imported from their own worlds. And so it is that some Bible translations and even academic commentaries identify the four as the paralytic's "friends."[2]

The sight of a man being carried was common enough in the first century: the wealthy were carried by their staff on bobbing sedan chairs and beds. For elites, being carried in the fresh air counted as exercise; some physicians even prescribed it as medicine. But the practice was also used to transport anyone who was sick or unable to walk. The siege-machine engineer Artemos, who was unable to walk, acquired the nickname *Periphoretus* (literally "borne about") because he was carried everywhere on a litter.

It's possible that the four people carrying the paralyzed man were indeed his friends—but there are reasons to doubt it. The man is transported on a *krabbatos*, a term that covers everything from a mat to an ornate couch, but the fact that the *krabbatos* is sturdy enough to be lowered through a roof—and that no fewer than four men carried it—suggests that it was on the heftier side, perhaps something more like a litter. The man is paralyzed, but he may also have been rich.

It is far likelier, therefore, that the four were enslaved workers—and so it is especially significant that Jesus' focus is on them, rather than on the man they have brought to him. Jesus notes that their *pistis* ("faith" or "loyalty") has saved them. The authors of the story want the reader to notice that these men are here and that—either through loyalty to their enslaver or through trust in Jesus—they have saved themselves.

An early-third-century depiction of the healing of the paralyzed man from a baptistery in Dura-Europos, Syria. For the scene to be identifiable to the viewer, the krabbatos *had to be prominently featured, but note that it is not a simple mat.*

Jesus' first words to the man known only as the paralytic, on the other hand, take a different tone. He first forgives the man's sins. (We do not know what these sins were, but one might think that the destruction of a neighbor's or tenant's roof was among them.) Then he issues a somewhat barbed command: "Take up your bed and walk." And the man, who was more accustomed to giving orders than following them, does. That he can carry the couch, which in this view is a heavier litter, does not necessarily lead to the conclusion that it was a humble pallet and, thus, that he was impoverished. The *krabbatos* is now empty. The story takes place in the world of wonder; impressive displays of strength are not out of the question. What this reading does change is our understanding of the instruction: having identified and forgiven the man's sins, Jesus tells the now able-bodied enslaver to do his own work.

In antiquity, digging was seen as one of the most arduous and artless of enslaved tasks. Burrowing through a roof, however, is more complicated; perform it incorrectly and you take a tumble. It requires at least a tacit knowledge of engineering. It is possible that the paralyzed man directed the labor, but this does not mean that the work of the four was mindless. As cognitive scientists have argued, group labor distributes agency among its members. No one is irrelevant and no one is fungible. This much is obvious from the story: it is the four's work that is seen and acknowledged by Jesus.

☩

Reparative work is in the gaps, in seeing and acknowledging those whom despotic curricula, history, and culture encourage us to "see through." For almost two thousand years, readers of the New Testament have agonized over the interpretation of every detail of the Jesus story. Christians have excavated participles as if they were precious relics. The goal of the historian has been to understand the meaning of ancient texts in their original contexts. The more optimistic have attempted to uncover the intent of the authors who wrote them, by attending to the authors' presumed religious beliefs, experiences, social mores, and ethnicities.[3]

Not everyone reads the Bible as a historian. It is possible to read the New Testament for the benefit of marginalized groups without thinking about enslaved authorship and history. But if historical reconstruction has merit, and as some of the New Testament's coauthors were invisible and servile, then those who do care about history should read the literature of the Jesus movement with this in mind. It may not be possible to credit low-status collaborators with specific interventions, but just as with tunneling through a roof, agency should be ascribed to everyone in the group.

The story of the paralyzed man, and the history of its interpretation, encapsulate how it is that people have translated and interpreted the New Testament without enslavement in mind. This is the case even though, we should assume, one of the authors was enslaved or formerly enslaved. Traditionally the story has been read as an encomium to friendship and a lesson about "standing on one's own two feet." Read it with an eye to enslaved collaboration, though, and the message is quite different. The attention that Jesus pays to the four men for their actions, the way he distinguishes them from their enslaver, his focus on their (coerced) loyalty, the way that it contributes to their salvation, and his brusque response to the formerly paralyzed man change its meaning entirely. It becomes a subtle rejoinder to those able-bodied members of the enslaving class who unnecessarily exploited their workers.

What is true of this story is equally true for the larger tale of the man from Nazareth. How might thinking with the interests and experiences of enslaved collaborators broaden our view? In many instances, as with this story, the answers reside in what is not said. Jesus does not seem to have been enslaved, but his story resonated with and drew upon the experiences of those who were. Enslaved coauthors were not in a position to change the whole story, but in their selection of language, and in their omission of certain details and the emphasis they place on others, fragments of enslaved interests might persist.

There are good reasons to think that enslaved coauthors were involved in the composition of all four of the canonical Gospels. This is true even for those who hold the most conservative views of the authorship of the Gospels. The earliest layers of Christian tradition present Mark as a servile translator and secretary who took dictation from Peter. The same early Christian writers relate that the Gospel of Matthew was originally written in Hebrew before it was translated into Greek. Given that these traditions do not name these translators, readers might infer that they were anonymous enslaved scribes. In the opening of the Gospel, Luke refers to the eyewitnesses and "underlings of the word" who handed on the traditions to him. Finally, the Gospel of John was written when the disciple John was so advanced in age that he surely needed to dictate his memories to someone else.[4]

To ancient audiences, the story of Jesus was both familiar and bizarre. Broadly speaking, it's a biography, one of many circulating about generals, prophets, and political leaders in the ancient world. Jesus is the kind of subversive protagonist ancient audiences almost never encountered. An accidental hero with an underdeveloped backstory, he bursts out of the River Jordan and onto the religious scene with exceptional powers as a newly proclaimed Son of God. He wrestles with a primordial demon in the wilderness and escapes unscathed; he bests a tempest that would have capsized most vessels. And yet, in the end, it is the quotidian exercise of human power that leads him to the most horrifying of deaths. There is no obvious boss fight or parting bang; his story ends with a series of whimpers. In this poignant detail, too, we might see traces of enslaved people.

In the Gospel of Mark, the earliest of the canonical Gospels, Jesus' story begins on the banks of the River Jordan. There he appears amid the mass of disillusioned young men who were looking to John the Baptizer for direction and purpose. At this juncture—before descending into the water for baptism—his only identity was that of acolyte. He is otherwise marginal and, in ancient terms, almost nameless.

Although, in antiquity, social status usually followed one's mother, Mediterranean naming conventions identified men as their father's sons. The Hebrew Bible teems with proud declensions of male lineage, and yet Jesus has no human father in the Gospel of Mark. His before-life is glimpsed later in the words of his former neighbors, the residents of Nazareth, who call him "the carpenter, the son of Mary, and the brother" of a cluster of siblings (Mark 6:3). In Mark, there is no reference to a biological or legal father, much less one called Joseph. In the Hebrew Bible, the only character identified solely as the "son of" his mother is Ishmael, the son of the enslaved Hagar. Historians scrape around for Jesus' father, but Mark does not want to give him up. To the ancient reader, the lack of a patronym is a suggestive social brand that marks him as status-less, illegitimate, servile.[5]

It is the baptism that summons Mark's Jesus onto the stage. He is named as God's son in a manner that evokes both the adult adoptions of imperial heirs and the manumission of enslaved workers. The scene also alludes to Genesis 22, in which God instructs Abraham to sacrifice Isaac. The echo of this event in the story of the baptism suggests that Jesus is no longer his mother's son; like Ishmael he is now the "beloved" child, like

Detail from a sarcophagus that shows Jesus being baptized by John. Note that Jesus is much smaller than John. In Christian art from this period, smaller figures were usually children or enslaved people.

Isaac. Despite being proclaimed into a filial relationship with God, Jesus' kinship remains fragile. His sense of place shifts from Nazareth to a "home" in Capernaum. When his mother and siblings arrive to see him, he does not recognize their relationships (Mark 3). Even as he builds a new set of powerful, sympathetic ties with his followers, a sense of his kinlessness and alienation remains.

Today the Bible's identification of Jesus as a carpenter's son (and perhaps a carpenter himself) connotes humbleness, albeit of an innocuous sort. But carpenters, or more accurately "construction workers" (the Greek noun *tekton* refers equally to stonemasons and bricklayers), were part of a class of marginalized workers who were often the subject of scorn and derision. Low-level subsistence workers (*penetes*), they struggled to make ends meet and did not always have more legal rights than enslaved workers. A trained builder was a step up from unskilled labor, but the whole endeavor was seen as morally suspect. While farming was considered grubby yet honest work, construction was implicated in the luxurious excess of superficial decoration and, simultaneously, associated with muck. Builders worked buried up to their knees and elbows in the mud and used animal manure as caulk to secure bricks. Their bodies weren't just dirty; they offended the senses. It's ironic, therefore, that in the place of a patronym, Jesus is known as Christos, the oiled or perfumed one. The lofty religious connotations are clear: Jesus is the anointed one, even if the person who anoints him before his death in the Gospel is an anonymous, low-status, potentially servile woman (Mark 14:3–9).

The other Gospels move away from fatherlessness and dirt, and with some reason. The absence of a legal father for Jesus might suggest that his mother was a sex worker, enslaved, or (more probably) both. Matthew places Jesus at one remove by making him the "son of a builder." Like Luke, Matthew supplies Jesus with a legal father, a royal genealogy, and a divine history. Even John's Jesus — so godly that some readers allegedly doubted his humanity — has a human father. These revisions to Mark's story erase the disrepute of fatherlessness but preserve the cloudiness of Mary's status. Matthew's genealogy names only five women in the lineage of Jesus; what the other four have in common is their liminal social status and involvement in sex work. He mentions Tamar, a widow who was forced to play the role of a sex worker after mistreatment by her in-laws; Rahab, a sex worker from Jericho who assisted Israelite spies; Ruth, a Moabite widow and non-Israelite who secured her future by persuading an older relative to marry her; and the "wife of Uriah" (i.e., Bathsheba), who was coerced into an adulterous relationship by King David. Luke's Mary calls herself "the slave of the

Lord," language that stresses the absence of bodily autonomy, but "slave" is habitually mistranslated in Bibles as *servant*. The pioneering South African academic Winsome Munro and the womanist New Testament scholar Mitzi Smith have argued that Mary's statement is suggestive. The language of slavery in Luke might be metaphorical, of course, but by that reasoning so might the language of kingship and divinity.[6]

Both in the Gospels and in their reception, those who weren't persuaded by Jesus' claims latched on to his ambiguous parentage. Even today, people irreverently joke that Mary stepped out on Joseph. The ancient version of this jest was loaded with violence. The pagan critic Celsus suggested that Jesus was the son of a Roman soldier and that he fabricated stories of a divine father to conceal the truth of his conception. Celsus here hints that Mary was a sex worker, or a victim of the kind of sexual assault that was common in times of military occupation (and that Roman emperors liked to brag about in their propaganda). Written around the same time, the North African lawyer Tertullian's judgment-day fantasies reveal that the terms "the son of the carpenter" and "son of the prostitute..." were bandied about as slurs. The language is socioeconomically coded, ethnically freighted, and deeply gendered. It does the same rhetorical work as cheap slurs like "whore." Later rabbinic traditions, drawing upon Celsus, would give the Roman soldier a name — Pant(h)era — and use "son of Panthera" to refer to Jesus, but none of these traditions represent special historical insights.[7]

Mary is not the only unprotected woman in Mark's Gospel. None of the women who approach Jesus for healing or forgiveness seem to be under the protection of a male family member. Neither the woman with the flow of blood, who approaches Jesus early in his ministry and heals herself by clasping the hem of his garment, nor the woman with the jar of nard who anoints Jesus before his death appears with male escorts. Women who moved alone through public spaces were seen as metaphorical as well as literal streetwalkers. The strength and resourcefulness of any unprotected woman in public might be read as sexual availability. If this is deliberate, then the condition of the woman with the flow of blood might have been read as the consequence of sexual violence and battery. The effects of her mistreatment as a sex worker are on full display.

I am not suggesting that, historically speaking, Mary was a sex worker or an enslaved woman who was sexually violated, but rather that the Gospels create the possibility for this interpretation. Many people, including Christians, have read them this way. The second-century *Protoevangelium of James*, an apocryphal account of the birth and childhood of Mary, shows Mary growing up in the Temple as a virginal handmaiden. She is not a sex worker, but the text utilizes the broader practice of enslavement to pagan deities to explain her upbringing and position as "the slave of God."

To stay within the canonical New Testament: the most conservative position on this matter is that Mark, the first evangelist, omitted all reference to a human father in order to make his primary theological point that Jesus is the Son of God. If this biographical gap is theological exposition, then it is arresting that, in a bold rejection of every social norm, the authors of Mark were willing to allow space for even the possibility that Jesus was enslaved or illegitimate. This is the kind of thing an elite author and follower of Jesus might want to eliminate, and yet there it sits, in plain sight, gleaming with interpretive possibility. Perhaps an enslaved secretary, who might ordinarily have tied up such loose ends or clarified vague points, introduced or left fatherlessness in the text for their own personal reasons.

The traditions about Mary and the absence of male protectors for women in Mark may reflect the lives lost and destroyed after the fall of Jerusalem and the experience of what historian of slavery Orlando Patterson calls "natal alienation." In the aftermath of the First Jewish War, Jerusalemites and other inhabitants of Judea found themselves violently separated from their families, fatherless, and enslaved. The Gospel of Mark, which was likely written during this period of enslavement and forced migration, preserves traces of that trauma. The predicament that faced the woman with the flow of blood and the woman who anointed Jesus for burial makes the casualties of war visible to the readers.[8]

Poverty, subsistence workers, social illegitimacy, and enslavement did not, however, exist only in the exceptional circumstances of war. The hints of servility in Jesus' backstory and the social exclusion he experienced as a result speak powerfully to those experiencing many forms of social marginalization. The authors of Mark—both named and unnamed—present Jesus as called from invisibility and integrated into the family of God as beloved Son. Mark's point, subtly put, is: it was the marginal, fatherless child who was chosen. Jesus was once Ishmael. To the coauthors of Mark (either Peter and Mark, or, more likely, an author and secretary, one of whom was likely named Mark) and the audience members deprived of biological family and forced to the margins of society, that was a powerful message. To elite enslavers it might have been barely recognizable.

If Mark only hinted at the servile origins of his hero, then Paul made his case more boldly. In Philippians 2:5–11, a passage some believe was adapted from an ancient hymn, Jesus transitions from the "form of a God" to the form of a "slave" (*doulos*) at his birth. This servility is not only implied by his origin stories and death, but also glimpsed in snatches in his words and deeds. At the Johannine Last Supper, Jesus washes the feet of the disciples, a service that in elite households was performed by servile workers. Jesus himself draws out the servile connotations of his work, explaining to the disciples that "slaves are not greater than their master, nor are messengers [literally, apostles] greater than the one who sent them" (NRSVue John 13:16). Though Jesus is clearly understood as the "master" in John, and discipleship is cast as friendship rather than service, the self-abasement of his actions here and the humiliation of his impending crucifixion are understood as "slavish." Even in John, the evangelist least amenable to the idea of a servile Jesus, Jesus engaged in behavior that is unexpectedly low-status. The enfleshed God could not escape the shadow of "slavishness," precisely because the structures of enslavement undergirded the world of Jesus and his earliest chroniclers. This was as true for the way that Jesus lived and preached as it was of the way he was born— and, as we shall see, how he died.

The most widely read, translated, and illustrated ancient Greek author is not Homer or Plato: it is the fabulist Aesop. When the printing press was invented, Aesop's fables and a copy of his biography were quickly bundled together and published. The historical Aesop, however, was less popular with his contemporaries in the sixth century BCE. He met his demise, according to legend, after he antagonized the residents of Delphi and they forced him off a cliff. Aesop's biography morphed in the hands of successive authors and editors, but the most consistent detail is that he was enslaved. In one first-century CE version, an unsavory trafficker described him as an "ugly slave," comparable to a turnip with teeth.[9]

By the time of Jesus, Aesop and his fables were experiencing a renaissance, regardless of his appearance to human traffickers. His fables had always been popular and were a staple in childhood education, but in the early days of the Principate he received an extensive biographical treatment. According to tradition, two men, Phaedrus and Babrius, collected, translated, expanded, and revised Aesop's oeuvre, though the fables were always fluid and in a state of continual revision. Perhaps one reason for the flexible deployment of Aesop's fables was his status as a formerly enslaved man. The first two centuries of the Common Era were a period in which elites were beginning to define and reify authorship and the status of the author as the domain of the enslaving elite man. Men without their education and status, they argued, lacked good judgment and the power to author literary texts. In this view, they weren't "real authors," and thus their words were seen as malleable and unprotected. Just as enslaved people were unprotected and used in flexible ways, so too the fables were seen as open to revision and expansion.[10]

It is thus significant that Jesus' favorite teaching method, the parable, has much in common with the fables popularized by Aesop. He speaks in pithy allegorizing stories with a moral takeaway. The best-known New Testament examples, like the parable of the sower, involve agriculture, but others are predicated on economic and social arrangements, divisions of labor, and royal banquets. In their basic shape and concluding applications, Jesus' teachings have much in common with the veiled speech of fables. Although the most ancient Aesopic fables involve animals, many incorporated human actors and often, as the Gospel parables do, concluded with a pithy moral application. One utilitarian sound bite, from a first-century collection, reads: "Brotherly love is the greatest good for all....Even the humble are exalted by it." It almost sounds biblical.[11]

Whether Jesus spoke in parables because he was socially disenfranchised, or simply because they were a popular and effective teaching method, does not really matter. What is more significant is the effect that this rhetorical strategy had—and what it signaled about his identity.

Ancient audiences associated Jesus' mode of speaking with enslaved teachers. Phaedrus, the Latin poet who rewrote many of Aesop's fables and was reportedly once enslaved himself, wrote that enslaved people cannot speak plainly, but must learn to speak obliquely to survive. The fable, he wrote, could only have been devised by an enslaved person. Thus, even though all kinds of elites learned and read fables in antiquity, in the minds of ancient readers, the fable was seen to represent the popular morality of those, both free and unfree, who were disempowered or exploited. It represented, spoke to, and spoke for outsiders. A fabulist, like Jesus, was assumed to be at most sub-elite—if not actually enslaved themselves.[12]

Setting the teachings of Jesus in the bucolic world of the servile fabulist can help explain the flexible ways in which early Christians used parables and Jesus sayings. As historians have noted with respect to non-Christian fables, the moral of a story sometimes stands apart from and even in tension with the fable itself. This concluding moral, known in Greek as an *epimythion*, often stems from the compilers. Different compilers—in this case, Matthew and Luke—can draw diverging conclusions from the same vignette. Sometimes, as is the case in the parable of the ten virgins, these conclusions might seem to modern readers to be at odds with the moral of the parable itself. The story involves ten young women, all of whom fall asleep while waiting for the bridegroom, but the moral of the story is to "stay awake" (Matt. 25:13). The disconnect between the moral and the story has troubled Christian interpreters for almost two thousand years. Why is the moral of the story "stay awake" when some of the young women who fell asleep went unpunished?

As contradictory as this might seem, the practice of drawing different moral lessons from the same story was a fundamental part of the world of fables. In supplying diverging interpretations, the evangelists acted in lockstep with ancient practice. The recognition that Jesus speaks in fables, a manner of speech associated with the disenfranchised and the enslaved, explains two puzzling elements of the parable traditions. First, it clarifies why the conclusions to these stories occasionally conflict with the stories to which they were connected. Second, it illuminates why Matthew, Luke, and subsequent generations of interpreters have Jesus respond to the same parabolic material differently. Interpretive fluidity is a feature, not a bug, of early Christian literature. That openness to varying interpretations was, in turn, connected to the liminal status of the speaker: it was precisely because Jesus was speaking in a "slavish" manner that he could speak so broadly and expansively.

Not only did Jesus speak in a "slavish" fashion, in ways that have troubled generations of readers; he sometimes appears to resemble an enslaved overseer himself. In the minds of enslavers, overseers were proxies who were selected for their loyalty, their character, and their ability to command others. Often they were "home-born" and thus potentially the biological sons of the enslaver. As representatives and extensions of the enslaver, they were supposed to possess the "masterly" knowledge needed to maintain order. Yet there was one thing that overseers did not know that can explain troubling gaps in Jesus' knowledge.[13]

In Mark 13:32, amid a flurry of devastating predictions about the end of the era, Jesus straightforwardly states that "no one knows about that day or hour, not even the angels in heaven, nor the Son, but only the Father." There are many things Jesus does not know in Mark, but Matthew preserves this as a rare moment of ignorance. Luke steadfastly excises it, and the Gospel of John softens its impact by repeatedly stressing that Jesus does know the timetable of his earthly work, his "hour."

The *eschaton* (end of days) is coming, it is only the schedule that is unclear. The first Christians lived perched on the edge of their seats, but as urgency gave way to a wait of undetermined length, they settled into the cushions. All the same, and even from this more agreeable position, the ignorance of Jesus on this point was no small matter. It was clear to ancient and medieval readers of the Bible that the temporal architect was God. From the exemplary workweek in Genesis 1 to the still-under-construction plan for the end of time, a divine tempo and time-table organizes the world. Jesus himself, however, does not appear to have been in the loop.

Jesus' ignorance was a critical element in the protracted debates about Christ's divinity: How can Jesus be God if he doesn't know his own schedule? The question was far from aca-demic. Centuries later, Hilary of Poitiers, a revered Doctor of the Church, narrowly escaped being labeled a heretic over pre-cisely this point. It took a forged retraction to put concerns about his orthodoxy to bed.[14]

The explanation for this situation lies in the world of enslave-ment. Absentee landowners wrestled with the challenge of over-seeing distant estates. Their solution was to capitalize on the discomfort of not knowing. The *dominus* (master) amplified the tension by ensuring that no worker, even the enslaved overseer who served as his proxy, ever knew when they would arrive. Knotty anticipation would keep the worker in a state of busy-ness; no one wanted to be caught on break. Withholding this information even from higher-status, more trusted managerial workers had a practical purpose: if an overseer was taking advantage of their position, the landowner would be able to catch them out. This much is clear from the agricultural para-bles of the Gospels, where tenants and overseers took advantage of the absentee landholder (God). It was the landholder's ability to arrive unexpectedly that kept people on their toes. Even today, Christians recognize the utility of temporal uncertainty in producing good behavior: a raft of semicomic bumper stick-ers warn, JESUS IS COMING, EVERYONE LOOK BUSY.[15]

With a few courageous exceptions, most interpreters give the undeniable language of Christly "slavishness" a wide berth. Here, though, perhaps enslavement can illuminate an otherwise puzzling passage. Perhaps Jesus, like the angels (who are, by all accounts, servile figures), is being presented as God's overseer. He works in the material world far removed from the distant *dominus*, God. As God's representative who was chosen, in accordance with ancient slaveholding practices, precisely because he embodied all the virtues and characteristics of the landholding deity, Jesus acts in God's stead and manages as God would manage. The thing he does not know is exactly the thing that an overseer should not know: the timing of God's return.[16]

Jesus' ignorance of the timing of the resurrection does not — in the world of slaveholding at least — compromise other cherished beliefs about Jesus' identity. In the layered collage of images used by the evangelists, Jesus can easily and logically be enslaved while also being God's only biological son. More than one ancient funerary inscription refers to a deceased "son" who was also "enslaved." Jesus could also be, in the mentality that made all enslaved people part of the body of the "master," seamlessly coterminous with God. Just as a scribe was figured as the hand of the enslaving author, so too an overseer was part of their "lord" (*kurios*). We might — we should — object on ethical grounds, but the despotic interchangeability of the body of the enslaved person and their slaveholder offers — in ancient terms — a philosophically useful explanation of the relationship between Father and Son. Divine identity is incompatible with enslavement only if one thinks that enslaved people are less valuable than other people.[17]

We might contrast this information gap with Jesus' deft — and equally "slavish" — control of time and space elsewhere in the Gospel of Mark. In journeying to his death in Jerusalem, Jesus meanders around the ancient Galilee. The circuitousness of his route is so striking that some scholars have argued that the authors of Mark must have been foreigners who did not know the geography of the region. But there is another explanation. As recent scholarship on transatlantic slavery has argued, dawdling and meandering are forms of hidden resistance to power and domination. Given Jesus' reluctance to die, we could view his actions as a mild form of servile resistance. It is an attempt to follow his own rhythm. The meandering of Jesus is done quietly: it flies under the radar, as the art of enslaved resistance must if it is to go unpunished. He arrives on time and accedes to the will of his Father in the Garden of Gethsemane, but the footsteps that others are supposed to follow do not chart a straight course. This is the "rival geography," as American feminist historian Stephanie Camp has called it, of enslaved autonomy. Enslaved agency may reside in such subtle details: the authors present a Messiah who navigates the structures of enslavement, resisting them where he can. Though Jesus is obedient to the will of his Father, God, his reluctance is on full display. In recognizing this, Mark foregrounds an ambivalent model of enslaved obedience and highlights the violence of the approaching crucifixion.[18]

Most readers of the Gospels, including most ancient readers, already knew that Jesus met his end on the cross before they heard his story read. As familiar as crucifixion might seem, the horror of it is lost on modern readers. Crucifixion was engineered to create the maximum amount of pain and suffering as a spectacle for others to watch. Among humans (for the Romans sometimes crucified dogs), scourging and crucifixion, the tortures endured by Jesus, were reserved for enslaved people as well as traitors who, through their actions, had forfeited the rights of a freeborn person. A case in point: after Jesus, arguably the best-known instance of crucifixion was the mass execution of the followers of the self-liberated Spartacus a century and some earlier. As a punishment for disobedience, crucifixion is gro-tesquely apropos: its obscene mechanics manipulate the victim out of humanity and into a legible form of the torturer's choos-ing. The preacher who meandered through the Galilee is now pulled taut on the straight and narrow beam. The meaning of the writing was clear: the powerful would make crooked things straight. Immobilization forestalled the possibility of resistance as the last gasps of breath — and any residual revolutionary potential — were squeezed from an exhausted frame. Like an insect in the hands of a collector, Jesus was stripped, pinned, labeled for consumption, and mounted high for display. This is the Roman way to kill: in a public display of power that compul-sively constrains, humiliates, and creates order.[19]

Crucifixion thus had a special place in the despotic toolbox. As a euphemism for intense pain in both Latin (*cruciare*) and English (*excruciating*), it was only selectively employed for the worst kinds of agony. There was a begrudging, or perhaps wary, respect for its particularity. It was used for the most heinous crimes, like treason, as well as more petty "crimes" committed by enslaved people. Historically speaking, Jesus was likely found guilty of sedition by Pontius Pilate, but for those who read his story, this demeaning death was more vividly associated with enslaved people. By the first century CE, the phrases "go hang on a cross" and "cross-bearer" were insults bandied between enslaved characters in Roman comedy. Historians have hypothesized that the writing and performance of these comedies were one place in which enslaved actors exercised agency. Humor metabolizes atrocity.[20]

The resonances with enslaved people's suffering run deeper, however. The shape of the Gospel of Mark has been described as a passion narrative with an extended introduction: it gallops through the healing stories and teaching moments only to slow as the reader reaches Jesus' final days. To most ancient (and many modern) audience members, Jesus' final words from the cross sounded defeated and disillusioned. Of course, this was the point: manufacturing despair was the purpose of this form of punishment. What proved problematic for some Jesus follow-ers and pagan critics of Christianity was Jesus' demeanor through-out his trial and torture. Roman heroes—the kind worthy of marble statues and lasting memorialization—ended their lives with composure and self-control. They appeared immune to the efforts of their torturers. Even Iphigenia, the daughter of Agamem-non, after being tricked into becoming a sacrificial offering at Aulis, is said to have bravely embraced her fate as she awaited her death. Jesus, by comparison, ricocheted between passivity and despair. During his trial he stayed silent—almost as if, like an enslaved person, he had been trained to hold his tongue.[21]

As he journeys from the trial to the crucifixion, reality moves into view. Jesus feels. Having been flogged, he needs help carrying the cross to Golgotha. His final words in Mark—"My God, my God, why have you abandoned me?"—are a desperate cry. If anyone could have expected cosmic partiality, it was Jesus, and the deadweight of expiring hope tugs at the scene. Jesus does not die with a clever parting quip, like Socrates, or with steely self-control, like Iphigenia; he dies without composure, absent strength, and seemingly in the throes of an existential crisis.

Although some interpreters—like Latin American libera-tion theologian Jon Sobrino and Black liberation theologian James Cone—have heard and digested this message and con-nected it to their own experiences of violence and precarity, most do not. Appalled by the violence, scholars try to slip under the text's skin to root around in the historical innards: to dis-cuss the evangelist's sources, historical practices, scriptural intertexts, and theological messages. Readers busy themselves with this important work as they hurry past the face of despair. Even the bystanders—who are there for the raw show—can't tolerate the sound of unglued subjectivity. Did they mishear? Did he call for his God (*Eloi*) or was he asking the biblical prophet Elijah (*Elian*) for help?[22]

This is the barbarism that the coauthors of Mark insist that readers directly confront: not, as Susan Sontag has written, at a remove, as passive "tourists of reality," experiencing "the suffering of others at a distance, denuded of its raw power." Some have argued that Mark is the product of collective memory and, if so, the crucifixion was seared into the template. Mark wants to communicate the pain with shocking honesty: he wants readers to smell the condemned man's sweat and blood and to notice the vultures circling above his head. Jesus is no sanitized literary hero whose lack of sensibility distances him and the reader from suffering. He is, instead, a palpable example of the effects of torture. For enslaved people who had witnessed, experienced, or feared such mistreatment, the death of Jesus in Mark is striking for its willingness to speak the bloody truths about their mistreatment. The Gospel, and its likely enslaved coauthor, do not draw a veil over the unpleasantness.[23]

On the contrary, to the readers and auditors of the Gospel, the splitting of subjectivity is immediately mirrored by fissures in the sacred and natural order. First, the temple curtain—the material barrier between the sacred temple spaces occupied by priests and the dwelling place of God's presence that, Josephus writes, was embroidered with an image of the cosmos—was torn in two. Then the sun darkened. The eclipse is a sign, legible to those who read signs, that the seemingly stable work of creation was being upended. The crowning achievement of God was torn apart by the injustice. Looking back on things, the Gospel was always about splitting: the opening quotation from

Isaiah speaks of a path dividing the valleys. The heavens ripped open at the baptism and transfiguration anticipate this moment. Just because you have foreknowledge, as the Markan Jesus and the audience of the Gospel clearly did, doesn't mean that you are prepared. That's the point.

Eclipses are dramatic events, even more so to ancient people, who saw them as divine communication. God responds. But even the darkening of the sky could not overshadow the potency of the crucifixion. The audience remains in the stickiness of torture's horror. It spoke from, to, and with them. In specifying that the bodies be removed that day because of the religious holiday, Mark once again obliquely refers to the fate of enslaved victims. Unless they died swiftly, as an inscription from Puteoli made clear, unfree men and women were routinely left on display overnight. Had it not been a holiday, Mark hints, Jesus might have been treated similarly. Anyone who heard of his demise would have associated his scourging and crucifixion with criminality and slavery: his story makes visible and large the liminality and dehumanization of enslaved people. It tells an unthinkable history in which marginalized, enslaved death overpowers even a celestial event.

For the audience, the fissure in the cosmos creates space, a moment for real mourning: for Jesus and for the thousands of enslaved deaths that were never grieved, marked, or even recognized. Enslaved Romans, particularly women, were active participants in the funerary rites of enslavers. They were called upon to wail and lament for others even as they were deprived of the same emotional space for themselves and their loved ones. But these coerced displays of grief provided opportunities for the expression of other sorrows and traumatic experiences. The gospel story and its coauthors here create a vacuum for readers and auditors to do the same: to craft their own spaces for mourning and belonging.[24]

The idea that some early Christians, like Mark, who were themselves likely enslaved, used the structures of enslavement to talk
about who Jesus was, will worry some readers. What does this
mean, some might wonder, for theological claims about his identity? Does the potential presentation of Jesus as "slavish" at
various junctures compromise anything about the way later generations of Christians, including modern Christians, have
talked about his status as God and the Son of God? It is worth
noting at the outset that the more familiar language that is used
to describe Jesus has its own problems. As womanist biblical
scholar and Episcopal priest Wil Gafney has shown, in antiquity the language of kingship—both for God and for Jesus—
invoked the unrestrained power of men who slaughtered
without conscience. In the present, it gestures to an arbitrary
elitist paradigm. Divine monarchs should concern readers as
well.[25]

Later generations of philosophically inclined Christians
pressed into the metaphysical difficulties that a God-man presents; could God become a human being without compromising
something about its God-ness? Could humanity and divinity
blend into a single person? How would this process work? As
they did so, the idea of a servile Jesus and, indeed, many human
moments in Jesus' biography became increasingly difficult to
reconcile with divinity. But for the evangelists and their enslaved
collaborators, the importance of the "slavishness" of Jesus was
persistent. For modern readers, as one scholar has argued, it
may do valuable ethical work. In the parables of the Gospel of
Matthew, God is unambiguously an enslaving estate owner and
Jesus is his son and thus an heir. That Jesus is presented as both
slaveholder and enslaved complicates how people think about
slavery. It resists the ethically questionable impulse to naturalize

the barbarism of slaveholding as an organic feature of the created world. No one can straightforwardly claim that God is a slaveholder or that slaveholding is part of the divine order when God chose to become incarnate as a servile member of society.[26]

These are theological questions, not historical ones. Historically speaking, it is famously difficult to piece together facts about the life of Jesus of Nazareth from the Gospels. What is clear, however, is that he was remembered and memorialized in this way by early generations of followers who themselves may have been enslaved and trafficked. This is particularly true with respect to the Gospel of Mark, the first life of Jesus. It is not insignificant that Mark himself was remembered as a servile secretary. But even if the Mark of tradition is a fiction, there was someone like Mark who helped write this story, just as there were servile collaborators whose talents and voices helped craft all early Christian literature.

The role of these enslaved collaborators in shaping the New Testament, moreover, was not confined to the act of writing itself. Inscription gave the message and story of Jesus a kind of permanence, allowing it to move apart from any individual apostle or Christian teacher, but the gospel still needed people. The written gospel only spread and survived because there were people to carry it, copy it, and read it aloud in performance for others.

PART II

MESSENGERS
AND
CRAFTSMEN

CHAPTER FOUR

MESSENGERS OF GOD

If fortune favors the bold, then history tends to turn its nose up at the cautious. Perhaps it is for this reason that the apostle Thomas has a mixed reputation. A bit player in the Gospels as a whole, he became a central figure in the Gospel of John's account of the chaotic days after the crucifixion. Thomas was absent when the resurrected Jesus first appeared to the disciples in the upper room and was, understandably, skeptical about the claims of his friends. Maybe Thomas thought they were in denial, that their judgment had been distorted by grief, that they had seen a ghost, or that they were simply mistaken. But whatever his reasoning, the more reserved Thomas needed something beyond the effervescent excitement of his friends to believe in a resurrected corpse. Even though, upon being confronted by the risen Christ, he instantly believed, the nickname Doubting Thomas has stuck. This turn of events seems particularly unfair given what legend says happened to him next.

A second-century narrative known as the *Acts of Thomas* imagines a scriptural afterlife in which Thomas traveled to India as a missionary. After Jesus' resurrection, the apostles drew lots to see where each would go next. Thomas, finding himself assigned to India, was immediately resistant. His first excuse, that he was too physically fragile, quickly wore down to a question: how could a Hebrew preach among the people of India? At the time India was considered—at least by those in the Roman Mediterranean—to be both the farthest limit of the world and a valuable long-distance trading partner. It was well-known for luxury spices, dyes, and precious stones, and was equally renowned for celebrated specialists in medicine, philosophy, and magic. Though Thomas claimed he was worried about xenophobia, he had reason to feel intimidated. He had good material—the marvelous exploits of the gospels radiate in their retelling—but he still worried. In a land where griffins roamed and monkeys were said to harvest pepper, Thomas's message about a resurrected wonder-working savior would not necessarily look so special.[1]

Jesus' response, according to this second-century source, was to sell Thomas, marketing him as a carpenter. His new owner was an Indian merchant named Abbanes, an agent of Gundaphorus, king of India, and the sale was a formal one: Abbanes paid in silver and Jesus wrote up the deed of sale that certified the transaction. This Jesus is a lawyer, as well as—quite shockingly for us—a human trafficker.

The story is a testimony to Thomas's faith that his sudden enslavement by Jesus did not dampen his devotion. When Abbanes conscientiously confirmed that Thomas had not been kidnapped, the apostle could only reply, truthfully and in words that revealed the messiness of language about God, "Yes, he is my Enslaver." (The word *kurios* or "lord" was used for enslavers, as a title for Jesus in the New Testament, and as a name for God in the Greek translation of the Hebrew Bible.) By the following morning, Thomas was resigned to his lot as an enslaved person. Channeling Jesus in the Garden of Gethsemane, he promised to subsume his wishes into those of his divine "master": "I will go where you will, Lord Jesus, your will be done."

Though it was possible to journey from Jerusalem to India in the first century CE by caravanning overland through the highlands of ancient Iran, following the footsteps of Alexander the Great, it was a prohibitively expensive trip. Elite appetites for Indian goods had forced open the mouth of the Red Sea ports such that by the first century there was a bustling maritime trade. For centuries, Arabian sea captains had known how to ride the monsoon winds all the way to the western coast of India. Roman traders had caught on. By the time Thomas was sold into slavery as a carpenter, merchants took the spice route from the port of Myos Hormos in Egypt, down the channel between Egypt and Ethiopia, around the Arabian Peninsula, and across the Arabian Sea to India. If the winds were favorable, as they were for Thomas, they could carry you from the silt-laden ports of the Indus delta to the southern tip of the Indian peninsula, where the highest-quality ivory, stones, and pearls could be found. Travel was dangerous—pirates, shipwrecks, bandits, hunger, and thirst were real threats—but India's most delicious export, the rough pearls of the humble black pepper, made the risk worthwhile.

A scene from a third-century CE sarcophagus showing the dangers of traveling on turbulent seas. A man in the center has been tossed overboard.

Enslavement was thus only the beginning of Thomas's travails. Once he docked in India—in the otherwise unknown royal city of Andrapolis—Thomas found himself an outsider. Unlike his apostolic peers in Aramaic-speaking Syria or Greek-speaking Turkey, he couldn't cobble together phrases, much less preach in the dominant language. As an involuntary immigrant, he did not wield the social cachet that, say, an educated Greek could in first-century Rome or that an English immigrant to the United States can today. Today, travelers encounter new space both through the experience of travel and through their carto-graphic memories of the world. Thomas, however, was concep-tually adrift. He was not equipped for linguistic or cultural translation. There were no mental maps to orient himself: Ptol-emy, the inventor of longitude and latitude, had located much of India east of China in what is currently known as the Pacific Ocean. Thomas was in uncharted territory and here—as every-where for enslaved people—there were dragons.

Wherever they found themselves, enslaved messengers abroad were exposed and vulnerable. With no enslaver from whom to derive a modicum of protection, they might be harassed, abused, or assaulted. When Thomas reached India, he was seated at a dinner party at which an enslaved Hebrew musician performed for the group. Flutists were sexualized in antiquity and the apos-tle demurely averted his eyes. An enslaved cupbearer slapped him for the perceived insult, but none of those present responded. There is no empathetic wince or narrative pause for the out-of-place Thomas; thoughtless violence against liminal individuals was altogether unremarkable.[2]

The story of Thomas is unusual, however, because it makes enslaved messengers visible to Christian readers. Though the survival of the story is predicated on his status as an apostle, it reveals an often ignored truth about ancient communication and the spread of Christianity.

Over longer distances, it was servile letter carriers (*tabellarii*) and merchants, only some of whose names are known to us, who fostered contact between different groups of Jesus followers and disseminated the literary artifacts of early churches. Specially trained envoys, both enslaved and freedmen, served as interpreters of the message. These people nurtured the connections between itinerant leaders and their flocks. As they did so, their words flowed freely into the reservoir of Christian interpretive tradition. They were vital connections between senders and recipients, the people whose work held together the various outposts of what would later be called the Universal Church.

There is a lengthy intellectual tradition that attempts to plot the expansion, rise, and spread of Christianity from its beginnings in the Galilee to its recruitment of the emperor Constantine and the related "conquest" of the Roman Empire. The improbability of Christianity's success has always been part of its rhetorical power; how could this small group of poorly educated misfits have succeeded against such odds without divine favor, supernatural support, and an indisputable conviction in the truth of their message? I cannot pretend to have the whole answer, but the story of the spread of Christianity as it is conventionally told in its many forms is too narrowly focused: it loses sight of all but the chief (mainly male) apostles and intellectual figures. Anonymous people are replaced by important texts. Yet Christianity did not only succeed because of authorized delegates, it was spread by tavern-keepers, construction workers, barmaids, dry cleaners, delivery girls, elementary schoolteachers, and merchant sailors. Though some of these had social credentials, many did not. Some, perhaps most, of these invisible actors were enslaved, formerly enslaved, or socially disenfranchised. Read the earliest life of Jesus closely, and it is clear that it was the unofficial evangelizing efforts of anonymous bystanders and former patients who did the most to spread the good news. They resisted even messianic attempts to constrain their speech and social structures that denied their personhood. These people were surely among the first Christian missionaries.

Thomas was trafficked abroad, but the same dangers faced those who worked as couriers and official messengers over shorter distances. Recognizing this, some sent multiple messengers bearing the same set of instructions, to ensure that at least one copy reached its destination. Though official envoys were supposed to be well received, the warmth of their reception depended on the political climate. A Greek translator who conveyed the wishes of the Persian embassy to the Athenians was put to death for daring to put the audacious demands of the "barbarians" into the "eloquent" Greek tongue. An apocryphal tale about Alexander the Great reports that he came close to crucifying messengers from the Persian ruler Darius. Some suffered as collateral damage. In the first century CE, a wealthy merchant from Puteoli petitioned for compensation when his ship was pirated, his merchandise stolen, and his freedmen executed.[3]

Even when entangled in the smaller stakes of personal diplomacy, messengers were in a precarious position. A tale involving incest told by Ovid finds an innocent courier physically threatened and accused of wrongdoing simply for delivering a love letter. According to some rabbinic texts, a man who divorced his wife was permitted to inscribe the *get* (certificate of divorce) on "the hand of the slave" who delivered it. As the "document" had to remain in her possession, the enslaved worker did as well. She may have been pleased by the gift, but she might equally have been enraged. Trans-historically, people have tended to use unwelcome messengers for target practice.[4]

In the parables of Jesus, kings, landowners, and powerful men dispatch enslaved workers to their subjects, acquaintances, and tenants, who brutalize, beat, violate, and kill them. In the Gospels, these are blink-and-you-miss-them moments: the messengers are narrative devices whose deaths advance the plot. The story does not linger on the broken bodies of the messengers or explain the logic of the violence. The brevity of description shows us that ancient audiences did not balk at such stories. With such blasé accounts of the perils of his vocation, it is no wonder that Thomas worried.

More generally, travel was unpleasant. No amount of money could shield you from the uncomfortable jerkiness of a litter, the sharp changes in temperature and climate, the stickiness of the journey, or the dustiness of the road. While friends and family members might have served as letter carriers if they happened to be going that way, subordinated workers were the backbone of the communications system, sometimes traveling up to fifty miles a day. The unpleasant tasks of debt collection, securing rents, and collecting remuneration were outsourced. Household staff protected the time of enslavers by delivering messages around town, issuing invitations to dinner, and shuttling between the market and the home. News, both personal and public, was relayed through a network of enslaved workers who shared stories in the marketplace, delivered messages, transported goods, and advertised the professional services of others. Messages and messengers jostled unceremoniously along between imported fabrics and fish oil.[5]

To us, both "good news" and "gospel" (both translations of the same Greek word) have a proprietary Christian flavor, but to ancient hearers the resonance was very different. It conjured ideas of an official proclamation, or news report: the kind of information that was dispatched to the major cities in the Empire and hammered into stone to announce military victories, political developments, or administrative innovations. The universalism of these proclamations masked an imperial undercurrent.

These were the kind of messages to which one *had* to attend. In the hands of second-century Christians, the term began to crystallize in another form as the title of the literary biographies of Jesus, but it retained a certain flexibility: the gospel was also the message enshrined in the texts. It could be delivered orally from memory or from a written text, but whether carried on the person or in the mind, it was conceptually the same announcement.

Thankfully for Thomas, Jesus had prepared the disciples for a life on the road. He called them to be not just students (or disciples) but also messengers (or apostles), and though the terminology carried connotations of ambassadorial work, it was clear they were on a different path. Alongside other members of the Twelve, Jesus gave Thomas power and authority to spread the news of the coming Kingdom. In Luke 9–10, he sent first a small group of messengers and then a larger mass of seventy to lubricate the wheels of sociability in advance of his arrival. The task asked of his disciples was, by Jesus' own admission, a difficult one: He likened them to "lambs among wolves" (Luke 10:3). They were expected to travel simply — no staff, change of clothes, or money was permissible — but they would receive, as was customary for messengers, sustenance and (presumably, though it is not noted in Luke) housing for their services.

According to one early Christian text known as the *Teaching of the Twelve Apostles* (or *Didache*), Christian travelers were supplied with no more than two or three nights of food and lodging. This hospitality, while generous, was only extended to those travelers who had been accredited with letters of introduction and personal recommendations. More charismatic apostles, who prophesied in the Spirit, and were received as if they were "the Lord himself," were swiftly ejected from the community. The text is clear-eyed about the risk of financial exploitation, and thus the good missionary, like the caricatured "running slave" of Roman literature, was constantly on the move.[6]

Religious messengers were hardly a Christian innovation. In his second-century satirical biography of the wonder-worker Alexander, Lucian of Samosata described something similar. Alexander dispatched representatives, who were almost certainly enslaved, to advertise the shrine he had established to the snake-god Glycon. Though Lucian depicted this oracle as nothing more than a sock puppet, Alexander was a genuine ancient celebrity whose portrait graced local coins. Like the Seventy in Luke 10, these emissaries relayed stories of Alexander's prophetic gifts; bragged about his ability to identify "runaway slaves" and robbers; and celebrated his successes in curing the sick and raising the dead. If these representatives had been Christians, they would surely be called missionaries. To the casual ancient viewer, however, both they and Christian apostles were messenger-heralds and part of a larger network of people who disseminated news at the orders of others.

Sometime in the summer of 116, a Christian by the name of Burrhus was sent by the assemblies of Christians in Ephesus and Smyrna to meet the elderly bishop Ignatius of Antioch. Formally, he was dispatched as a letter carrier and perhaps also a secretary. Ignatius had been sentenced to death and was being transported to Rome, the Eternal City, under armed guard. The bishop was a prisoner en route to his execution, but in his own mind Ignatius saw the journey as something more. He pictured himself as an ambassadorial figure modeling Christ for the Christians he encountered along the way, but that lofty sentiment was not shared by his captors. Thus, what would have been a short sea voyage became a protracted overland journey as they stopped to accomplish other tasks. Over several months, the ten soldiers who had custody of him zigzagged across central Turkey, picking up other prisoners and pausing to conduct other business. Though the stops in Smyrna and Philadelphia slowed the soldiers' progress, Burrhus still had to rush to intercept his fellow Christian on the road. He relied on his navigational and networking skills to locate the group, all the while mentally rehearsing both the messages he was supposed to deliver and the directions he had received. Having found Ignatius and the rest of the party on the northern road that ran through Philadelphia—rather than the southern route, which Burrhus surely thought would have been vastly more convenient—he settled into his role as amanuensis, courier, and general assistant to Ignatius. Certainly he was good at it.[7]

We do not know much about Burrhus, but his name hints at servile origins and status. What is clear is that he was able to distinguish himself in Ignatius's eyes; so much so that his role in the composition and delivery of two extant letters is noted in their conclusions. Though an agreement between the Ephesian and Smyrnaean Christians had covered the cost of Burrhus's travel to Smyrna (if not also the income lost by his absence), money was tight. Ignatius's *Letter to the Ephesians* includes a request that Burrhus continue to stay with him because the Smyrnaeans were not willing to foot the whole bill. That Burrhus could not make the decisions for himself might suggest that he was not at liberty to do so. Perhaps he did not have the requisite financial resources or, perhaps, as a servile worker, he was not in control of his own movement. Though it might seem as if enslaved readers would have used the opportunity of long-distance courier work to liberate themselves, this rarely occurred. Not only was the punishment for "running away" severe; enslaved letter carriers had friends, romantic partners, and children to whom they wished to return. In either case, Ignatius presented Burrhus not as an individual, but rather as a reflection of the communities that financially backed him: he is a "word [or pledge] of honor" and a "copy" of their love. The Ephesians must have agreed to the request, as Burrhus accompanied Ignatius at least as far as the northern port of Alexandria Troas, an almost ten-day journey on foot. It is there that his trail goes cold.[8]

Burrhus was not unique. Once he joined the party, he met Crocus, the probable carrier of Ignatius's *Letter to the Romans*, but unlike some of the anonymous messengers, neither of these men were just couriers. Their roles were expansive and intimate—Ignatius says that they "refreshed" him "in every way." The delicate vagueness of the language obscures the range of practical assistance they provided. Presumably they arrived with a meager amount of money that they used to support themselves and to improve Ignatius's circumstances through bribery and the acquisition of provisions. Burrhus had to form contacts, scout the local markets for food and writing supplies, negotiate with the soldiers who guarded Ignatius, and identify travelers who might be sympathetic and reliable enough to pass on messages in Antioch, Ephesus, or Smyrna. If they stayed in one place and money ran short, then he, like those who accompanied college-aged elites to advanced education in Athens, would have found work to support them. All these roles required ingenuity, diplomacy, and a subtle understanding of timing. If Burrhus approached the guards at the wrong moment, say after a long night of drinking, they might cut off access to their prisoner or confiscate food and writing supplies.[9]

Ignatius was an old man when he was arrested, and the journey—even by donkey or an unglamorous oxcart, if such a thing was permitted for a shackled prisoner—was difficult. It is likely that he needed physical assistance and that every form of refreshment included more intimate caretaking tasks that were embarrassing to speak about. This was heroic work.[10]

Burrhus's companionship in Ignatius's final months was a luxury that placed something of a financial burden on the

This early-third-century relief from Smyrna (modern Turkey) shows an enslaved prisoner being transported in chains by Roman soldiers. Ignatius refers to himself as shackled in several of his letters.

assemblies in Ephesus and Smyrna, but this was one of many contexts in which it was preferable to have a well-educated worker serving as a messenger. Children could deliver goods, dinner invitations, or brief messages inscribed on ostraca (clay shards), but a more experienced messenger was important when it came to exchanging books or delivering letters. The letters that followed and preceded Ignatius's arrivals and departures were copied and shared between different assemblies, and this process involved literary skills beyond locating the correct address. Although Ignatius might appear to be a special case, some ancient elites acquired their books by sending copyists to consult and duplicate editions owned by their friends. The writer of a fifth-century CE letter from Hermopolis in Egypt noted that he had sent Elias, "the school master's slave," to return a book. As he also requested copies of a collection of hard-to-come-by commentaries, it is likely that Elias remained there to identify the books and, possibly, copy them himself. Roman elites were voracious collectors and book exchange worked as an ancient form of publication. As a result, these well-educated messenger-copyists might work locally or over great distances as part of a network of long-distance lending libraries.[11]

If travel was dangerous for the courier, publication was not risk-free for the sender either. What if the recipient did not like the work or, worse, misunderstood it? Even among friends such things could happen. After a night of adrenaline-filled and alcohol-fueled co-writing with his friend Calvus, Catullus (circa 84–54 BCE) rose, exhausted, and composed one last poem alone. The sudden shift from collaborator to lone author elicited a burst of self-doubt: what if Calvus hated his poem? What if, as Catullus and Calvus had so often done to their friend Suffenus, Calvus scoffed at his offering and mocked it with other members of their circle? In the harsh light of day, the competitive barbs that dotted the mantle of Roman elite friendship were easy to make out; Catullus felt remorseful about publicly sharing his work.[12]

Peeking out from under the surface of ancient Roman conversations about writing are worries about control. Just as enslaved workers were shared among friends for use or pleasure, so too could books be shared within a trusted circle of friends. Once written, however, the book went out into the world independent of the author. The "master's" oversight ended at the doorway. This is one reason that Roman elites sent or even gifted enslaved workers along with their writings.

There was a distinct advantage to sending a piece of writing along with an enslaved messenger. Beyond the normal social benefits derived from gift-giving, the two—book and enslaved reader—were mutually reinforcing. The letter-carrier-turned-reader could be schooled to read the book with the correct intonation. Then, armed with information about the sender's intentions, they could watch for the furrowed brows of confusion and disagreement and, after the reading, provide their audience with additional examples and any sensitive information that might strengthen the message.

The role involved more than supplementary information and messages. Channeling the sender was a full-bodied exercise. Non-Christian writers pictured oral delivery as a kind of performance, a form of what might be called method acting. Cicero, for example, reported to his friend Cornificius that the mutual acquaintance who delivered his letter—not an enslaved person, as far as we know, but a messenger who fulfilled the same function here—"did more than convey to me your thoughts and words; I swear to you, there was not a single expression of your face that he did not make vivid to me."[13]

For our condemned traveler and his companion, the same process of imitation and translation now played out. After some time tending to Ignatius's needs, observing his facial expressions, and absorbing his speech patterns, Burrhus was prepared to serve as an impersonator. He was already, Ignatius said, a "copy" of Ephesian devotion, so Ignatius likely trusted him to mirror his intentions with equal skill.[14]

✝

Like Ignatius, the apostle Paul was not universally well-liked and found himself competing with and undermined by other Christians. The situation made trusted couriers like Burrhus essential to his work. Paul's message of salvation was complicated and the groups to which he wrote had disappointingly short attention spans. It seemed to him that as soon as he left one city, his followers there immediately latched on to the next missionary to come along. The reports of communities that had fractured or deviated from his instructions were lodged in Paul's mind. Though his sights were set on Rome and Spain, and he felt com- pelled to push further westwards, he also felt torn: the disagree- ments in his assemblies burrowed into his conscience. A letter only worked if the messenger could close the gap that now sepa- rated him from his assemblies.[15]

Only the most trusted of messengers could manifest Paul's presence and intentions to the groups of early Christ followers whom he had once shepherded, but who were now at some remove. Then as now, tone was hard to convey from a distance, especially in the context of a strained relationship. If Catullus had reason to worry about embarrassment after his night of wine-soaked writing, Paul—and Ignatius along with him— were in more delicate situations. In due course they would emerge as titans in Christian history, but in the moment they were innocent of the future.

Amplifying the problem was the sense of urgency that coursed through Paul's veins. Judgment Day was just over the horizon, and, in his own mind, Paul was part of a final generation freneti- cally working to the last minute to reach as many potential con- verts as possible. A frantic missive that was supposed to be conciliatory might accidentally inflame tensions further. A good messenger, someone who knew and understood him, could smooth any unintended sharpness, conjure the fiction of his presence, and act as a living and breathing copy of his arguments and emotions. If the messenger did their job, it would be almost as if Paul himself was there in body as well as spirit (Col. 2:5).

For the couriers themselves—Timothy, Titus, Onesimus, Tychicus, Epaphroditus, and Phoebe—the task was a form of imitation and self-erasure. The good messenger lived a kind of life of mimicry that allowed the audiences to imagine themselves in the presence of the sender. For Paul, they were part of a hierarchical chain. Each messenger represented the ultimate authority: God sends Christ, who in turn sends Paul as his ambassador (2 Cor. 5:20), who himself dispatches emissaries. As the reader passes down the chain, the social status of these human ciphers grows obscure, but their role remains the same.[16]

The work of these messengers was not mechanistic; it was active and responsive, and involved an ability to translate texts into different cultural registers. Some recipients may have preferred digestible summaries to the dense letters; others may have needed some extra help unpacking their meaning. Just as today ministers guide the interpretation of impenetrable or confusing biblical passages during their homilies, so too did messengers in ancient times serve as interpretive guides for audience members. They were not just couriers; they were leaders who cemented emotional ties. They conjured the presence of the author with their voices, expressions, and hand gestures. They authenticated, validated, and answered for the message itself. In a very real sense, the messenger was the message.[17]

Though letter carriers could help secure the meaning of a written text, ancient messenger services were slow, and they had faster, low-status — even "slavish" — rivals that worked, in some ways, to Christianity's advantage. Until the invention of the telegraph, messages, whether oral or textual, were tethered to the material world. They could not move faster than the messenger. A relay, such as that devised by the Persians, or the imperial post (an invention of the emperor Augustus that allowed a single messenger on official business to change horses) could expedite things slightly. Roman engineering produced an extensive web of roads that knit the Empire together, but the message still could not move faster than human conveyance. Anchors, hooves, and feet could drag; winds could rebel; bodies grew sick; and grim obstacles presented themselves. Upon arrival, however, the tempo changed, and the message was no longer tied to the steady rhythm of the messenger's footsteps: It metamorphosed and took flight. Once ships docked in the harbor, writes Plutarch, words were carried away on the breath expelled by lips. The ships that anchored at Alexandria in Egypt, or Ostia in Italy, carried textiles, grain, and rumors unloaded by merchants and sailors eager to share their colorful stories in local taverns.[18]

The contrast between the belabored journey of the authentic official messenger and the breeziness of word of mouth was a source of frustration for ancient elites. They fantasized about more efficient modes of delivery and imagined supernatural winged couriers like Hermes and Gabriel, but in truth only low-status forms of communication like rumor and gossip could act with anything approaching the efficiency of a mythical being. Somehow news of wartime victories and defeats moved ahead of official messengers, spontaneously spreading through the crowd before melting away. Handwritten letters authenticated by reliable couriers might be the gold standard, but they were weighed down by their own materiality. Rumors, on the other hand, were unencumbered. Authorless words flew throughout the ancient city, were scratched onto walls as graffiti, and were whispered between errand boys on the street.

In the poetry of Virgil, a personified Rumor (*fama*) was described as a monstrous bird covered in eyes, ears, and tongues; she delighted in spreading reports of things that both had and had not happened. And this, to those in positions of authority, especially, was the problem: Rumor had no source or author and was impossible to examine. It was not that Rumor—or her sisters, Hearsay and Gossip—were necessarily wrong, but that they had no authority to back them up. Gossip was associated with women, "effeminate men," the elderly, and unfree people. It was connected to moral failings like drunkenness, overindulgence, undereducation, and frivolity. Those who cannot handle the rigors of philosophical conversation, wrote Plutarch, steer the conversation to foolish talk. This, he added, is the kind of thing that "slaves and silly women of the streets do." The rhetoric of gossip is clear: anyone who engaged in it was morally suspect and incapable of good judgment.[19]

Hidden beneath the social networks of elites, therefore, were alternative social circles in which unsanctioned conversation could flourish. They were built up over time during exchanges in the marketplace, in bookstores, in courtyards, in perfumiers' shops, or at street crossings. Perhaps Paul, who trafficked in animal skins, traded stories with the enslaved bookmakers who browsed his holdings as they shopped for raw materials. The errands that took enslaved workers out of the house allowed them to form small sympathetic alliances, intimate bonds, and looser social ties.

Hints of these relationships appear in a dark first-century anecdote from Martial. An emaciated boy whose corpulent enslaver had dislocated his ankle appealed to four muscular and branded funerary workers for help. The boy's meager thighs could not support the man's weight alone. The attendants unceremoniously dropped the corpse they were carrying, hoisted the slightly injured enslaver onto the bier, and proceeded on their way, presumably to the funeral pyre. Readers are left to infer that the slaveholder met an unpleasantly hot and smoky end. The farcical story reflects elite fears that workers plotted among themselves, but it may direct us to a lived reality: like any of us, unfree people formed unpredictable relationships. A chance encounter at a market stall could blossom into something substantive. Those accidental relationships were critical to the spread of Christianity.[20]

According to pagan critics, the Christianity of the first and second centuries was the superstition of "women and slaves." The

philosopher Celsus depicted Christianity as the product of precisely the kind of illicit conversation that enslavers feared.
According to him, it was spread by low-status and poorly educated teachers who targeted women and children, whispering
that they should reject the authority and values of their fathers
and formal instructors. It spread in the storefronts of cobblers,
launderers, and woolworkers, who, he implies, evangelized when
they made deliveries to private homes and villas. These were
professions that employed a high proportion of enslaved and
formerly enslaved workers. While fulfilling their day-to-day
professional obligations, Celsus alleged, some members of the
urban service industry delivered Christian philosophy along
with laundered garments.[21]

In Celsus's imagination, Christianity lived in the doorways
of artisanal workshops and in the unmastered spaces of the
home. In non-Christian households, perhaps these spaces were
the small pockets that were out of the sight line of the enslaver
by day, or the flexible communal spaces that domestic attendants slept in at night. Tacitus suggests that enslaved public
workers—those in charge of caring for the temples and such—
were housed together; Pliny the Younger had literate children
spend their nights on the floor of the school he had built on his
property. Archaeological evidence suggests that some spent
their nights in subterranean chambers underneath the Forum of
Nerva in Rome, and excavations from Pompeii hint that some
domestic staff were housed on the outskirts of the city alongside
the farmhands. Many more roomed together in the tinderbox
apartments above workshops or on the floors of the stores themselves. Though enslaved workers had little free time, the complaints about the so-called laziness of urban workers suggest
that there were opportunities for conversation, religious engagement, and love. Funerary inscriptions attest to the romantic
relationships that blossomed between enslaved members of

different households. An inscription set up in the first century CE by a baker named P. Ponticus Iucundus, a freedman of Publius, celebrates his "wife" (*contubernalis*), Gavia Lyncis, who had formerly been enslaved by a different man named Quintus. Iucundus's selection of the word *contubernalis*—a word typically used of the relationships between enslaved people—here suggests that this was a lengthy relationship formed in bondage. Finally, the elite caricature of truant staff day-drinking in taverns may gesture to defiance and self-medication, but also sociability. It was in these moments of human interaction that Christianity found its footing.[22]

Celsus is a tricky source, and his vigorous dislike of Christianity makes him untrustworthy. He exploits the intellectual snobbery of elite men with stock arguments about the perils of womanly or "slavish" influence. Any man who might be persuaded by the Christians, he implies, is a "bucolic yokel" who listens to fabulous nonsense. The polemical benefits of this line of argument for Celsus are clear: he could claim that Christianity was a frivolous fabrication crafted by unreliable actors. The question is: is there any truth to his description of early Christianity?

Many academics have demonstrated that women were an important force in the spread of Christianity, and the same logic holds with respect to enslaved Christians. The rhetoric of "slavish" rumors helps map the geography of what is usually called early Christian "missionary" work. Gossip takes place in locations associated with servile people: in corners of the home, in storefronts, on street corners, and at the gates of the city. Rumor and Gossip dart through space with the confident familiarity of the local messenger, and they vanish without a trace as if they have something to fear if caught in the act. They also emerge among certain groups of people: between foreigners who spoke with accents, among women whose movements were restricted, and among those "who have no general education but practice rhetoric on a street-corner level without method or art." As personified beings, Rumor and Gossip move like enslaved people. If, for Roman elite writers, the author was an elite freeborn man, Gossip was an enslaved woman.[23]

We do not have to trust Celsus to know that Christianity spread by word of mouth. It is part of Christian tradition that the first followers of Jesus spread their message orally through the representatives sent by Jesus and Paul. In the Gospel of John, the Samaritan woman Jesus encountered at the well used gossip to "witness" her encounter with Jesus (John 4:39). In the Gospel of Matthew, the enslaved woman who accused Peter of being a disciple in the courtyard of the High Priest could only have learned of Jesus' arrest via the servile coworker who had been assaulted in Gethsemane only hours earlier. Matthew does not explain how she learned of the arrest so quickly, but he doesn't have to. The "gap" in the story is filled in by the fast-paced movement of information among enslaved workers.[24]

Unsanctioned speech is a neglected part of the official history of Christianity, but it is central to the story of Jesus. The Gospel of Mark charts the geographical expansion of the Kingdom of God through back alleys as well as broad avenues. The Gospel opens as an imperial proclamation of "the good news of Jesus Christ." Jesus' activity was announced by a herald, John the Baptizer, who prepared for his arrival. Reports of Jesus' activities emerge immediately and yet, as he wound his way through the Galilee and Judea, Jesus was reluctant to endorse the spread of news about him. He regularly instructed those he healed to keep quiet. Yet despite his best efforts, his attempts at information management are ignored. Though warned, the man with the skin condition who was healed by Jesus at the beginning of Mark's Gospel "began to...spread the word" (Mark 1:45). As a result, Jesus was unable to enter urban centers without attracting attention.

In the world of the gospel story, news about Jesus spread through networks that linked the lowest and highest members of society and connected rural sections of the Galilee to the regional capital city of Jerusalem. Though Jesus tried to restrain these social networks, he also consulted and celebrated them: he asked the disciples what people were saying about him and predicted that the woman who anointed him at Bethany would be spoken about throughout the whole world (Mark 14:9). He also worried about and was victimized by the effects of gossip: In Mark 13, Jesus warned his disciples against listening to rumors that the Messiah had returned. At his trial and in its aftermath, it was rumors stirred up by the chief priests that led to his condemnation and to the liberation of Barabbas (Mark 15:11). Frustratingly, the women who encountered an angel in the guise of a young man dressed in white did not pass on to the disciples the message that Jesus had gone ahead to Galilee (Mark 16:7).

This last episode—the aborted angelic message in Mark 16—has elicited a great deal of conversation. There is no shortage of scholarly theories and subtle condemnations of the women's behavior. That they failed to convey the information out of "fear" seems a flimsy excuse to some comfortable modern readers. Passing on communications from supernatural beings was not inherently dangerous: Lucius Domitius, an ancestor of the emperor Nero, once carried the news of a military victory to the senate at the behest of two radiant youths. But as with so many things, status matters. The conduct of the women can be at least partly explained when they are viewed as servile. When an enslaved barber was identified as the source of a military rumor and could not name his informant, the assembly was so outraged that they called for him to be tortured for fabricating such a tale. For women, who were not considered reliable witnesses, and for low-status women, who were liable to be tortured, situations like the one in Mark 16 were precarious. And yet, for readers of Mark's Gospel, it is clear that the women did share this information with someone, because the reader is hearing about it. It is almost as if the servile evangelist is covering for them. That the story exists is not, as some have argued, a hole in the Markan plot, but a hint. Instead, the news of the resurrection spread in the same way as news about Jesus spread during his lifetime: through the comparatively safe, anonymous channels of Rumor and Gossip.[25]

In Mark, the good news is a multivalent message delivered in various registers and proclaimed against the constant background noise of unsanctioned speech and gossip. Its growth, however, is down to the latter. In his treatise on gossip, Plutarch wrote that rumor grows like wheat multiplying in a jar. The Kingdom of God, Jesus said, grows similarly: it is like a mustard seed that starts small and suddenly appears everywhere (Mark 4:30). Though some of the agents who spread news about Jesus are identified, others are not. The strange tension between Jesus' instructions about secrecy and his rapidly growing reputation—something that scholars label the Messianic Secret—reflects the uncontrollability of unsanctioned speech in antiquity and the anonymity of the speakers. Enslaved gossip and rumor cannot be repressed; they are obstinately durable. The Greek poet Hesiod characterized rumor as divine precisely because it could not be restrained by human means.[26]

The same frenetic quality is ascribed to the Jesus movement after the crucifixion. In the Pentecost event of Acts 2, the Holy Spirit descended with a rush of wind and settled on the apostles like small serpentine tongues of fire. The apostles could now speak in a variety of foreign languages. The shift is instantly effective: the crowd of religious tourists who had come to Jerusalem for the Passover were amazed to hear the Galilean disciples addressing them in their own languages, prompting an explosion of interest in the Jesus story. Three thousand people were allegedly converted on that day. The story does not use the language of hearsay, but the focus on rapidity, the description of the fiery rushing of the gale-like Spirit, and the presence of the crowd are the hallmarks of the quasi-miraculous windlike reports that sped around and across the Mediterranean. Though early Christians, like other ancient writers who wrote in Greek, condemned slander and idle talk, the Jesus movement itself was carried along by the current of these unregulated servile waters.[27]

The formative role of missionary messengers was not only felt in the delivery of letters: gospels, apocalypses, theological treatises, apologies, homilies, and every other genre that lined the shelves of the proverbial early Christian library also had to be moved to be made public. No Christian church council could have convened without messengers, and no Christian canon could have been formed without their work. Without the practices of trade, travel, and book exchange, all early Christian literature would have remained local and parochial. It is only because of the messengers who participated in the exchange of Ignatius's letters that his collection—or, for that matter, Paul's—survives today.

It was not only formal messengers who carried the gospel to other people. Both pagans and Christians claim that the gospel spread rapidly and surreptitiously: it wove its way through marketplaces, followed tradespeople through back alleys, and hung in the air at gatherings of leatherworkers, fabric dyers, and weavers. This is not to say that Christianity emerged as some kind of agentless spontaneous eruption, but rather that it hitched a ride on grain ships, kept time with the rhythms of day laborers and seasonal workers, and accompanied enslaved boys and girls as they completed their errands. It was, in ancient parlance, the unauthored gossip of the masses, of women, and of enslaved people.

Wealth always hovered in the background, though, sponsoring the upkeep of teachers and preachers, supplying and paying the expenses for the couriers who delivered letters, and, most important of all, financing the copying of Christian texts. For no text, however cherished, could be disseminated beyond its initial recipients without being copied. Copying, unlike writing or taking dictation, was nominally the task of reproducing a text. As the least enviable of ancient literary chores, the work of the copyist was almost always relegated to servile actors. No person of means would choose to copy their own writings; it was simply too much work. Copying, however, only aspires to precision. No text was ever copied perfectly, and handwriting can be idiosyncratic and difficult to follow. Those involved in the duplication of texts had to make decisions about words they were replicating. Copyists, therefore, were among the first and most influential interpreters of Christian scripture.

CHAPTER FIVE

CURATORS OF THE WORD

The oldest surviving Latin Gospel book, Codex Bobiensis, currently lives at the Turin National University Library. The religious pilgrims who flood the city each year often overlook it, preferring to visit the famous Shroud instead. Perhaps they can be forgiven for their oversight; having been damaged during a fire in the early twentieth century, the book was dissected, and mounted on cardboard frames. It is a humble presentation for a document that is, next to the illuminated manuscripts of the medieval period, quite undistinguished. But Bobiensis, which is designated as *k* in modern editions, is beautiful in its simplicity. Although the letters have faded through years of neglect, they are even and clear; the resulting text is rather straightforward to read.

A manuscript that dates back to the late fourth or early fifth century, Codex Bobiensis survived an odyssey of sorts before reaching its current resting place in Turin. The book was brought to Turin in the eighteenth century from a monastery in Bobbio, northern Italy, when the Duke of Savoy decided to unify collections from the city's university and incorporated Bobbio's treasures in this collection. It had come to Italy from North Africa, for reasons unknown, and was erroneously associated with the missionary Saint Columba by Irish monks. Though it preserves only portions of Matthew and Mark, enough material has survived that there is a lively academic debate about its age and contents. Some place the book's origins in the third century and connect it to the kind of Bible used by Cyprian, a famous Carthaginian bishop, who converted to Christianity in 246 and died as a martyr in 258.[1]

As is so often the case with ancient manuscripts, the identity of the copyist who made the book is unknown. While their fingerprints are all over the manuscript, reconstructing who they were is a difficult process of deduction and educated guesses. The copyist's excellent handwriting eliminates at the outset the possibility that they were an amateur. No nonprofessional could have produced a manuscript this delightfully uniform. The copyist might have been male or female, as enslaved women were sometimes prized for their excellent handwriting. Unlike dictation, copying rarely took place in the household or presence of the author, or even owner, of a text. Perhaps the copyist was enslaved in a wealthy household and copied the text for their enslaver either at home or at the residence of an equally affluent friend. Alternatively, perhaps they labored in a workshop for a freedman bookseller who had been commissioned to make some kind of Gospel book. In either instance, the copyist would have been a servile or artisanal worker. Anything else about them can only be inferred from idiosyncrasies in the manuscript itself.

Despite its lofty heritage and ties to a hero of the early church, Bobiensis has peculiar features. In the preserved portions of the Gospels, sections are missing. Almost every page contains an unexpected reading of the text. One such detail is found in the story of the empty tomb. In Mark 16:4, a lengthy (and novel) sentence explains the mechanics of the resurrection: "At the third hour of the day, darkness came over the whole world and angels from heaven descended and, as he was rising in the brightness of the living God, at the same time [the angels] ascended with him..." Older versions of Mark do not describe the resurrection, much less the comforting presence of angels. One wonders what the copyist pictures here. The angels are critical to the scene, but how? A noncanonical ancient Christian text may help us imagine it. In the second-century *Gospel of Peter*, which was written roughly a century after Peter's death, a Roman sentry reports seeing three extremely tall men departing from the sepulcher "with the two supporting the other one."[2]

In nineteenth-century artist Edouard Manet's Dead Christ with Angels, *two celestial beings prop up Jesus.*

Is this what the copyist of Bobiensis imagines? That a resurrected but still recovering Jesus was helped out of the tomb and off the mortal coil by angelic assistants? It is possible (but extremely difficult to prove) that the scene comes solely from the imagination of the copyist. Leaning on the bodies of family members or enslaved workers for support was how people managed temporary weakness and immobility. This is how a wheezing Pliny the Elder rose from his bed on the final day of his life. It was such a common image that "leaning on one's slaves" became a metaphor for intellectual dependence in the writing of Lucian. If this is correct, then we here glimpse how one scribe pictured the resurrection: a miraculous event that involved the helpful arms of angelic beings who performed—as they did on so many occasions—servile tasks. If we imagine that the copyist was enslaved, then we might conclude that this was somewhat personal to them, as enslaved workers were called upon to perform all kinds of assistance. It is possible that the angels reflect not just people of the copyist's social status, but roles that they themselves had performed. Angelic assistance makes a theological point as well: Jesus was resurrected with the same body that was crucified on Good Friday. His recovering body is a sign that he is not a ghost or an apparition.[3]

Even if Bobiensis was produced by a Christian copyist embedded in the rich religious climate of North Africa, as one talented scholar has recently argued, the resulting text has a different shape than the one found in modern Bibles and all other known gospel texts from antiquity. Either explanation brings us to the same point: copying manuscripts alters them, sometimes in significant ways. Bobiensis is one of thousands of examples of the textual variety that flourished in the early church.[4]

Often scholars see the textual variation produced in the act of copying as evidence of ecclesiastical conflict. In this view, the activity of copyists mirrors theological disagreements or discord within pockets of Christianity: each line marks a theological divide and strikes a blow against a perceived heresy. But neither of the explanations for Bobiensis's distinctiveness described here invokes this kind of agonistic context. Instead, it speaks to the lives and experiences of enslaved and otherwise low-status artisanal workers.

Copyists were part of a larger set of literate workers who were responsible for duplicating, organizing, repairing, and preserving ancient literature. Though copyists have often been blamed for the "mistakes" that crept into ancient manuscripts, they are as likely to have repaired and preserved texts as harmed them. Despite the bad reputation they developed among ancient elites and modern scholars, they were textual curators and physicians. Their work was indispensable to the dissemination and survival of Christian texts, a fact that is all the more interesting given that some of them—like the copyist of Bobiensis—are unlikely to have been Christian at all.

Copying is hard work. Even if some ancient elites thought that composing by hand had sentimental or intellectual value, duplicating a text was something else entirely. It was relentlessly demanding and—to Romans—not even the kind of manual labor that inspired begrudging respect. Cornelius Nepos, a friend of Cicero's, remarked that the scribes charged with copying documents and maintaining archives were looked down upon as quasi-mercenaries. Although the knotty bundle of Roman attitudes about labor renders cultural translations almost meaningless, one might call the job that copyists performed blue-collar literate work, something like data processing or clerical work. Even in governmental contexts, where the stakes were high, the grunt work was performed by anonymous enslaved people.[5]

The task was so cumbersome that with the arrival of the printing press in the early modern period, even monks, who had dedicated their lives to God and austerity, had to be cajoled and flattered into continuing to copy texts by hand. It is one of the distinctions of early Christian book culture that the hardship of hand-copying texts takes on a kind of personal religious significance. In a short epilogue attached to the account of the death of Polycarp of Smyrna, one of Christianity's first martyrs, the copyist wrote that he "gathered [the pages of the text] together, now almost worn away by time, so that the Lord Jesus Christ might bring me into his heavenly kingdom." For the copyist, Pionius, this act of textual resuscitation was tied to personal resurrection.[6]

For most early Christian copyists, however, curating, collating, and reproducing manuscripts was less a spiritual calling than a job. It was physical work that took place in a material context that, just like the copyist themselves, affected the character and quality of the manuscript that was produced. The drudgery of the work meant that it was regularly performed by enslaved and freedman workers who often worked in the households of wealthy private collectors. If a rich bibliophile wanted a copy of a famous text, they only had to send a copyist to the house of a friend to make it.[7]

It is likely that Christians of the first through fourth centuries utilized a variety of methods in obtaining copies of their books. They relied on private networks of copying and distribution, requesting copies of books from fellow Christians or correspondence partners, searching for desired volumes in bookshops, or hiring copyists who were moonlighting from their day jobs in bookstores or bureaucratic offices. Artisans and merchants who had some literary skills themselves, or employed others who did, may well have copied texts in their homes. What was true of pagan elite homes and bookshops, however, was true of early

Christians as well: wherever you find repetitious work, you find enslaved and formerly enslaved workers.

Enslaved people were represented elsewhere in the ecosystem of Roman book production. If judging a man's status by his name is more reliable than judging a book by its cover, then most booksellers were freedmen—and thus it is likely that many booksellers began their careers as enslaved literate workers. In either scenario, they were likely well-read and educated. By virtue of their position, they had to know both their clientele and their market: in a world before Google searches, it was booksellers who had the most expansive knowledge of the contents of private collections, the inventory available at the stores of their competitors, and the latest news about the arrival of new books in their city. They, like librarians, were human card catalogs.[8]

Most of the evidence for bookshops and booksellers comes from Rome, where, the physician Galen tells us, stores were clustered together in friendly competition just off the Forum. Book buyers seem to have been interested in a wide array of genres: some bought the poetry of Horace and Martial; others sought out scientific treatises by Aristotle, the medical textbooks of Galen, or the speeches of Pliny; still others acquired Quintilian's multivolume manual on training in rhetoric. Booksellers' wares represented a broad array of interests, and even those who could afford to have books copied at home would occasionally dispatch agents to commercial vendors to sniff out hard-to-come-by works.[9]

The quality of material available at a bookstore varied widely. Formally the cost of a manuscript was based on two factors: length and quality. Copyists—or their enslavers—were paid by the line and their fees were sometimes fixed by legal decrees. In 301, the emperor Diocletian standardized the rates for copies at twenty-five denarii for one hundred lines in the best script, twenty for less high-quality handwriting, and ten for functional

writing. Even apart from the varying quality the pay scale produced, a number of ancient literary sources complained about
false advertising. The attractive snippets of text placed on display outside the bookstore could be a far cry from the error-
laden manuscripts that lay nested inside. In an ideal world, each
text would be proofread and corrected; evidence of such corrections persists in manuscripts that have survived from antiquity.
But the thin profit margins of bookselling and the pressure to
work quickly affected the quality of the copyist's work. It is
tempting for scholars to see the caliber of an ancient manuscript
only as a reflection of the skills of the copyist, but the budget of
the customer and financial constraints of the vendor also affected
the final product.[10]

When people, both ancient and modern, notice copyists and
comment upon their work, it is almost always when the copyists
make mistakes. "Good" copyists were and are invisible: they
performed their work so perfectly that they wrote themselves
into nonexistence. "Bad" copyists, on the other hand, leave
traces of themselves and it is the presence of this additional layer
of human agency and error that is thought to have perverted and
corrupted the text. This conceptual binary is much too simplistic, of course: "originals," even final drafts, were tolerably imper-
fect, and copyists and correctors (whether employed in bookshops
or in private libraries) were supposed to emend grammatical
mistakes, orthographic errors, and other infelicities. And yet
readers, both ancient and modern, tend to disparage copyists
for their "corruptions," rather than praise them for their creative contributions. Scholars speak of scribal error and rarely of
scribal expertise.

Many surviving manuscripts from the early Christian period
are in a "documentary" hand, an informal style used in book-
keeping and administrative work. Some historians have seen
this as evidence that early Christian copyists were (freeborn)

amateurs. An informal style of copying, however, does not equate to an unprofessional copyist. Nor do beautiful books always equate to careful work. One deluxe copy of Virgil's *Aeneid*, for example, was quite carelessly produced. Careful analysis of ancient manuscripts reveals that the people who copied Christian manuscripts wrote in handwriting that bears traces of both literary (formal) and documentary (informal, for correspondence, shopping lists, accounting) styles. These texts were copied not by amateurs, but rather by those who had experience copying texts. Considering the skills and agency of enslaved workers might further complicate the relationship between copying, calligraphy, training, and status. What if copying a text beautifully (as required by an enslaver or customer) but poorly (with many errors) was a form of resistance? What if copying a text accurately but in an informal (documentary) style is evidence of a copyist who took satisfaction in their work?[11]

When viewed in this light, Codex Bobiensis yields interesting clues about the identity of its creator. Many people make accidental changes when transcribing and copying texts—our best guess for professional copyists is about one per page—but some of those in Bobiensis are substantive differences that are challenging to explain. There is a mistake in the Lord's Prayer, for instance, which in this manuscript does not read "Let your kingdom come," but "I have come to your kingdom."

What kind of Christian does not know the Lord's Prayer? A non-Christian, or at least this is the conclusion at which some specialists have arrived. If this is the case, then perhaps Bobiensis was commissioned from a bookseller. Book manufacturing, like any kind of luxury-goods industry, was an expensive business and not a very profitable one at that. Papyrus—or, in the case of Bobiensis, parchment—was costly, and literary workers were expensive to train. It is easy to imagine that a pragmatic bookseller, painfully aware of his bottom line, instructed his copyist to omit certain portions of the Gospel book that he was creating: the less paper used, the greater the bookseller's margins. While the person who commissioned the Gospel book was likely a Christian, the enslaved people responsible for copying and making this text may well have had different priorities.[12]

Copying always involves decision-making. The base texts could be ambiguous or difficult to read. They might contain mistakes that needed clarifying or correcting. It should be assumed that (almost) every ancient manuscript contained evidence of prior correction and that, consequently, the copyist was adjudicating between different options. Manuscripts also contained material that was not, strictly speaking, part of the content of the book. Tables of contents, headings, indices, and marginal notes all shape how readers think about texts and affect their interpretation of it. These paratexts, as they are known, were usually added by sources other than the primary author, but they played (and continue to play) a huge role in determining how we think about texts.[13]

Early Christian manuscripts are full of paratexts: abbreviations, corrections, and marginal notes that gloss, explain, or correct a text. Some are quite snippy and issue stern rebukes to those who might copy their manuscript incorrectly. Perhaps the most famous is the story of the woman caught in adultery (or *Pericopae adulterae*) found in John 7:52–8:11. The story is something of a fan favorite: a woman caught in flagrante was brought to Jesus by scribes and Pharisees. They asked Jesus for his opinion: should the woman be stoned to death in accordance with Mosaic law? At first Jesus ignored them and wrote on the ground, but when they continued to challenge him, he replied:

"Let anyone among you who is without sin be the first to throw a stone at her." The crowd slowly dissipated, and Jesus told the woman to go on her way and sin no more. It's a classic story of forgiveness and suspended judgment. But its renown makes the story's provenance all the more remarkable.[14]

The earliest manuscripts of the Gospel of John (P66 and P75) were written in the second and early third centuries and bear no trace of this story. The earliest surviving copy that contains it is Codex Bezae (circa 400). When the story is found in manuscripts, it appears in a variety of locations: most scribes placed it after John 7:52, one at 7:36, some appended it to the end of the

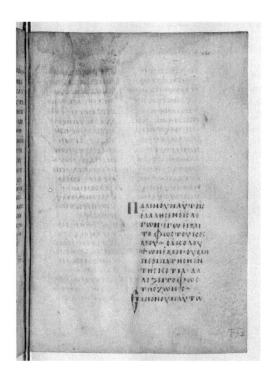

Codex Regius (700s CE) shows a space between John 7:52 and John 8:12, suggesting that the scribe knew of a story—the woman caught in adultery—that belonged there.

Gospel of John, and still others placed it in the Gospel of Luke. One copyist inserted a series of dots in his text where the story would have appeared, suggesting that he knew of the manuscript tradition but didn't judge it to be authentic. Other copyists left a blank space in the Gospel of John where the story would have been located. References to and variants on the popular story are found in many Christian authors from the second century onwards, and from the fourth century it was popular among Latin-speaking Christians.

One theory maintains that the *Pericopae adulterae* migrated from the margins of John into the body of the text. Another sees it as reflecting an oral tradition that found favor with Christian interpreters and was incorporated into the body of the Gospel of Luke before eventually ending up in John. What is clear, however, is that the process of placing this beloved tale in the text required copyists.

It might seem at first blush that, to copyists, the world of adultery felt far removed. (Enslaved people were not allowed to form legal marriages and thus could not be found guilty of adultery— although they were nevertheless liable to sometimes fatal mistreatment for their sexual behavior.) The administration of sharp (in)justice, however, would have been painfully familiar to any enslaved literary worker. Under Roman law, beatings and crucifixion were the forms of violence most regularly visited upon enslaved bodies, but in Jesus' parables, enslaved characters also find themselves targets of unsanctioned vigilante violence like stoning (Matt. 21:35). Second chances were a rarity for enslaved workers. The story of the woman caught in adultery may, for those who first incorporated it into the margins and body of the text, have resonated with their experiences of the inequitable administration of justice. Just as women were held to account for adultery in ways that men were not, so too enslaved people had no opportunity to defend themselves. Alternatively, perhaps these literary workers—like so many readers since—simply loved the story.

Some copying decisions might have been shaped by the materiality of the workshop itself. Take, for example, the well-known Jesus saying that it is "easier for a camel to go through the eye of a needle than for someone who is rich to enter the kingdom of God." Since antiquity, the hyperbolic statement has caused interpretive problems: the messy image is tantamount to a radical exclusion of the wealthy. A well-worn medieval myth maintains that the "eye of the needle" is in fact a small gate in Jerusalem through which pedestrian foot traffic could enter after hours, but there is no archaeological or historical evidence to support this claim. The manuscript evidence is complicated, but at least one tradition, represented in a cluster of manuscripts known to scholars as Family 13 and associated with the city of Caesarea Maritima in Palestine, assumed that the saying contained a typographical error. Instead of *kamelos* (camel), the copyist reasoned, the text was supposed to read *kamilos* (rope or ship's cable) and so they made a small change to the manuscript.[15]

If accurate, this emendation—like the myth of a pedestrian gate—would soften the hyperbolic impact of the saying, but perhaps the alteration of the text was about the material context of copying as well as broader social values. Copying, whether in homes, workshops, or dedicated bookshops, was part of both editorial activity and artisanal bookcraft. When ancient codices (as opposed to scrolls) were made, stacks of folded leaves called quires were sewn between leather covers (or bindings) with a thick, cordlike thread. A variety of sewing techniques, similar to those used in rope-making, basket-weaving, and even the manufacture of curtains, were used to secure the leaves to the leather cover, from a basic stitch to more elaborate patterns. The copyist may or may not have been involved in the binding of the codices, but they were almost certainly aware of the techniques by which writing objects were made, and familiar with the multisensory work that it involved. Viewed from this perspective, this version of the eye-of-the-needle metaphor emerges out of the lifeworld of the bookshop. The needles sat alongside writing implements, rulers, knives, inkwells, and papyrus as tools of the trade. A copyist embedded in this setting, catching a glimpse of cord out of the corner of his eye, may well have been inspired to emend the saying.[16]

Bookshops were not explicitly religious spaces, much less Christian ones. In Codex Bobiensis, there are junctures where the copyist uses nonstandard abbreviations for the sacred names of God, Lord, and Jesus. Where Christian manuscripts would normally have read IHS (derived from IHSOUS, the Greek for Jesus), Bobiensis has HI[S]. There are several places where the copyist has substituted, perhaps inadvertently, the names of pagan deities Helios (the sun god) and Jove (Jupiter) instead of the words for *Elijah* and *sheep*. A reader might, as some have, see these as the signs of an inferior copyist. Many texts contain atypical or inconsistent abbreviations or spellings, and scholars often attribute such features either to incompetence or to the splicing of different manuscripts in the copying process.

In many cases this analysis is undoubtedly correct, but studies of the behavior of workers engaged in repetitive literate work in more recent periods suggest other explanations. They describe varying their language as a form of play and self-protection: it kept them entertained. Others report that they left clear errors in documents because they were not supposed to think. Following instructions to the letter was, thus, a form of resistance.[17]

Perhaps the scribe of Bobiensis understood these impulses; the fabulist Aesop certainly did. According to one first-century CE biography, he regularly used the vagueness in direct orders to subvert his enslaver Xanthus's demands. On one occasion, Aesop exploited a grammatical ambiguity in the instruction to "make a lentil pot," to carefully prepare a single lentil for his enslaver's dinner party. (In ancient Greek, the word for a singular lentil could be used to refer to a whole meal.) On another occasion, Xanthus told Aesop to bring an oil flask and Aesop did, without first filling it with oil. Perhaps ancient copyists were no different; they craved variety, autonomy, and creativity. Asserting themselves in this way was an act of self-preservation, what anthropologist David Graeber calls a "spiritual act." Their bids for agency and entertainment are misunderstood as incompetence precisely because they are not seen at all.[18]

Copying, as research into low-status literate work from other periods shows, is never mindless. Clerical and data-processing workers from the twentieth century report changing how data was entered simply as a means of alleviating boredom. The physical savvy of bookwork has always involved adaptability and sustained attention. A loud noise, a sudden jolt, deficient ink, and rougher materials all affected the copyist's work. If, as some scholars have argued, textual alterations are an index of Christian concerns and interests, then those interests were also informed by the immediate physical contexts and skills of bookwork. These skills only grow more important if some Christian copyists were artisans. Texts do not copy themselves, and copyists are not just instruments for the powerful. Some of the choices made by copyists in booksellers' shops and private homes were related to economic efficiency and consumer interests; others were grammatical and aesthetic; others still were about clarity, historical accuracy, theology, or perhaps just boredom. Perhaps some interpretive decisions were the result of top-down instructions from powerful slaveholders and ecclesiastical leaders, but the influences at work also include conversations between enslaved workers in various households and vibrant internal monologues. Any and all of these could have shaped Christianity in ways that we have yet to fully appreciate.[19]

In the spring of 56 BCE, an emotionally battered Cicero returned from exile and proceeded with the intimidating task of putting together the pieces of his political and public life. Of key importance to him was the reassembly of his personal library, which had been damaged and had fallen into chaos. Cicero solicited the assistance of Tyrannio, a *grammaticus* (grammarian) and mutual friend of Atticus's, and engaged him in the job of setting things right. The enormity of the project was overwhelming, and so he also asked the wealthier Atticus to lend him two *librarioli* (enslaved library specialists) to help with the task. With all the subtlety of a neglected parent, Cicero engaged in some emotional manipulation, writing that "if you [Atticus] love me, be attentive about the library slaves." The additional staff, he explained, were needed to repair the manuscripts with glue, add title tags to the scrolls, and build custom shelving to house them.[20]

Given that Cicero was in the process of reassembling his life, the urgency of his demand is understandable: a psychoanalyst might say that the library was a metonym for his life. Cicero himself goes much further; he wrote to Atticus of his delight in the book tags that now "adorn" his library. After Tyrannio (and, though Cicero does not credit them, the enslaved library specialists) arranged his books, "a soul (*mens*) seemed to have been added to my house." All was right with the world now that Cicero's library was in order.

Tyrannio, the executor of Cicero's vision, might have had a different perspective on the work of the two enslaved librarians—for although only briefly, he had once endured bondage himself. Tyrannio was a manumitted Greek scholar. According to Plutarch, he had been captured during the Mithridatic War, in the first century BCE, and was immediately liberated on account of his erudition and learning. He was the kind of formerly enslaved figure whose unavoidable intellect threatened the fragile conceit that freeborn Romans were superior to those they had conquered; thus, though socially inferior, Tyrannio was treated with respect and as a kind of confidante.

Cicero readily admitted the instrumental role that Tyrannio played in the repair and organization of the library and conceded that the two *librarioli* were a necessary part of the process. The work of this trio was more than pasting and elementary carpentry. Some of the books would have lost the colophons that identified them; the librarians thus had to identify the text by its contents. When people do that today, they are called scholars. Indeed, even in the ancient world, this was an academic task. Galen tells a story in which a "learned man" used precisely this skill to identify a fraudulent work.[21]

Like Tyrannio and his enslaved collaborators, the literary workers who labored over early Christian texts had to make crucial organizational decisions that altered the shape of the canon. The modern New Testament begins with the canonical Gospels of Matthew, Mark, Luke, and John; teases the reader with the ensuing Acts of the Apostles; moves through the frenetic correspondence of Paul and other apostolic heroes; and ends with the cosmic bang of Revelation. In the second and third centuries, however, it was not at all obvious that this collection should contain twenty-seven books, what order they should appear in, or even what a New Testament would be. An early sixth-century Latin codex of Paul's letters, for example, contains a text known as the *Letter to the Laodiceans*, after Colossians. Most scholars think that the text is a fabrication, but the decision to include it in this collection—one that might have been made by a low-status copyist or bookmaker—places it on the same level as canonical Pauline epistles.[22]

Even among those who agreed that there should be four Gospels and that those Gospels should be Matthew, Mark, Luke, and John, there was some disagreement about the order in which they should be arranged. Even the letters of Paul are organized according to a particular interpretive scheme. Today our Bibles place them not in chronological order but rather, broadly speaking, in order of declining length and—in the view of many—declining theological importance. When the collection is read from beginning to end, it is Romans, the weightiest of the epistles, that governs our understanding of those that follow. But the now-traditional ordering of Gospels and Epistles emerged gradually, and we know of dissenters. Marcion, a religious teacher active in Rome in the second century who spurned the Hebrew Bible entirely, placed Galatians—the sharpest rejection of Jewish customs—at the head of his Pauline letter collection. Order matters.[23]

The clearest example of how collecting and organizing affect the New Testament is 2 Corinthians. Most scholars will tell you that it is a composite text, assembled from several shorter letters (anywhere from five to six, depending on the model). These shorter letters were later blended to form a single whole, but the ragged literary seams in the text—changes in tone and subject matter, repetitions, and inconsistencies—offer clues that this isn't a single work. Some of these shorter letters might have been written on a single sheet of papyrus, others on scrolls, but at some point they were pasted together into a single roll. This is how people kept records of letters that they had sent and received. The archaeology of ancient letter-writing quickly reveals the idiosyncrasies of ancient organizational impulses. There are pasted rolls of letters—easily identifiable from the different handwriting of the scribes—among the caches of documents found at Oxyrhynchus, an ancient Egyptian town that lay to the west of the Nile. Sometimes received letters were copied onto fresh rolls, and not always in chronological order. In one such instance, the individual letters are numbered but one has been omitted. In another roll of collected letters, some of the customary closing statements (the ancient equivalent of "Best wishes") have not been reproduced. Perhaps the text known as 2 Corinthians came to life in the same way, through the practice of gathering and ordering texts.[24]

When scholars discuss the birth of 2 Corinthians, they often assume that the text emerged in one of two ways: either through the unintentional actions of a copyist, or through the deliberate intervention of an editor. But this demarcated language of editor and copyist is misleading: the process of copying, trimming, pasting, and arranging was performed by literary workers, many of them enslaved. It is their work that shapes how we read these letters today.

To be sure, these are consequential decisions, but that does not mean that they were made by high-status individuals. This is as true of the shaping of the Pauline letters as a whole as it is the compilation of 2 Corinthians. While some think that Paul himself had editorial oversight and control, the process of assembling letter collections in antiquity almost always involved enslaved workers. This was at least partly because of how difficult it was to manage a variety of different book rolls and papyrus sheets at once: to use them simultaneously, you needed multiple people.

Sometimes the arrangement of letters and texts privileges some individuals while obscuring the contributions of others. As classicist Mary Beard has written, it is because one book of Cicero's collected letters is dedicated to his secretary that Tiro emerges in full color. Had the collection been organized chronologically, Tiro would have faded into the background. There were other enslaved workers in the letters who were equally critical to Cicero's life, but the structuring of the collection pushes them into the background. As Cicero's literary executor, Tiro may have edited the letters himself. But whether he is responsible for it or not, it is the structure of the whole that makes Tiro prominent and others invisible.[25]

The organization of letters tells us how to read them, highlights certain themes and individuals, and occludes other ideas and people. For Roman literary elites, organization was an authorial task. Reorganization, therefore, might be seen as a kind of resistance or at least a departure from some prior authorial intention. In the case of Paul, this may not seem that important. The case can and has been made that Paul never pictured his letters being read in any particular order or even as a collection. In the case of the Gospels, on the other hand, the sequence of narrative events is critical.

The authors—both named and invisible—of the Gospels presumably had an order in mind when they wrote their narratives. But once texts moved out into the world and into the hands of others, they could be and sometimes were reframed and thus revolutionized. This is where paratexts—tables of contents, indices, church lectionaries—that segment and reorient our reading can become subversive and liberating. More often than not, those responsible for the creation of paratexts were enslaved or formerly enslaved workers. They provide an alternative pathway through the text. Rather than reading from beginning to end, people can hunt and peck between the bindings or meander like Jesus on his way to Jerusalem.

Among contemporary Christians, this kind of nonlinear reading is particularly utilized in the case of the Gospels. Though people read them as novels—from beginning to end—we also consult them as we might a recipe book, cross-referencing different versions of the stories. I have done this myself throughout this book when I point to versions of the same story in different Gospels. This feels very natural: the evangelists are telling the same life story, so pausing our reading of one Gospel to compare it to another version of the same story makes a certain amount of instinctive sense.[26]

Christians did not always read the Gospels this way. Though many agreed that there should be four Gospels, and even grounded this assumption in the natural order of the universe, they did not read the Gospels in parallel. Fourfold Gospel reading was encoded into our reading practices and Bibles with the fourth-century historian Eusebius of Caesarea. In a period before chapter and verse divisions, Eusebius and his team of servile literary assistants divided the canonical Gospels into numbered sections and produced a set of coordinating reference tables that allowed readers to cross-reference versions of the same story in other Gospels. In doing so, Eusebius and his team inaugurated a trend that has dominated how Christians have read the Bible ever since.[27]

The enormity of Eusebius's innovation is hard to see precisely because it has become so ubiquitous, but a great deal of decision-making went into the production of this reading scheme. First, the team had to decide on unit divisions: what is a unit, where does it begin, and where does it end? While today church services have designated readings, early Christians often read for as long as time permitted. In segmenting the Gospel, the Eusebian team were cementing informal distinctions about what constituted a particular story, episode, or passage in the life of Jesus. Each unit had to be correlated to the corresponding units in the other Gospels. Some decisions seem easy: Jesus feeds five thousand people in all four Gospels, for example (Matt. 14:13–21, Mark 6:32–44, Luke 9:10–17, John 6:1–15). But there is an additional story, relayed by Matthew and Mark, in which he feeds four thousand people (Matt. 15:32–39, Mark 8:1–10). What about those? What about chronological discrepancies? In the synoptic Gospels, the incident in the Jerusalem Temple, where Jesus gets into a physical dispute with moneychangers, occurs in the final week of his life; but in John, the incident kicks off his ministry (Matt. 21:12–13, Mark 11:15–17, Luke 19:45–46, John 2:13–17). Are they the same story? Did Jesus "cleanse" the Temple twice? These were and indeed are live questions for Christian readers, but Eusebius et al. provided definitive answers by means of a simple chart. A great deal of interpretation and theological work happens in the construction of the tables, but they seem to be factual accounting. Instead of argumentation that makes itself open to disagreement, there are only beguilingly agentless lines and numbering.

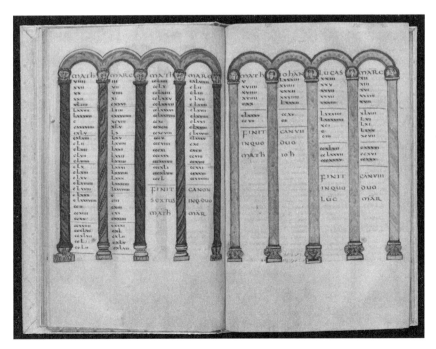

Eusebian Canon Tables in a ninth-century Gospel book

This kind of schematization might seem to be the ancient equivalent of administrative or clerical work. Indeed, it drew upon technologies and practices from ancient administration, mathematics, astrology, medicine, magic, and culinary arts. But at least one set of ancient readers disagreed: one of the oldest illuminated Gospel manuscripts in existence, a sixth-century Ethiopian Gospel book, includes an image of Eusebius alongside those of Matthew, Mark, Luke, and John. The portraiture conveys that in the construction of the tables, Eusebius too is an evangelist.

The Ethiopian images capture an often hidden truth: schematization is theological work. Dividing the Bible into chunks and mapping its contents in new ways created interpretively significant connections. By setting them in parallel, and thus connecting the story of divine creation from the prologue of the Gospel of John ("In the beginning was the Word...") to the genealogies of Matthew and Luke, the Eusebian team could underscore the divine and human origins of Jesus. Equally important, they instructed the reader to read the Gospels in a new and particular way: a way that reoriented the original organization. In this way, Roman reading practices, which often focused on the author, were disrupted by a new scheme that moved people's attention away from the intent of the individual evangelists and toward that of Eusebius and his team.

If this shift seems unimportant or intuitive to us, it is only because we have so thoroughly absorbed it. While Eusebius himself was neither enslaved nor invisible, he utilized the skills of invisible workers for this technological and administrative project—and he himself remains largely uncredited for his influence on how we read the Gospels today.[28]

Tyrannio, the formerly enslaved scholar who restored Cicero's mutilated library, had done this kind of curatorial work before. According to the Greek geographer Strabo, on Aristotle's death, his library passed through a sequence of underresourced and careless hands, from Aristotle's students to wealthy bibliophiles, sticky-fingered Roman generals, and lazy copyists. At one juncture the works were stored in a subterranean tunnel, where dampness and moths ate away at their contents. It was Tyrannio, an admirer of Aristotle, who finally gained access to the deteriorating collection and used his curatorial skills to produce superior copies.[29]

Strabo's story might be anecdotal, but it reveals a great deal about the afterlives of books. Literature was constantly imperiled, by the intellectual ambitions of imperial actors, by the corrosive effects of moisture and insects, and by the sloppiness of copyists. In antiquity, books were treated like enslaved people: defaced, deformed, captured, imprisoned, inherited, or sold on the open market.

Neglected and unprotected, however, books will rot — especially in Rome, which, as anyone who has visited the city in the summer knows, is a swamp. The dampness that filled the air in Roman villas was exacerbated by an elite love affair with impractical moisture-producing fountains, which fed a constant drip of water onto the paving stones of the best homes. Even in the ancient world, humidity was known to be a problem. Stumbling upon a bookseller's stall near the harbor, Aulus Gellius remarked that the books were filthy and damaged from neglect. In the third century, an absent-minded military doctor wrote a panicked letter home from Alexandria, asking his wife to shake out his medical texts so that they wouldn't be destroyed by dust, insect larvae, or damp. (He had neglected this task before he left.)[30]

Insects are underrated as cultural predators. Though today popular myths blame zealous monks or philistine barbarians for the destruction of the Library of Alexandria, the truth is quite different. It was, in fact, the humbler but more numerous armies of bookworms that laid low this fabled bastion of human knowledge, slowly eating away at the metaphorical foundations of ancient learning. Bookworms were not picky eaters: they consumed book bindings, papyri, parchment, leather bindings, animal skin, glue, and, in a pinch, less erudite offerings like wood or textiles. Their gastronomic pursuits turned them into editors; Galen complained that a theta (θ) becomes an omicron (o) when an insect munches through. Technically speaking, bookworms are the larvae of insects—flies, moths, or beetles—who eat through texts during pupation and chew their way out on their path to maturity. It is often the negative space produced by the passage of the larvae that manuscript experts find themselves studying in museums and libraries: the choppy holes and lacunae are not simply the work of time's hands, they chart a larva's life well-lived.[31]

Just like bedbugs or head lice today, bookworms were erroneously thought to offer a social commentary on the cleanliness and diligence of book owners and curators. They were a challenge, but one that any competent servile library worker was expected to meet. Trimalchio, the antihero of Petronius's *Satyricon*, threatened to burn his attendant Stichus alive if mice or moths touched his clothes, and we can imagine that at least one bibliophile enslaver cruelly delivered a similar threat to his librarian. Conceptually the issue was one of care. Like human bodies, the literary corpus needed attention: to be depilated, rubbed, and exercised. Rolling and unrolling formed the foundation of an energetic regime that was supplemented with reparative practices of trimming and gluing frayed edges, and rounded out with the application of natural insecticides like saffron and cedar oil. Books were clothed in a leather roll that protected them from the elements. Even wax tablets, the hardiest of ancient writing devices, needed maintenance; if the wax was not regularly massaged, it would harden, crack, and become useless. Aging skin and neglected books were known to crack, too. Cedar oil served double duty as a depilatory that kept the skin of enslaved teen boys from appearing adolescent. As with human bodies, keeping books youthful involves a great deal of work.[32]

There was a distinct tension between curation and use. With no small amount of sexual innuendo, the Roman satirists Horace and Martial joked that their books would be passed around and worn out like sex workers. Rough treatment and group reading, the early rabbinic authors warned, can "tear and damage a book scroll"; the scroll should be unrolled and aired once a month, but never by more than one person at a time. This manhandling was appropriately gendered. Martial pictured book rolls growing frayed beards from frottage against torsos, both clothed and unclothed. In the same way, delicate papyrus and even more expensive parchment were damaged by men who had never been known to respect bodily boundaries.[33]

When modern readers think of an ancient library, they should picture not a quiet room with silent readers, but a textual surgery bustling with activity and filled with people. Delivery boys flowed in and out; janitorial staff swept the floor, deciding which pieces of fallen papyri to reuse as patches on old books; therapeutic tools and sticky substances perched on work surfaces; and a cast of librarians, curators, and copyists attended to their patients. When the remarkable survival of ancient papyri is discussed, people should credit not only good fortune or the arid soil of ancient Egypt, but also the enslaved workers who worked as textual physicians and therapists. Just as books do not replicate themselves, they also do not organize, assemble, or preserve themselves. The making of the Bible is not just about copying, it is about the arts of crafting, curation, and care.

Though copyists were also curators who repaired and preserved human knowledge, this is not how they have been remembered. From antiquity to the present day, those invested in ancient texts—from academics to modern Christians—have worried about what took place in the bookstores of antiquity. The concern is fraud, deception, and what is broadly described as "textual corruption."

It is a matter of fact that the manuscripts of the New Testament that have survived from antiquity all differ from one another. They were produced by hand in a culture that was acutely aware of the impossibility of perfect duplication. Even coins, the metallic backbone of commerce and trade, were struck by hand and thus differed from one another. In general, ancient people had a tolerance for variation that we do not share. When egregious errors were made, however, both ancient and modern analysts have tended to blame copyists. Much like enslaved workers in general, artisanal workers were an easy target for undeserved accusations of forgery, corruption, and distortion. An elite line of argument, grounded in little more than classism and shared by some early Christians, saw those who manufactured books as uneducated tradespeople and potential forgers. The caricature has, unfortunately, stuck.

The problem was essentially spatial. Ancient curators performed their work in workshops and bookstores: spaces that were typically out of the sight of enslavers and customers alike. In antiquity, this made their work inherently suspicious. Lucian, in his criticism of the celebrity wonder-worker Alexander the False Prophet, lists the textual specialists that Alexander employed as part of his fraudulent empire. Alexander would instruct paying visitors to write their questions for the god on scrolls, which were then sealed and taken into the inner sanctuary of the temple. Secreted away, Alexander and his team would unseal the scrolls, read them, formulate a response, and carefully reglue the seals. The prophecies Alexander delivered to the desperate pilgrims were just a sham perpetrated by a group of literate artisans (Lucian lists researchers, oracle writers, oracle curators, clerks, seal manufacturers, textual interpreters, and translators among them). The same skills that preserved the ancient library, Lucian imagined, could be used to forge a new one. So too one rabbinic text warned that the raw materials of the bookshop — worn-out manuscripts and semi-finished parchment — could easily benefit the forger. Unless they were willing to spend each workday hovering over the workbench, elites could only imagine the subversive and deceitful uses to which the artisan's skills might be put.[34]

The negative characterization of copyists is not only an ancient prejudice. The impulse to return to the "originals" — the original events, the original intentions of the authors, and the original texts that they composed — has animated academic conversation about the Bible since the Renaissance. These interests were nurtured by a scientific turn during the Enlightenment and constantly reenergized by the discovery of new manuscript fragments in Egypt, Israel, and Palestine, and private and public collections. In an era of conquest that styled itself as discovery, scholars saw themselves as plucky adventurers rediscovering the Truth. Truth, of course, is elusive when great distances are involved. Though textual criticism has broadened its focus and many scholars now wonder about whether it is even possible to speak of an "original text," the prospect of an unstable and fragmentary Bible continues to trouble many religiously invested readers.[35]

Often, however, the scholars undertaking these reconstructions of the textual history of the New Testament are considerably less interested in the social status of the people who copied the manuscripts than in the manuscripts themselves. As a result, if scholars identify a difference between manuscripts (what scholars call a textual variant) and assess that difference to be theologically meaningful, then the copyists are often implicitly assumed to be elite representatives of various ancient theological positions. In these reconstructions the copyists were either "orthodox" Christians or heretics with axes to grind. For religiously invested readers, the thought of a Bible corrupted by copyists is deeply unnerving.

When scholarly focus is trained on the social status of servile workers, however, this picture of textual corruption seems less uniformly likely. Some interventions were theologically motivated, but the recognition that many manuscripts were copied by servile workers should reshape how people think about the character of their work. Perhaps some of the changes in the manuscript tradition derived from the workplace of the copyist, their interior lives, and their experiences, rather than a desire to reinforce a particular theological position. The copyists who toiled in ancient bookshops in the first and second centuries were not the conspiratorial figures some have imagined them to be. In some instances, it is impossible to know whether these copyists were even Christians.

Ancient intellectuals were intensely aware of the problem that diverging copies of the same text presented, and they seem to have enjoyed debating which copy was the most accurate. The second-century writer Aulus Gellius got into fierce debates about the wording of texts and espoused the importance of collating manuscripts and securing copies produced by well-respected copyists. The third-century exegete and philosopher Origen of Alexandria, whose *Hexapla* and *Tetrapla* reconciled the various versions of the Hebrew Bible, regularly referred to different copies (*antigrapha*) of biblical books. Like Aulus Gellius and one of his contemporaries, the physician Galen, Origen may have been a pedantic intellectual outlier. Most early Christians did not concern themselves with diverging copies, and most Romans likely did not either.[36]

Even to those intellectuals who cared, it is not clear that the existence of differing manuscripts was always problematic. For some, the existence of multiple manuscripts, all containing slightly different versions of the same text, may have been a welcome opportunity to display their own good judgment (*iudicium*). The ability to evaluate manuscripts separated the well-educated Roman man from the servile boy. It was in these moments of textual adjudication that the pseudo-intellectual was exposed, and it is debatable whether the existence of different versions of the same text was entirely negative. Like the grit that irritated the oyster and produced a pearl, a variant could unmask an imposter while also revealing the truth.[37]

In those cases where differences between manuscripts became deeply troubling to ancient writers, it was usually because of differences that, in their view, were the fault of servile or low-status workers. Galen, for example, obsessed over unauthorized and inaccurate versions of his work that circulated on the Roman book market. For Galen, these illicit and erroneous copies of his work had their origins in the hands of servile, mercantile, incompetent, and—to his mind—duplicitous notaries, copyists, and booksellers.[38]

When early Christian intellectuals worried about major alterations to scripture, they, like their peers, portrayed those textual meddlers as servile artisans. Referring to the textual work of their "heretical" counterparts, orthodox Christians summoned the same elitist prejudices to delegitimize certain forms of interpretation and editorial work. In short, they depicted "heretical" editors as bad readers.

In the memories of orthodox Christians, there were several early teachers whose interests in textual collation and emendation were seen as dangerous, aberrant, and servile. The first, Theodotus the Cobbler, worked in an unimposing leatherworking store in Rome in the latter half of the second century. On a worktable more accustomed to the incision and stitching of leather, Theodotus analyzed logic, compared manuscripts of Christian books, and waxed philosophical. According to our meager sources, Theodotus was an influential figure until Victor, Bishop of Rome, excommunicated him. One line of thought claims that Theodotus was from Byzantium and thus a drop in the steady trickle of Greek-speaking immigrants who dripped into Rome from the eastern provinces in the second century. Though he was a cobbler by trade, even his critics conceded that he was "very learned in argument." Perhaps he was less a shoemaker and more the kind of business owner whose success infuriated the old money of Rome. In any case, he was not the first leatherworker to achieve distinction as an intellectual.[39]

It is likely that Theodotus's store, like that of other successful shoemakers, was located south of the Forum, in the same area that housed the bookstores frequented by Galen and Aulus Gellius, close to the temples where intellectuals stored their libraries and engaged in erudite skirmishes. Perhaps it was here, in the company of books and bookmakers, that Theodotus learned to correct manuscripts. Eusebius noted that Theodotus was a devotee of geometry, philosophy, and medicine, and hypothesized that it was this misdirected attention that led him astray. His philosophical training meant that he approached the divine scriptures not — as he should have — using the "rule of faith" but with formal logic. The Greek word translated as "rule" here is *kanon*. In its most literal meaning, it referred to a rigid bar that could be used to measure and keep things straight. Rulers were such a regular part of bookwork that they have been found in tombs as part of stationery kits. *Kanon* could also refer to grammatical standards, models, guides, and even, in metaphorical contexts, to people. Cicero, for example, referred to Tiro as his writing's *kanon* (ruler, standard, or guide).[40]

According to his critics, it was the absence of this Christian interpretive rule and the use of the "skills of unbelievers" that led Theodotus and his followers to "recklessly [lay] hands on the holy writings, claiming to correct" them. The language of correction or, more literally, making straight was technical terminology for editing manuscripts. It is impossible to make things straight, though, without an equally upright guide and it showed. Ironically, the manuscripts produced by Theodotus and his disciples all differed from one another. Rather than clarifying texts through correction, as they claimed, they introduced differences and obscured the meaning of the scriptures. By their own standards, they were failures. The root of the problem lay not with correcting manuscripts—all manuscripts had corrections in them, after all—but rather in how they approached and misread scripture itself. You cannot straighten a text unless you have the rule(r) of faith as a guide. Theodotus and his disciples misunderstood what they read, these heresy hunters argued, and altered it to make sense of it. The biting irony is that a man devoted to geometry did not possess an interpretive ruler.[41]

A similar weakness, we are told, afflicted Marcion, a teacher who, some said, started his career as a shipowner in Pontus, on the Black Sea. He breezed into Rome in the middle decades of the second century with enough wealth and charisma to win him supporters in the Christian community. A sizable donation to local religious leaders—perhaps as large as 200,000 sestertii—cemented his position on the Christian social circuit.[42]

The animating principle of Marcion's textual machinations was his rejection of the Hebrew Bible. To Marcion, the God of the Hebrew Bible appeared flighty, inconsistent, and immoral, and thus Marcion elected to dispense with this foundational set of scriptural texts. In their stead, Marcion placed his own Bible: a single gospel and a collection of ten Pauline letters, beginning with Galatians, the letter that is most easily read as a rejection of Jewish texts and traditions. Though it relied heavily on Luke, Marcion's gospel was unattributed and unmoored from the apostolic traditions that (by this time) connected Matthew, Mark, Luke, and John to Jesus. It was this unnamed gospel that scandalized his peers. Perhaps Marcion audaciously wrote his own version of Luke in the way that others had rewritten Mark, or perhaps—as Irenaeus and Tertullian suggested—Marcion had merely mangled Luke through bad editing.[43]

In their characterizations of Marcion's work, Irenaeus and Tertullian pictured him as an immoderate, disfiguring editor who claimed to have "corrected" and "recovered" the Gospel of Luke when in actuality he had produced a falsified version. Tertullian began his vicious attack on Marcion by comparing him to the curator's professional nemesis, the mouse. "What Pontic mouse," Tertullian asked, "is more ravenous than the one who has gnawed away the Gospels?" Having "mutilated" Luke and produced his own fragmentary gospel, Marcion proceeded to dismember the epistles of Paul, removing those sections that undermined his own belief system. Just as with Theodotus, Irenaeus and Tertullian saw Marcion's theological commitments as the precursor to his voracious editorial campaign. Before he produced his version of the Bible, he wrote his *Antitheses*, a philosophically informed theological work that juxtaposed the moral natures of Christ and the creator God. This work supplied the critical basis for his rejection of Judaism and the Hebrew Bible.[44]

In Tertullian's scheme, the "barbarian" assumptions of Marcion's *Antitheses* formed the heart of Marcionite heresy and drove his misguided analysis of scripture. Armed only with heretical arguments, Marcion wielded not the full toolbox of the copyist, but only a knife. Tertullian went even further: the problem wasn't just that Marcion was a textual butcher and—given his nautical background—a pirate, he was also a bad reader. Tertullian's polemic traces the origins of Marcion's errors to Jewish readings of scripture. The language of mutilation Tertullian uses to describe Marcion's editing is the vocabulary of circumcision. Marcion, he alleges, is acting like a Jew. Here both irony and bald-faced anti-Semitism punctuate the criticism. The teacher who scorned the Hebrew Bible was himself a textual circumciser whose anti-intellectual butchery is shaped by Jewish reading practices.[45]

The stories of these Christian thinkers come to us through opponents who were unashamedly uncharitable (as well as anti-Semitic). What they reveal, however, is that when early Christians thought about the ways that editors and copyists might potentially "mangle" the Christian Bible, they utilized broader cultural biases against low-status work and workers. Against Marcion, Tertullian deployed the same ethnically coded judgments that elite Romans tossed around about artisans and early Christians. In his response to Celsus, Origen refused to concede that so-called true Christians ever produced versions of the same text that varied from one another. That was something only "heretical" and low-status Christians did.[46]

When orthodox Christians portrayed their rivals as ill-educated textual meddlers, they contributed to an enduring caricature of artisanal book workers as incompetent and destructive. For at least the first two centuries of the Common Era, almost all copying and correcting was done by servile people whose work was more curatorial and editorial than ancient polemic admits. They were not the partisan monks of late antique and medieval monasteries; they were scratching out a living in workshops. The idea of copying as corruption is an inherently enslaving idea that misrepresents the character and interests of copyists and other book workers.

Even as some early Christian theologians used classist tropes to defame the reputation of the "heretical" teachers with whom they disagreed, they were, broadly speaking, less concerned about the small differences between copies of the texts than are their modern counterparts. Instead, their focus—much like that of Roman elites in general—lay on "reading well." Differences between texts were unavoidable because they were produced by human hands. For Christian intellectuals like Origen, Irenaeus, and Tertullian, these differences might be benign and easily corrected by the properly educated Christian reader.

A professional copyist and corrector could comb a manuscript for errors and catch many small fractures, but it was the interpretive act of reading that was decisive for setting the text's meaning. It is precisely because manuscripts were inherently flawed that discernment and judgment were seen as playing such an important role in securing the meaning of the text. For people of the enslaving class (which included Christians), a person whose judgment had been improperly shaped (that is, a non-elite person) was seen, by definition and nature, as both morally deficient and incapable of reading well. Thus it was bad judgment that turned Marcion, Theodotus, and their followers into textual parasites and corruptors. It was often poor judgment, not the textual variants themselves, that distorted the meaning of scripture. Ultimately, it was bad readers, not bad texts, who were the heart of the issue.

Textual variety has elicited no small amount of hand-wringing among modern readers, but its centrality emerges out of a particular set of contemporary commitments. Some modern Christians worry that they cannot access the "real" New Testament if they do not know what it originally said; but a second-century Christian might respond that in worrying about the state of the manuscripts, people have run ahead of themselves. What does it matter what the text says, if the person reading cannot understand it anyway? For early Christians, reading was an interpretive and moral act that straightened the meaning of the text. If good reading is more important than perfect texts, it is, thus, of inestimable importance that many of those doing the work of early Christian reading and interpretation were enslaved.

CHAPTER SIX

THE FACES OF THE GOSPEL

Sometime in the early second century, an enslaved reader was reviewing a copy of the Gospel now called Mark. That evening, the reader's enslaver was hosting a dinner party for his friends. The wine would be free-flowing and the food, prepared by a slightly nervous cook, included delicacies like crawfish and pig's liver. And, at some point, when eating had slowed to grazing, the reader—let's call him Felix—would be asked to read the Gospel for the guests.

Even though some of the guests would likely be drunk, and the floor littered with the detritus of the costly meal, Felix's performance had to be close to perfect. If he stumbled over a turn of phrase, lost his place in the blur of letters, or mispronounced a word, he could lose the audience and might even be heckled—or worse.[1]

Felix had a problem. The Gospel of Mark wasn't long or difficult to follow, the Greek was easy enough, the sentences short, and it was helpful that the miracle stories had been tidily collected together towards the beginning. If he lost his place or accidentally skipped one, there was a chance that no one would notice. But how to finish? The story seemed to end midsentence.

The final word of the Gospel of Mark was the conjunction *gar*, meaning *for*. It wasn't wrong, exactly, it just wasn't well-written: an audience would expect a more emphatic ending. Reading events were supposed to spark conversation, and exotic stories of foreign marvels in far-flung lands were usually quite good for that. Mark, however, was not. Its ending didn't sound like an ending.

Felix would have prepared by reviewing the text at least half a dozen times, planning out his facial expressions, verbal inflection, and hand gestures in advance. He had likely jotted some light marks in the margins as a guide, but he kept returning to the unsatisfying conclusion. Even if he did everything right, there was the possibility that at the end of the performance he might be greeted with expectant faces wondering why he had stopped. Reading was an energetic, disheveling, and sweaty activity even without the additional concerns that subpar material elicited. *Maybe I'll just get a tongue-lashing*, he might have thought. Perhaps the group would get distracted and fixate on the original meaning of a word. Elite intellectuals were known to get into fierce debates over such things: a well-timed verbal carcass tossed to the pedantic wolves could draw their attention away.

There was another way around the problem. Perhaps a few sentences mentioning some postmortem apparitions and miraculous deeds could wrap things up nicely? Felix was already quite familiar with such stories from other versions of the gospel he had encountered. And he knew how to do it: expanding traditions, paraphrasing works, and imitating the words of other authors was something that he, like others, had learned in school. A swift summary that embraced the gastronomic setting of the reading and had the apostles recline alongside the audience would make for a more impressive performance. Framing all of this with the marvelous—a favored talking point for the educated—made for a wonderful conversation starter.

The plan went much better than Felix could have hoped. It had been fortuitous that the dinner included figs that he could gesture to during the otherwise quite befuddling fig tree episodes. The dinner guests were delighted by the culinary and literary feast. As they stumbled out into the streets, their pathways lit by handheld lamps and steadied by helpful arms, everyone agreed that the enslaver threw excellent dinner parties. One guest had taken a notary, Rhodion, to record the evening's reading. Felix's expansions now had textual form. Rhodion's shorthand notes on the Gospel were fleshed out into a fresh copy.

Between the two of them, Felix and Rhodion had created a new expression of the Gospel of Mark, one more suited to this occasion. It was hardly the first time either of them had done this; Felix regularly reorganized sentences in his performances to make them more elegant. Crafting morsels for the ear was one of his talents. Neither one of them could be said to have changed the written text either solely or jointly: Felix had performed it with emendations, as was customary, and Rhodion had transcribed what he had heard, as he was tasked. Improving works for performance was part of Felix's remit, and even if this longer ending was a bit creative, it was a paraphrase of other episodes of the—at the time—rather fluid life of Jesus.

So far as I know, there was never a Felix. Though each detail in this story rests upon some ancient and academic foundation, it is of my own imagining. I invented Felix, Rhodion, and the situation that gave rise to the additional endings to Mark (the episodes known today as Mark 16:9–20). In many ways this is a necessity: the Roman documentarian spirit, unlike the more familiar forms of bureaucracy that emerged in the aftermath of the French Revolution, did not pretend to represent, or document, every person and every thing. Those who did paperwork did not always leave paper trails. Though my account is narrative rather than argumentative, it is not markedly different from other scholarly explanations for the longer ending. Alternatives that identify the intentions, ambitions, and even theological allegiances of the individuals who transcribed the longer ending also assume unmediated access to the (un)consciousness of far-removed others. They just don't always tell us that.

If you consult a study Bible today, you can see the questionable status of the longer ending (Mark 16:9–20) marked, usually in square brackets, by a modern editor. Scholars agree that it is a later development in the textual history of Mark, even if they disagree about who was responsible for it. Most analyses credit copyists or editors with the innovation. My own historically informed fabulation privileges the reader (*lector*), a figure who is largely absent from traditional accounts of the rise of Christianity. Though they might also have sometimes taken dictation or inscribed texts themselves, readers (*lectores*) were those who read aloud from manuscripts written and copied by others. In doing so they built upon the work of the copyist and shaped the interpretation of the text and dramatically advanced the spread of Christianity in ways that no other literary worker could.[2]

At gatherings of Christians it was the servile reader who brought the gospel alive. Their animated performances guided the group's understanding of each passage and coaxed them through difficult passages. The same story, in the hands of a talented reader, could be reshaped through emphasis to speak to a variety of different concerns, to offer damning commentary, or to unify a group and marshal a consensus. For many Christians in the ancient world, it was in these moments of communal interpretation that the Bible sang, came to have meaning, and became relevant to their lives.

✝

Ancient literacy was a spectrum, not a binary. While today the word *literate* tends to refer to those who can both read and write, there were in the past — as there are in the present — many who can read, to varying degrees, without being able to write; who are numerically literate but unable to get to grips with dense philosophy; or who can read and write at elementary-school levels — enough to copy something out — without being able to compose something elegant or grammatically correct. Even those without access to books would have scrutinized the letters on coins, epitaphs, and imperial inscriptions; might have had to enter into a legal contract, or make a will; or would have encountered visual references to literacy in artwork, graffiti, and physical objects. Literacy was a sign of social status and erudition, and thus books, whether within arm's reach, on bookstands, or in engravings, conveyed status. And as status symbols, books were legible to all.[3]

In English, "reading" refers quite exclusively to the act of running one's eyes over the letters of a book and soaking in their meaning. Ancient taxonomies were blurrier. The language of "reading" could equally refer to the translation of written script into mental or vocalized ones or the practice of listening to others read aloud. Many ancient Christian authors refer to the latter as "hearing" a text read aloud, or being "hearers of the gospel," but conceptually there was no bright line between listening to a text being read and reading the text oneself as skills. What was more important was whether one had understood what was read.

Whether one reads Greek, Latin, Hebrew, or any other language, reading is interpretative. When children learned to read in antiquity, the teacher would often ease them into the difficulties of textual decipherment by dividing words, inserting punctuation, and crowning important letters with breathing marks, but highly literate adults were generally expected to navigate the relentless stream of letters with ease. Hebrew offered additional complexities and possibilities; not only were characters often written continuously, but ancient Hebrew was written without short vowels. Even once letters were sorted into words, the reader had to adjudicate between many additional possible vocalizations and meanings for each word.

Consider, if you will, how people might pronounce the vowels in "read." Whether it is pronounced like "red" or "reed" determines whether the action took place in the past or in the present. Some words have antithetical meanings that can only be determined by context. The word *sanction*, for example, can mean both approval and censure; it is only our understanding of the context that supplies its meaning in any instance. Now imagine how much more space there was for interpretation if a word had no vowels, as was usually the case in Hebrew writing. To give an imprecise analogy using English: *read* would be written as *rd* and the reader would have to determine if the word was *read* or *raid*. One might label this skill decipherment.[4]

The challenges of decipherment and reading aloud meant that those who read publicly, like Felix, had to prepare. In many cases, they rehearsed so well that reading merged with recitation from memory. In the context of public readings, many Jews who read scripture aloud in Hebrew were performing a hybrid of reading and recitation. Some became specialists in particular texts. Later rabbinic opinions differentiated expert instructors in Ecclesiastes from those with facility in Proverbs. Repetition was also the ethos of Roman education, and specialists in particular texts or authors were well-known. The ever-critical Aulus Gellius once encountered a would-be grammarian who claimed to be the foremost expert on Varro's *Satires*. Aulus Gellius made (by his own account) short work of the upstart, but a true specialist had the ability both to defend their knowledge against detractors and also to elevate the quality of their intellectual engagement. The Greek-speaking orator Dio Chrysostom advised his audience that to read the comic poets carefully, you should not casually read them to yourself, but instead have trained experts read to you.[5]

Although there is a stubborn myth that ancient people could not read silently, those who learned to read by vocalizing aloud, as children still do today, could read silently in their heads without recourse to the spoken word. This does not mean, however, that silent reading was their preferred modality. A great deal of ancient reading was a participatory social affair, and most descriptions of it seem to envision reading aloud. There are exceptions, of course; both Quintilian and Pliny lauded the intense and generative silence of solitary nighttime work. But even when elites talked about solitary reading, they did not necessarily mean that they were reading alone, but rather that there was a smaller audience. A restless Augustus, for example, would summon readers to his chambers in the witching hours. It was, Dio Chrysostom said, more enjoyable to have things read to you by men who know just how to render the lines properly: the effect of a text is enhanced "when one is relieved of the preoccupation of reading."[6]

Many ancient city-dwellers attended reading events where texts were performed. I say *performed* because reading was a physical activity that was accompanied by a carefully choreographed vocabulary of bodily gestures and facial expressions that conveyed the emotion and tone of narrative moments. You could follow the pathos of the work even if you were hard of hearing. Speaking and acting were species of communication, and while ancient educators did not exactly want their charges to imitate enslaved actors, they begrudgingly acknowledged that they operated in the same sphere. For us moderns who examine the skeletal remains of these performances on the page, there is much that we miss. The statement of the centurion at the crucifixion, that "truly this man was Son of God" (Mark 15:39), might have been delivered with a straight face, or it might have been loaded with irony and accompanied by a hand gesture or expression that functioned as modern scare quotes do. There was no fixed interpretation, and no way for us to access it if there had been.[7]

Depending on the angle from which it is viewed, Christian reading can appear either as a subset of Jewish religious reading or as part of the broader world of the ancient Mediterranean. Talented scholars have argued for both sides (and various options in between) but there are commonalities between these overlapping groups. In almost all cases, the group utilized the services of a trained *lector*. By the second century, Christians were gathering in one another's homes for meals and reading aloud from scripture in settings reminiscent of Greek and Roman *symposia*, ancient clubs and associations, and the scriptural readings of the Jewish community based at Qumran, by the Dead Sea. Christian readings preceded the meals, wrote the Christian philosopher Justin, and went on for as long as time permitted. A reading was followed by an address that explained the content and developed its moral themes. A description of this kind of exposition survives in the novelistic *Acts of Peter* 20–21, in which Peter entered a dining room, rolled up a scroll, and explained the meaning of what was just read. The length of readings and their subsequent interpretation were determined not just by the whims of the host or the intentions of the expositor, but also by the punctuality of the guests, the cook, and whichever household attendant was responsible for timekeeping.

Many of the texts read aloud at Christian gatherings were from the Hebrew Bible and the Gospels, but Paul and the author of the Apocalypse of John (the final book of the Christian Bible) clearly expected that their works would be read publicly. Performing this service had a personal benefit to the *lector*; the opening of Revelation stipulates that the one "who reads these words" to the group is "blessed" (Rev. 1:3). By the third century, the role of the *lector* in what would loosely be called Christian services began to be formalized as a low-status but official rank in the nascent church. The role of *lector* exists today in many Christian denominations, having evolved into a more codified official role.

Before this period and, in many cases, during and after it, it is likely that enslaved or formerly enslaved readers were the most proficient candidates available: they were trained copyists, notaries, readers, bookkeepers, and so on. They may not all have been enslaved or freedpersons, but, as already discussed, young servile workers served in this capacity at Roman, Greek, and Jewish reading events. Many Christians were also enslavers, and we should assume that they used enslaved people in the same way.[8]

Even apart from social events, like those held in private homes or synagogues, where it was expedient to have a professional or trained reader, there were practical reasons why someone literate might use a *lector*. Readers could assist with editing a composition. They could read a text back to the author or a small group of trusted friends. Delegating reading to others mid-composition meant that an author could consult several different works simultaneously, accelerating the work of research by cutting out the lengthy, repetitive process of rolling, unrolling, and locating one's place in a text. It also allowed one to "read" and "write" at the same time. It's impossible to imagine that Pliny the Elder's encyclopedic *Natural History* could have been composed without his staff of omnipresent enslaved workers. While some took dictation, others read the relevant portions of books and notebooks aloud. It was a synergistic project that depended upon readers and writers working in concert with one another. The fact that we associate the end product with Pliny alone says more about the system in which the work was created than it does about the authorship of the work itself.

Assistants were almost certainly used by Christian writers as well. Modern scholars of the New Testament agree that there is a literary relationship between Matthew, Mark, and Luke. The three synoptic Gospels contain many of the same stories and sayings, which they often produce in the same language and order. The overlap between them suggests that at least one, if not two, evangelists were using another Gospel (almost always identified as Mark) as a source when they composed their Gospels. Some speculate that other hypothetical texts, enigmatically known as Q, M, and L, were in the compositional mix. If Matthew or Luke used more than one text in their research and writing, then it would have benefited them to have had at least one if not multiple readers (to say nothing of secretaries) to assist them. Origen's voluminous commentaries on biblical books and his multi-source *Hexapla*, a critical edition of the Hebrew Bible produced in six versions and multiple languages, involved a team of enslaved assistants whose reading and translation skills were, as already noted, critical to the production of these works.

For those who did not have writerly aspirations themselves, readers could serve an accommodative purpose: enslavers who wrestled with congenital or age-related loss of visual acuity needed to use readers to participate in business as well as literary culture. Nighttime reading is increasingly difficult as people age, which is one reason why ancient people worked in the bright light of the morning.

The bodily strain of reading meant that the *lector*, whether enslaved or not, was likely to have been young. Romans were aware that the senses of children do not tire as easily as those of adults, and this observation can explain why young children were regularly employed in bookwork. From the third century onwards, when Christians began to formalize the role of the *lector*, children feature prominently in the evidence. The use of enslaved readers and children may have put them in harm's way. In remarking on the persecution of Christians in late antique North Africa, Victor of Vita noted that among "those who were exiled were many readers who were little children." In the mid-third century, Cyprian elevated a child named Aurelius to the position of reader because he had stayed true to the faith when he was put on trial. In the late second century, a Christian martyr named Speratus, a common name for enslaved people, was brought to court while carrying a bag containing copies of Paul's writings. It is reasonable to suppose that he, too, was an enslaved *lector* or messenger.[9]

The use of readers not only enabled those with bodily impairments to read, they also permitted women, whose education was generally less extensive, to have access to erudite works and elevated philosophical conversation. Though some influential scholarship argues that women in the ancient world were, by and large, illiterate, it overlooks the ways that literate workers helped everyone bridge the literacy gap. This applies to women as it did to low-status attendants and musicians who were present at dinner parties and reading events. Nor did one need to attend a symposium or private recitation to gain access to new ideas and classic stories: public readings and poetry competitions were popular, and Dio Chrysostom recalls that when he strolled through the Hippodrome, the sound of people telling stories and reciting poetry filled his ears.[10]

Even without the mediating assistance of a reader, some women could and did read, sometimes in a professional capacity. An inscription from Rome records the name of an enslaved *lectrix* called Sulpicia Petale. A relief from Trastevere (near ancient Rome and now in the city) shows a well-dressed butcher's wife doing accounts, and a mural from Pompeii depicts a woman holding wax tablets as she draws a writing implement to her lips. Literate women like the servile Grapte and aristocratic Perpetua appear as readers, teachers, and authors in early Christian narratives; the concern about female, enslaved, and young reader-reciters found in rabbinic texts suggests that women did work in this capacity; and later Christian hagiography lists numerous literate women who had access to and cared for sizable libraries.[11]

Second-century CE *funerary relief showing a woman, possibly the wife of the butcher (right), working with tablets while her putative husband chops meat*

Funerary evidence, too, suggests that women participated in literary culture in various ways. Women's graves in Italy, the Netherlands, Germany, and Britain are accessorized with ink-wells, styli, writing tablets, knives, rulers, and spatulas for smoothing the surface of a wax tablet. This inexhaustive list of evidence is considerably shorter than comparable data for men's literacy, but to dismiss it all as performative would be special pleading. Moreover, and unless one wishes to argue that all ancient women were deaf, any woman within earshot of an enslaved *lector* would have been an auditory reader. In all these ways, the message of Christianity would have reached—and in turn been shaped by—enslaved women as well as enslaved men.[12]

Though the servile *lector* mediated and shaped the meaning of the written word for the audience, they worked in a synergistic relationship with the copyist, the written text, the audience, and their environment. The imagined performance that opened this chapter showed a notary and a reader coauthoring a new version of the gospel. But there are better-documented examples of the ways in which literate workers worked in concert with one another, and how they shaped the foundational texts of Christianity in the process.

Jewish readers, for example, who regularly recited Hebrew scriptures from memory in the synagogue, were at liberty to insert memorized words or phrases in their oral recitation even if those words were not in the manuscript to hand. Similarly, some rabbis suggested that omitting a word or paragraph was allowable for a reader so long as the transition was imperceptible to the accompanying translator, who made the Hebrew intelligible to Greek- or Aramaic-speaking members of the congregation. Even editing on the fly was defensible if it made risqué passages a bit more family-friendly: thus, sexual intercourse became "lying down." Just as modern travelers expect that films are edited for airplane viewing today, so too rabbinic authors accepted some subtle censorship. The limiting factor here was not exactly the text, nor always the audience, but above all else intelligibility.[13]

The relationships between different invisible actors—translator, reader, and copyist—can help readers understand the text of the New Testament itself. A prophetic vision about the impending apocalypse in Mark 13 is interrupted by the aside "let the reader understand" (v. 14). Many modern Bibles mark the phrase in parentheses. It alerted the *lector* to the fact that the preceding mention of the "desolating sacrilege" is an allusion to a vision in the biblical book of Daniel. As it stands in Greek, the quotation is grammatically unexpected. The aside calls for stress, or even a pause and brief explanation of the content here. It highlights the collaborative relationship between scribe and reader. Perhaps, in its inception, a readerly copyist wrote the note for themselves or for a colleague as a kind of reminder. In this instance it is possible that, like the story of the woman caught in adultery in John 7–8, it originated in the margins as a gloss and was promoted to the main text. The copyist may have flagged the grammatical infelicity and reference to Daniel, as if to say, "Heads up, you may get questions," or "Watch that you say this correctly," or even "Interpret this prophecy as you see fit." It is not necessary to see the gloss as an authorial power grab. On the contrary, it might grant the *lector* license to expound freely or offer them the kind of collegial warning shared between classmates during exam seasons.[14]

The synergic relationship between copyist and reader, seen in Mark's and John's textual histories, also existed between reader and audience. Ancient readers could read rooms as well as books. While the *lector* was the conductor, who influenced the auditors with hand gestures and expressions, they would also have responded to the mood of the assembled group and tailored their performance to the emotional climate. They drew the environment into the performance: architecture, furniture, and attendees all became props. Early on, the Gospel of Mark issues the repeated invitation: "Those who have ears to hear, let them hear" (Mark 4:9, 23). Like knuckles rapped against a desk, the call to pay attention, which resurfaces throughout the Gospel, may have been accompanied by gestures that beckoned liminal audience members into the reading. The tired and hungry enslaved waitstaff leaning against the walls for support, the kitchen workers who were close enough to overhear, the attendants at public events who were there to take notes or carry belongings, and the homeless beggars lingering on the dusty fringes of public events were all invited into a Gospel reading that in many ways was directed to them. With whom did the reader lock eyes when they spoke about those with ears to hear or those who hunger? To whom did they gesture when they read the instructions about widows, orphans, and the poor in Luke and the Epistle of James? Could the *lector* have produced spontaneous displays of generosity in his audience members? Did a reading of the story of the feeding of the five thousand—where

A mosaic showing the abundant food discarded at the banquets of the wealthy—a Roman artistic theme that was so popular it has its own name (asarotos oikos, or "unswept floor"). In the bottom-right corner, a dog snacks on the debris.

Jesus multiplied loaves and fishes and instructed people to gather up the abundant scraps into baskets at the conclusion — shame wealthier householders into gathering and sharing the picnic of discarded food accumulating on their floors with the destitute?

The argument of the Canaanite woman that Jesus should help her daughter (who was possessed by a demon) because even "dogs eat the crumbs that fall from the master's table" read differently at dinner parties where animals picked over the remains of the meal (Matt. 15:37). Merely through ambiguous gesture and emphasis, the *lector* had power to direct attention and shape interpretation.[15]

The relationships between reader and scribe and between reader and audience were unstable and irreplicable. Each reading produced moments of emotion-filled resonance that were as varied and shifting as the weather — and perhaps even affected by it. Each expression to the next called people to action in specific ways. Reading is thus never a simple act. Breath, vocalization, pauses, emphasis, and accent all translate the written word into something else. The reader was not just an authority figure — they were an author.

One of the perils of adapting a literary classic, whether for the big screen or for the small tablet, is that casting the role of a beloved character is sure to be controversial. The actor's physical appearance and their interpretation of the role inevitably confirm or clash with the vision of the cherished friend that readers already have in their minds. While those who grew up with the book might be disappointed, another set of viewers will be inexorably shaped by the presence on the screen. The coexistence of several cinematic portrayals of the same character means that, depending on their age, onetime audience members living in the same household might equally picture Shakespeare's Juliet as Olivia Hussey (from Zeffirelli's 1968 version of *Romeo and Juliet*) or Claire Danes (from Luhrmann's 1996 iteration). The overwriting of identities goes both ways: sometimes a TV or film character becomes so closely tied to a particular actor that it is difficult for audiences to see that actor as anyone else. More than one successful thespian has bemoaned the perils of typecasting—when a particular person becomes so intimately tied to a kind of character or work that they blend into one another.

What is true of modern cinema was also true of ancient servile *lectores*. When texts were read aloud in antiquity, it was a performance that utilized not just an individual servile reader's literate ability, but also their physical presence. For audience members, a reader who performed the text became the personification of the author. Their vocal intonation, hand gestures, and facial expressions led the audience on a journey. It was precisely because reading events skirted the line between emotionally beguiling oratory and theater that they were so powerful. The rhetorician Quintilian wrote that when a speech was performed aloud, the speaker (who employed a scroll) stimulated the auditor "by the animation of his delivery, and kindle[d] the imagination, not just by presenting a vivid picture, but by bringing us into actual touch with the things themselves." The performance was the invention of the speaker. Even if the speaker was themselves the composer of the speech, the performance was the "newborn offspring of imagination.... We are moved not merely by the actual issue of the trial but by all that the orator himself has at stake."[16]

Though oratory was distinctive, other modes of reading aloud used similar corporeal strategies. The reading of letters was also a question of transporting the auditor into the presence of the author. Many wealthy writers would have tried to direct the performance ahead of time. But at the moment of reading, and regardless of anyone's efforts at authorial impersonation, it was the reader who interpreted, shaped, and transmitted the emotions of the text and the presence of the author.

In this context, the letter-reader became the author, both for those who knew him and, more crucially, for those who did not. Most auditors of the Gospels were unacquainted with those who were said to have written them. Paul's first audiences may constitute a special case, but within half a century of his missionary journeys, there were few alive who could remember him, either. For this majority, the readers were the authors. They channeled not just the intentions of the authors, however tentatively those authors were sketched, but their presence as well. While enslaved *lectores* are invisible in modern histories of the Gospels, they were, to ancient audiences, the faces of the Gospel.

The ability of the reader to influence the interpretation of a text and perception of its author was not lost on ancient power brokers either. It is unlikely to have sat well with everyone. Hints of this live on in Pliny's report of the then-novel practice of dedicating portraits of celebrated authors like Homer in prominent public libraries. These portraits sparked an emotional response in viewers, who closely associated the books with the images. Whatever affective response the portraits elicited, they also served to police the role of the lower-status reader. By speaking for themselves, writes classicist David Petrain, the portraits "deprive others of the chance [to speak for them]. . . . Their arrangement fixes in place an authorized view of the literary tradition that . . . defended against individual, revisionist performances." This was an attempt to guard the text against subversive performance. It is a tacit admission of the power of the servile reader.[17]

In their own ways, Christian leaders were equally attentive to the power of the reader. Between textual variation, copyist errors, and readerly interpretation, the works that were read

aloud to Christian auditors might have drifted from the meaning of "the" gospel. Tertullian suggested that if you were to
travel to the churches founded by the apostles, in a manner
akin to the manuscript-hunting bibliophiles of ancient Rome,
you would find their "authentic writings" preserved there. In
Corinth, Philippi, Ephesus, and Rome, he wrote, these writings
were "recited, uttering the voice and representing the appearance of each of them." The situation he envisioned evoked the
antiquarian bibliophilic interests of his day, but also focused on
performance—the "voices and appearance" of the apostles themselves—as if not only texts but also their vocalization had been
handed down in an unbroken performative tradition.[18]

In more philosophical Christian circles, group reading was
seen as an almost mystical mode of communion. In describing
the higher-level meanings embedded in scripture, Clement of
Alexandria wrote that "the mysteries are transmitted mysteri-
ously in order that they might be on the lips of one speaking and
the one spoken to, or rather, not in the voice, but in the understanding." This passage might be seen to shift the intellectual
focus from voice to mind, and indeed it does that, but only par-
tially. For Clement, even the most elevated forms of elite spiritual reading were best described in terms of hearing: the ear is
the organ of perception with which Christians must listen
closely, "in a hidden way." Unlike the rhetorician Quintilian,
who distinguished between reading and auditing so as to draw
lines between the highest form of reading and other, inferior
forms, Clement maintained the auditory quality of superior
reading. For Clement, good Christians heard well, while the heretics heard doctrine "in a twisted way."[19]

On several occasions, Irenaeus, the second-century Bishop
of Lyon, worried about the influence of the reader. In a discussion of 2 Thessalonians 2:8, a passage about the Second Coming

of Jesus, he insisted that "if one does not pay attention to the reading and if [the reader] does not exhibit the intervals of breathing as they occur, there will not only be incongruities, but he will utter blasphemy when reading," by making it appear "as if the advent of the Lord could take place according to the working of Satan." Irenaeus issued an instruction that the *lector* must deliver the verse in such a way that "the apostle's meaning is preserved." The problem, Irenaeus openly admitted, is that Paul frequently transposed word order in his sentences. The language is technical, but the stakes are high: readerly interpretation might not only cloud the meaning of the apostolic text but also lead people into error. Readerly decisions could affect the liturgy as well. In a transcription of one of Augustine's sermons, a youthful, likely enslaved *lector* sang the wrong psalm during a service. Treating the error as an act of providence, Augustine delivered a homily on an unexpected topic and together they produced a new liturgy for the day.[20]

The decisions, interpretations, and indeed mistakes of readers have thus affected auditors of the New Testament who hear the Bible read aloud at church. Everyone from the graffiti artists of Pompeii to elite orators to Christianity's most celebrated theologians knew that readers had power. But here a fissure emerges between the realities of how people read and the rhetoric of what makes for good reading. For both ancient Roman literary theorists and early Christian theologians, there was reading and *reading*. Though a *lector* who mispronounced words or read haltingly was clearly a bad reader, the ability to vocalize without effort did not necessarily imply that they had understood what they were reading. Even as intellectuals exploited the skills of servile workers and children, they developed an ideology of "good reading" as an elite skill formed through education. Bad reading, on the other hand, was low-status and "slavish." The rhetorical representation of bad reading as servile is one of the reasons that enslaved readers are invisible to modern readers today.

For many Christian thinkers in the second century, the diversity of manuscripts and people was theoretically unproblematic. The symbiotic relationships between authors, messengers, and copyists were sustained by a unifying principle and a powerful force: the rule of faith and the Holy Spirit. The concept of the rule of faith, which persists to this day in some modern denominations, drew upon the implements of the humble workshop. Read properly with the powerful guidance of the Holy Spirit acquired at baptism and all will be well. The power of the text lay not just in the words on the page but in their interpretation. Readership and authorship were blended.

With the exception of some influential French philosophers and their intellectual heirs, most people would not categorize a letter carrier, copyist, or reader as an author. Yet all three played vital roles in the making of the Christian Bible and the early spread of Christianity. These uncredited missionaries, editors, curators, and meaning-makers were as integral to the survival and flourishing of Christianity as the authors or the apostles. The New Testament as it is known today came to have meaning through the assemblies of people, tools, and moments that have produced and nourished it. Often these interactions are invisible, but they are nevertheless meaningful. The living text of the Bible was constantly reproduced in ancient bookshops and butcher's stalls, as it still is in modern churches and lecture halls. This recognition should broaden the collective understanding not just of who we imagine was responsible for writing these texts, but also those with whom Christians imagine themselves reading.

Despite their best efforts, no one, from author to copyists to readers or bishop, was quite able to cement the meaning of the texts of the New Testament. The conceptual and linguistic raw materials on the page are constantly reproduced and reinterpreted. The language of enslavement, which was embedded in the earliest texts as a description of the Christ follower, was there from the very beginning, but its meaning was not fixed. Those who read and interpreted the New Testament in the centuries and millennia that followed were formed by this language, consciously or unconsciously, even as they reshaped it to suit their own circumstances, politics, interests, and ambitions. In this way, just as in the contributions of servile copyists and readers, Christian tradition still bears the mark of enslavement.

PART III

LEGACIES

CHAPTER SEVEN

THE FAITHFUL
CHRISTIAN

For nearly three centuries after the death of Jesus, until the
reign of Constantine the Great, the first Christian emperor,
Christians found themselves navigating turbulent social and
political waters. At various junctures and for a variety of reasons, they were socially marginalized and subjects of suspicion.
Upon occasion, general pagan distrust of Christians spilled over
into bloodshed: followers of Jesus were arrested, interrogated,
tortured, and sometimes executed. Though many Christians
grew wealthy and influential during this period, others knew
that if they found themselves in the wrong place at the wrong
time, things could devolve into violence. If they refused (on religious grounds) to sprinkle a few grains of incense in a fire, or to
swear an oath of allegiance to the emperor, they might find
themselves in figurative and literal hot water.

Most Christians, however, followed Jesus without experiencing any legal or social difficulties. This period, which is
romantically known as the Age of the Martyrs, was not a time
of constant persecution — but the memories of the deaths of the
few who were martyred altered the psychology of early

Christianity all the same. The stories of their final moments inspired the majority who remained: they were shared at gatherings and gravesites, in classes preparing converts for baptism, and in letters that crisscrossed the Mediterranean.[1]

In one such letter, written about 177 and preserved in the papers of a fourth-century historian, we learn of Blandina. According to her biographers, she was the finest of the celebrated martyrs of Lyon and the cheapest of enslaved workers. Though her name meant "winsome," it was something of a cruel joke. Everyone—even those who came to admire her—would negatively remark upon her physical appearance. Perhaps she would have been petite under any circumstances, but a lifetime of underfeeding and neglect had left her small and weak. Her complexion had a puffy quality to it, so much so that her facial features took on a pallid formlessness. The more compassionate might have wondered if she was sick, but others cruelly dismissed her as unsightly—if they troubled themselves to think of her at all. She would not have fetched much money on the auction block, nor was violence against her taken as seriously as it was for more valuable staff. She was, in a social economy in which corporeality was everything, easy to blame for anything that went wrong in the lives of those around her. As an *ancilla*—something like a kitchen girl—her work, and thus her worth, were barely recognized. She spent her days cleaning latrines, weaving, and cooking, invisible to her enslavers. And so, like that of Aesop and Shakespeare's Caliban, Blandina's perceived ugliness made her a regular target for verbal mistreatment and casual beatings.[2]

It is unclear why Blandina and her fellow martyrs were initially arrested. According to the story, animosity against Christians gathered heat during the summer of 177. Christians were excluded from the public baths and marketplaces, and an angry mob eventually dragged a group of alleged Christians to the tribune and accused them of the improbable crimes of incest and infant cannibalism.

The attention of the crowd, soldiers, and tribune fell upon a small group, whom they resolved to force to apostatize. Thinking strategically, they began with Blandina. To her torturers, she looked like easy pickings. Even fellow Christians wondered how she would hold up during the assaults. A small girl like that would surely struggle. The torturers reasoned that if they broke her first, they could use her mutilated body to threaten the others into recanting their beliefs. The men took turns assaulting her, from dawn to dusk. They tried every kind of torture, tearing clothes and strips of flesh from her so that her body was mangled and her insides were laid bare to the world. By sunset, as they stood hunched and panting, they realized their miscalculation. She was still breathing. A lifetime of ache had prepared her for this final trial.[3]

Seventeenth-century etching of Blandina bound to the stake. In the story, Blandina is described as hanging in the form of a cross.

Blandina was transformed: in the torture chamber, she was "filled with power." The rounds of torture that she endured brought her not pain but rest and restoration. After her tormentors had exhausted themselves, she was taken to the arena, where she hung in a cruciform pose, inspiring fellow Christians with her fortitude. As she hung suspended in the air, her spiritual siblings "looked...through their sister to the one who was crucified for them," and were persuaded by someone—either Christ or Blandina, the Greek is unclear—to believe "that everyone who suffers for the glory of Christ will have eternal fellowship with the living God." In a reversal of fortunes and cultural expectations, she whom society had deemed worthless was now a model for others—an enslaved Christian who led other Christians, an enslaved woman who was filled with power.[4]

Scholarly interpretations of this story have been divided. While Blandina is the one who dies, it is less clear if she is the one acting. On one hand, it is Blandina's prayers, her bravery, her love of Christ, and her encouragement that inspire her fellow Jesus followers. On the other, she is instrumentalized by the narrator and by Christ to make a point. When she is suspended on the crosslike stake, she seems to recede from view. Her imitation of Christ is so effective that she is subsumed into and by him. Christ was with(in) her, not in the kind of euphemistic way you can find on laminated bookmarks today but in a very material sense; acting in and through her. Almost thirty years later, the enslaved North African martyr Felicity, who was pregnant at the time of her arrest, spoke of her expectation that Christ would be with her in the amphitheater. During the vulnerable moments of childbirth, she told the guards who sadistically mocked her that when she suffered in the arena, things would be different: "Now I alone suffer what I am suffering, but then there will be another inside me, who will suffer for me, because I am going to suffer for him."[5]

To modern European and North American readers, and modern Christians in particular, the language of corporeal indwelling might seem strange or uncomfortable, but to these two enslaved women it was a source of comfort that drew upon ancient Mediterranean ideas about interactions between human beings and the mystical plane. Many believed that supernatural entities could inhabit human bodies, to cause them great harm, control them, endow them with great powers, or even provide them with comfort.

Blandina is relevant not only because she was enslaved and her story, too, was written by a (presumably enslaved) secretary, but also because she demonstrates the practical and lived realities of what it meant to be a Christian and enslaved. Martyrdom is the religious practice most regularly associated with early Christians, and had its origins in stories of Jewish heroes and in a wider Greek and Roman culture that valorized purposeful death. But to understand both the representation of Blandina and also why many early Christians embraced the idea of martyrdom as a feature of Christian identity in the centuries that followed the writing of the books of the New Testament, one must think about what it meant to be a "good slave" in antiquity.

What is true of the development of ideas about martyrdom is also accurate with respect to the emergence of Christian identity in general. To be a Christian often means to be enslaved to God or to behave as if one were enslaved to God. Even ideas like the indwelling of the Spirit, or the participation of the Christian in the body of Christ—ideas that live on in modern Christian denominations today and that are not conventionally seen as being "about" slavery—were built up around the conceptual scaffolding of enslavement. The logic of enslavement helps explain the activity of the Holy Spirit, the mechanics of baptism, the role of faith, and the demands of discipleship. Acknowledging that the language and logic of enslavement are present in these texts helps map the synaptic connections between seemingly unconnected and even incongruous concepts in Christianity. Though enslavement was not the only way in which people thought about the identity of Christ followers in the first few centuries after his death, it was a vital ideological force. It was, as South African historian of enslavement Chris de Wet has put it, "embedded in and constitutive of early Christian religious thought."[6]

The writings of the New Testament, but in particular the letters of Paul and Peter, are replete with the language of enslavement. The earliest Christian authors inaugurate a tradition that refers to all Christ followers as "slaves" (*douloi*) of God. Many people have read and continue to read this language of enslavement as a metaphor for the human condition or a euphemism for unquestioned devotion. But it was not a neutral metaphor for the enslaved collaborators who authored, copied, and read these stories. To them, and to enslaved Christians like Blandina, this language meant something. For the enslaved meaning-makers who had a hand in developing these texts, the description of all Christ followers as enslaved—regardless of social status—may have done democratizing work. In her study of the Petrine epistles (1 and 2 Peter), New Testament scholar Shively Smith has argued that the exhortation to enslaved Christians to embrace unjust beatings at the hands of their enslavers may have stemmed from an author or authors who themselves were enslaved. By comparing mistreated, enslaved people to Christ, they were both navigating a difficult space in which violence was unavoidable and subverting conventional hierarchies. In their account, it was enslaved people who were the most "Christly."[7]

The problem, as Smith is keenly aware, is with the ways in which later generations of Christians read these texts. Even as the general principle of enslavement to God was abstracted into a metaphor, these texts became tools of violent oppression in the hands of later generations of enslaving Christians. The theological idea that Christians should embrace suffering like Christ, for example—an idea that was rooted in scripture, that was embodied by Christian martyrs, and that flourished in the medieval period—has been used in recent history to coerce Black women into accepting violence and mistreatment.[8]

Understanding the legacies of the enslaved coproduction of the New Testament means acknowledging several entangled ideas: First, that enslaved coauthorship in antiquity shaped definitions of Christian identity in ways that have ramifications for people invested in these texts today. Second, that for almost two millennia, powerful Christians have interpreted passages about enslavement in the New Testament selectively and in ways that were fundamentally self-interested. Third, and relatedly, that in the hands of the powerful, certain violent principles governing how enslaved people should behave, be controlled, and be "punished" worked their way into the Christianity-shaped consciousnesses of Europe and North America.

This chapter and the next will explore how Christian identity was shaped by Roman ideas about "good slaves" and "bad slaves" and tease out some of the legacies of these ideas in the history of biblical interpretation. This final part of the book departs from the life course of the New Testament texts from inscription to reading, and instead investigates how these texts were read by the generations of Christians that followed. In the process, part 3 reveals some of the unexpected and violent ways that Christian identity rooted and rerooted itself in practices of enslavement.

✝

It was well-known to people in Mediterranean antiquity that they were surrounded by a densely populated supernatural world that worked almost indiscernibly alongside our own.

When Blandina browsed the stalls in the marketplace, a crowd of invisible spirits—some friendly and some vicious—jostled alongside her, threatening to break in. Some were psychic pick-pockets and home invaders; they probed the folds of human consciousness looking for a way in. Just as she had learned to navigate the streets of the city and to call upon trusted vendors and acquaintances, so too had she cultivated self-protective habits to shield herself from malevolent actors.

For an enslaved woman like Blandina, this practice was especially important. The human body was known to be porous: it was open both to spiritual penetration and bad influences. Moreover, it was sponge-like and formless: it contained spaces that, without psychic self-care, could be inhabited by the wills and selves of other external agents or within which negative forces could compete for control. Some bodies—especially those of women, those who were sick, or those whose bodies were sexually penetrated—were viewed as naturally porous. The squishy, sodden nature of the female body meant that it offered a hospitable climate for phantasmic guests. You could see examples on the streets of the city, where female diviners charged with spiritual agents could be consulted as oracles for a fee. Before her baptism, Blandina would sometimes stop to watch them, but afterwards she steered clear: she had to be on her guard.

Elite writers tended to scoff at the old-fashioned notions of *hoi polloi*, but they had their own deeply classist views about the psychic deficiencies of the unfree. It seems unlikely that an *ancilla* such as Blandina was reading high philosophy, but she may have overheard it or imbibed a pithier version through the philosophical adages that trickled into everyday life. If her enslavers were into self-improvement—and certainly her *domina* ("mistress") had found her way to Christianity in a period when

THE FAITHFUL CHRISTIAN

few Christians lived in the region—then Blandina might have heard various educational theories about the formation of the self.

In the broad principles of the ancient world, education was closely tied to despotic theories of enslavement. Children and enslaved people were unable to order themselves: they were internally unmastered, formless, or empty, containing space within them for both their own mind (their *nous*) and other entities, be they supernatural beings or unsettling negative passions. We hear a hint of this in Paul's Letter to the Philippians, where he says that even Christ had to empty and abase himself to take on the "form of a slave" (2:6–11). The role of education was, in part, to shape and cement the formless freeborn child into an impermeable, embodied self that was self-governing: to construct what Marcus Aurelius famously described as an "impenetrable fortress."[9]

In some ancient descriptions of human physiology, the existence of psychic space enabled certain people to be filled, as Blandina was at her martyrdom, with divine power. In the popular imagination, women and enslaved people were seen as especially possessible. This anatomical predisposition made them excellent oracles and was a marketable trait that some enslavers exploited. We see this in Acts 16, in the story of an enslaved woman who correctly and repeatedly identifies Paul and his companions as "slaves of the most high God." But this state wasn't limited to those whose bodies were spongy and plastic: just as anyone might become enslaved, so too anyone was vulnerable to invaders.[10]

A certain physiological openness underpins a great deal of ancient Christian thinking. Followers of Jesus were "temples" for the Spirit. For early Christians, baptism and the receipt of a Holy Spirit through the laying-on of hands utilized the same biological pathways as demonic possession. They labeled other kinds of supernatural actors simply "unclean spirits," a turn of phrase that implies that they are the same kind of entity as the one embraced in Christian ritual. For this reason, as in many denominations today, ancient baptism was prefigured by what is sometimes called a "minor" or "simple" exorcism. We do not know exactly how the ritual was practiced in southern Gaul at this time: Perhaps Blandina participated in an all-night Easter vigil and then went down to the river to be immersed in the cold waters of the mighty Rhône before dawn. Or perhaps, given her status as an enslaved woman, her baptism was a perfunctory affair, squeezed between tasks, in a courtyard fountain or part of a household baptism. Perhaps, as for the Christians of Rome, the preparatory rituals and baptismal practices were organized around a regime of spiritual hygiene. In Rome, before exorcism and baptism, catechumens (those preparing for baptism and full participation in the body of Christ) were prohibited from exchanging the ritual kiss of the peace, because their own kiss was "not yet pure." If they were unwittingly possessed by a hostile spirit, they risked infecting others.[11]

The physical nature of the instructions reveals something counterintuitive to us moderns: for many in antiquity, spiritual entities were themselves material. The imposition of hands and the ritual of baptism utilized the same biological pathways as any other kind of possession, but the model was reassuringly scriptural and even Christly. At his own immersion in the River Jordan, Jesus received the Spirit in the form of a dove. The practitioner, John the Baptizer, predicted that those baptized by Jesus would be baptized not with water but with "the Holy Spirit and with fire" (Matt. 3:11). The prophecy found its fulfillment in Acts, with the descent of the Spirit on the Apostles (Acts 2:1–4). In the Bible, the Spirit is a rhetorician as well as a linguist: Jesus reassured his followers that the Spirit would speak for and through them. Some early Christian thinkers theorized that the

Holy Spirit served as a kind of internal reading guide that worked to produce orthodox interpretations of scripture.[12]

Medieval imagining of the Holy Spirit descending with beamlike fire on the apostles at Pentecost

The Holy Spirit of early Christianity was educated but unassertive. In comparison to other supranatural entities—who exerted a tyrannical enslaving influence over their hosts—the Holy Spirit was relatively fragile and undeniably high-maintenance. It needed cultivation and did not tolerate malevolent housemates. As the *Shepherd of Hermas* puts it,

The Holy Spirit that lives in you will be clean, not being overshadowed by another evil spirit. But while dwelling in a spacious room it will rejoice and be glad about the implement in which it lives and will minister to God with much cheerfulness, having an abundance in itself. But if some irascibility comes, immediately the Holy Spirit, being sensitive, is confined because it does not have a clean place and it seeks to leave from the place.[13]

Some people found the idea of bodily invasion to be intolerably superstitious. One first-century pagan medical writer wrote dismissively that "in the old days" the "people" believed that disease was the result of an attack by the gods or *daimonia*. Certainly there were many philosophical types, including Christians like Origen, who found the idea of spiritual possession unseemly. Yet we should be wary of distinguishing too sharply between elite and non-elite views. Passions, which philosophical thinking maintained should be properly regulated, were often depicted as material entities that could enter and disquiet the self. Safeguarding oneself from internal, sometimes competing emotions—what the *Shepherd of Hermas* calls double-souledness—was thus an important aspect of the philosophical life. It involved a form of self-defense that protected the vulnerable self from bad influences: without a regime of good reading, repetitious engagement with scripture, and, arguably, spiritual sustenance through a diet of sacred food (the eucharist), the Christian biome is disrupted. Psychic self-care, therefore, appeared in multiple social locations: in the writings of the well-sandaled philosopher and theologian as well as "popular" ideas about demons and the spirit world.[14]

The mechanics of spirit possession raises some interesting questions for us about what it means to be a Christian. As one scholar describes it, the identity of Christ followers is inextricably linked to their being possessed by the Spirit. In turn, it is their openness to possession by the Spirit that makes them authentic members of the body of Christ. To be inhabited by the Spirit meant that a Christian must be obedient and submissive in ways that could not be mapped directly onto the male ideal of Roman education. It would be simplistic to say that anything that did not precisely conform to the elite male ideal was "feminine" or "slavish," but it is worth noting how spiritual possession applied pressure to the fantasy of manly self-control. In this vision, the ideal Christian—like enslaved people everywhere, and like Jesus resigning himself to the will of his Father in Gethsemane—had to allow themselves to become subject to the will of another.[15]

The fragile nature of Christian self-possession reveals something that the archive of slavery only begrudgingly admits; namely, that enslaved will and cognitive independence are always a reality. They cannot be exorcised. Enslaved loyalty and the power of the enslaving class are predicated on the *coerced willingness* of enslaved people to perform the will of the "master." Humanity is in our sights and will is never erased. The model of possession developed by Paul and his servile collaborators and interpreted by early Christians in the story of Blandina inscribes a different paradigm, one that unmasks the faulty calculations and unstable logic of enslaving epistemology by showing that the will of the enslaved person is omnipresent. The despotic mask slips, and the reader is confronted with the vulnerability of enslaving power and the reality of enslaved agency. If Blandina was an instrument of divine will, it is only because she allowed herself to be.

In an obedient host, however, the still-small voice of the Spirit could rise to a roar. In Gaul, one of Blandina's fellow martyrs, the lawyer Vettius Epagathus, who had initially escaped detection as a Jesus follower, denounced the injustice of the proceedings because the Spirit was inside him. Or again, in Acts 16:6–7, the apostle Paul and his companions were "forbidden by the Holy Spirit to preach the word in Asia" and prevented by the "Spirit of Jesus" from entering Bithynia (in what is today northern Turkey.) Here we see that possession was about both ownership and power. God extends his reach by incorporating people into his own body, the body of Christ. By becoming (to use Paul's language) a temple or vessel for this divine spirit, the Christian became a tool or body part through which God could act.[16]

Perhaps Blandina, more than the other adult martyrs of Lyon and Vienne—a diverse jumble that included Roman citizens, slaveholders, and lofty rhetoricians—was well prepared to be instrumentalized. She had spent her life filling in for others and channeling their desires. "Putting on Christ" was, for her, more like a change of clothing than an epistemic shift. Long before she encountered Christianity, she was a vessel for the will of her enslavers. Christian ideas about being inhabited by Christ or the Holy Spirit were based on the same logic of possessibility as broader cultural ideas about enslavers.

Though we cannot be sure that Blandina had heard Pauline epistles read aloud, we can be certain that many enslaved people were involved in their production and reception. Imagining ourselves alongside them as they listened, we might find ourselves reading Paul's language about the body of Christ in 1 Corinthians 12 with fresh eyes. In an attempt to manage the discord in the first-century Christ-assembly at Corinth, Paul turned to the frequently adapted image of the body in his attempt to reinstate harmony in the group. "For just as the body is one and has many members, and all the members of the body, though many, are one body, so it is with Christ" (1 Cor. 12:12). Paul claimed that all members of the community, regardless of their differences—whether they are "Jews or Greeks, enslaved or free-born"—were initiated into the same body when they were baptized (Gal. 3:23). Just as a body has many parts that contribute to the functioning and survival of the whole, wrote Paul, so too were individual members of the community essential to the body of Christ. The effects of this are twofold. Individual people cannot claim to be independent actors: "If the foot would say, 'Because I am not a hand, I do not belong to the body,' that would not make it any less a part of the body." At the same time, all parts of the body are important to the functioning of the whole: "The eye cannot say to the hand, 'I have no need of you,' nor again the head to the feet, 'I have no need of you.'" Paradoxically, the body parts "that seem to be weaker are indispensable" (1 Cor. 12:12–22).

At first pass, the image seems benign, even congenial. If there is a tension here, it echoes only the low rumble of friction between individual freedoms and communal interests that reverberates in all conversations about human rights and social obligations. Certainly the instruction is rooted in an egalitarian spirit of cooperation that would help Jesus followers get along with one another.

Yet perhaps to Blandina, and those like her, the partitioning of the body gestures to something darkly familiar: the ways in which she and others were imagined and described as biological appendages to the bodies of their "masters." They would have heard themselves described as — and sometimes even named after — hands, feet, and implements. Although Paul drew upon existing understandings of the city as body, his description also mirrored the social structures and fictions of enslavement. Extending one's reach, presence, and control by dehumanizing and subjugating others is a despotic stretch. One scholar has called this phenomenon "masterly extensibility." Absentee slaveholders viewed their workers as prosthetic extensions of their bodies, a means of expanding, through "human appendages," their purview and realizing their vision. For the enslaving class, an enslaved person was conceptually both an instrument and a part of the enslaver's body. One authoritative voice in the Palestinian Talmud pronounced that "the hand of a slave is like the hand of his master." As New Testament scholar Fabian Udoh puts it, the "faithful [enslaved worker] is defined by the symbiosis between him and the master, such that he knows, anticipates, and does the master's will."[17]

For those who had been trafficked on the auction block, as for those acquainted with the enslaving manuals of the day, the identification of enslaved people with body parts was familiar. "Slaves," a first-century management guide written by a man known only as Bryson opined, "resemble the limbs of the body, the actions of which the [slaveowner] has in his control. Those entrusted with the custody and the management of the estate fulfil the role of the senses.... Those entrusted with serving resemble the hands because it is with them that one succeeds in fetching something useful for the body. Those entrusted with [manual labor] resemble the legs because upon them rests the whole of the body and its weight." The possibilities for extensibility that enslaved bodies afforded to the enslaver allowed him to have multiple bodies (*corpora*): his own physical body, which was spared effort and strain, and a larger despotic body extended through the others by virtue of the "master's" will. This is where the logic of slavery binds Pauline images of the body together. Christ can have both a resurrected body and an extended body of followers. In the Pauline view, the Spirit coursed through Christ's circulatory system, channeling divine will through obedient body parts.[18]

While Bryson insisted that the enslaver "must protect his servants as he protects his limbs," enslaved people were not human beings in this despotic system, but were (ostensibly) interchangeable biological bric-a-brac. Moreover, ancient people were keenly aware that body parts sometimes had to be removed: the sharp instruments of war, the lack of antibiotics, and the frequency of workplace accidents meant that damaged eyes, hands, feet, and legs were regularly amputated to prevent infection. We should not assume that being pictured as a detachable body part protected anyone from injury. This is true even in cases of spiritual injury: wealthy Christians living during the reign of the emperor Diocletian, in the early fourth century, were able to avoid both persecution and religious apostasy by using enslaved members of their household as prosthetic surrogates. Diocletian had demanded that Christians perform a sacrifice to prove that they were loyal subjects, and some Christians sent enslaved people to perform the rite on their behalf. The enslavers escaped physical and spiritual harm, but their proxies, if they were Christian, were forced to apostatize and now faced eternal damnation.[19]

Even in the case of disability and physical dependence, there was no legal parity between enslaved "part" and enslaver. Studies in contemporary philosophy and the history of technology instead reveal the ambivalent relationships that people often have with their prosthetics. Prosthetic devices remind users of their own bodily limits and inadequacy. To be unproblematic, therefore, a person acting in this role must be absorbed into the personhood of the more powerful "user" or "head." Blandina and others in her position would have been familiar with the risks of this kind of relationship: they navigated their lives on tiptoes.[20]

Paul and his coauthor's intervention into the logic of possession and body parts in 1 Corinthians 12 might thus be read as an attempt to posit the importance of every "part" of the body of Christ. All members of the corporate body of Christ were relevant and important. Indeed, some have understood this passage as an optimistic reworking of an intrinsically harmful image. In describing the intentions of Paul and his collaborators, these readings may be correct. It hardly seems accidental that the body parts most associated in ancient thought with enslavers (the head) and enslavers' judgment (the eye as source of knowledge) were reminded of their dependence on body parts associated with enslaved workers (the hand, which did skilled work, and the foot, which did physical labor).[21]

Liminal readers like Blandina, however, were in no position to take chances. Nor should we. Enslaved people could not exert masterly will or aspire to the status of the head. As one ancient historian has put it, "It is not that slaves don't have heads, but that they don't count." Paul and his collaborators do not subvert this model, but it is significant that the hand—the body part used to represent secretaries and copyists—pushes its way through the mantle of control. Perhaps here we feel the influence of Paul's often invisible collaborators.

In Roman theories of enslavement, the "master" extended his reach through his enslaved workers. It was his will that they were supposed to enact, not their own. In Pauline theories of the relationship between Christians and Christ, similarly, it was the possessing Spirit that took up residence in the Christ-believer that bound these body parts together, incorporating all members of the community into a single masterly will. The flourishing of the united will of the body of Christ was predicated on the withering of plural voices, desires, and perspectives. Though 1 Corinthians 12 focuses on the importance of every "part," and resists the idea that anyone is fungible, it ultimately returns to a model in which the Christ-believer becomes a dehumanized vessel for the activity of God exercised through the Spirit. Similarly, 1 Corinthians 11:3 and the later compositions Ephesians and Colossians make clear that it is Christ who is the "head" of the Christian body politic. This is the logic of enslaving power: theories of enslavement dissolved the humanity of the person and transfigured it into an instrument or possession. It is also the logic that runs throughout the Pauline corpus; it is made more powerful by the fact that it does not name itself. Paul and his many interpreters used this idea to explain both the human relationship to Christ and the nature of Christian identity.[22]

In the Pauline scheme, then, human beings are possessions of God and subject to God's will, but in its reception this language and idea did not (and still do not) affect us all in the same way. An enslaved second-century martyr like Blandina was understood as a perfect Christian and perfect vessel, but later generations of Christians were less willing to cast themselves in this role.[23]

In the long history of interpretation, powerful Christians have always imagined themselves into the position of the divine head. The seventeenth-century Catholic priest and philosopher Nicolas Malebranche, for example, wrote of the hierarchy of the body politic: "Not all the members of a body can be its head and heart; there must be feet and hands, small as well as great, people who obey as well as those who command. And if each says openly that he wants to command and never to obey, as indeed each of them does, it is obvious that every body politic would be destroyed, and that disorder and injustice would reign everywhere." What is cast by Malebranche as a sensible, even pragmatic, argument is also tyrannical. It institutionalizes inequality. In the imagined space of the corporate body, knowing one's place is a spiritual discipline.[24]

This had, and continues to have, practical and felt consequences for those members of society who are deemed less important than others. Just as appeals to biology and physiognomy are sometimes used to naturalize prejudice, so too is it an oppressive move to root the idea that some people must agree to obey others—regardless of the injustice they face—in scripture. In the context of colonialization, the kidnapping and enslavement of human beings, and the development of racist theories of enslavement and social organization, the image of the body returned to its enslaving roots. Enslavement is no natural or neutral metaphor.

If enslavement provides the connective tissue that binds the believer to God and to others, we might wonder how else it has structured early Christian identity. How might Blandina — or anyone attuned to the power dynamics of the day, which is to say, anyone — have understood what it meant to be a follower of a movement so clearly modeled on the relationship between enslaver and enslaved?

For enslaved people, the passages of scripture that were read before dinner or at gatherings were, for them, working events. Most people did not have an understanding of what it meant to be a Christ follower that drew upon all of Paul's letters or an idea of discipleship that was assembled from multiple Gospels, so we will not attempt anything similar. Instead, we tug on the threads of language — the snippets overheard during readings, the longer passages explained in impromptu homilies, the material covered in religious instruction — that contained despotic potential.

For better or worse, some of the most straightforward and influential descriptions of what it meant to be a Christ follower come from the Pauline epistles — passages that also contain some of the Bible's most intractable language about slavery. Throughout his letters, Paul brought his readers to the slave market. He twice reminded the Corinthians that they were "bought for a price" and "are not their own" (1 Cor. 6:12, 7:23). Paul described himself as a "slave of Christ" and labeled the faithful "slaves to righteousness" and "enslaved of God." The assembly of Christians in Corinth, he wrote, was "purchased" by their new divine "master." Those who were enslaved to human slaveholders were now imagined either as freedpersons, manumitted through Christ's intervention, or instead as newly enslaved to their divine "master." These two metaphorical threads intertwine in the Pauline corpus. For inhabitants of Corinth—a pivotal port in the Roman slave trade—the structural resonances were obvious. They were enslaved to God, and their lives were no longer their own.[25]

Divine slaveholding was a familiar concept in the Greek-speaking world of Paul's day. Inscriptions from Delphi, Leukopetra, and the Bosporan kingdom on the northern Black Sea attest practices in which enslaved people were sold or dedicated to gods. Some inscriptions are ambiguous, and might suggest that the sale or dedication of a person to a deity was a pathway to freedom. Yet often these dedications required that the unfree person remain with their human enslaver until the latter died. Even manumissions that granted the recipient freedom of movement still obligated them to work at specific temples, shrines, or Jewish synagogues. It is easy to see these dedications as fictions: how could Apollo, Zeus, or the Autochthonous Mother of the Gods actually enslave someone? To those who had been dedicated to synagogues and found themselves sweeping the floors and maintaining the buildings, the reality of their condition was not in doubt. Enslavement to a god was much like enslavement to a human "master." Divine beings could act as theo-economic agents, with practical consequences for those enslaved to them.[26]

People in Paul's assemblies who found themselves negotiating the demands of multiple enslavers were not in a unique condition. Ancient papyri and inscriptions reveal that enslaved workers were sometimes jointly "owned" by multiple members of the same community. This was not, then, about the passage of the Christian from enslavement to freedom, but rather the introduction of a new relationship of dependence and obligation. The articulation of the Christian condition as enslavement

was thoroughly compatible with other, more theologically popular language like "child of God" or "heir." One funerary
inscription for a sixteen-year-old boy from northern Greece
described the child as both "home-born slave" and "son" of
the manager of a local tavern. Paul could tie enslavement and
sonship together because, legally, enslaved people could pass
from the status of an enslaved person, to a freedperson, and to
eventual adoption as heir. Exactly this model was proposed
in the *Shepherd of Hermas*, where a retelling of the parable of
the vineyard had a loyal enslaved worker become co-heir with the
vineyard owner's son.[27]

For readers of Paul, therefore, the prospect of manumission
and social elevation was a familiar one. Roman theories of social
control emphasized the importance of providing enslaved workers with the hope (however fleeting) of freedom and future
reward. In one work, the Roman playwright Terence has a freedman exclaim to his patron, "All our hope lies in you.... You're
the only person we have, our patron, our father." Hope incentivized the unfree to work harder and more obediently. This caused
a problem when, in 4 CE, the emperor Augustus passed legislation preventing "bad slaves" (that is, those who were shackled,
tortured, and found guilty, branded, or consigned to the mines)
from being manumitted. The Elder Pliny observed that the quality of the work of chained (and thus hopeless) workers was poor.
Almost a century earlier, Cicero had noted that "it would be
utterly intolerable for slaves if some hope of liberty were not
held out to them."[28]

For Paul, this hope was the resurrection, the juncture at
which the "slave of Christ" would be raised and adopted as a
co-heir with Christ. The hope that the Jesus follower felt had a
specific target (i.e., resurrection and inheritance) and was linked
to other servile virtues like "patience" and "perseverance" (Rom.

12:12). One imagines that to Blandina, to Onesimus, and to the crowd of silent witnesses that edged around freeborn congregants at gatherings, Paul made relatable promises. One day the deity—who, unlike human enslavers, could be trusted to make good on his promises—will elevate you to sonship and inheritance. At this juncture in the merger of metaphysics and law the structures of domination would change.

The character traits that Paul exhorted his addressees to embody overlapped with those qualities that enslavers tried to cultivate in their workers, most notably loyalty. Though many enslavers ruled their homes with fear, they were aware of its practical limits, and they worried about the internally rebellious worker who was only outwardly compliant. The preferable model, they knew, was obedient love that generated loyalty. In Roman literature and drama, the preeminent virtue for the enslaved worker was *fides* (Latin) or *pistis* (Greek). Those reading English translations of the New Testament tend to encounter *pistis* as "faith" or "faithfulness" but it had a broad semantic range in antiquity and could be elastically deployed in a wide variety of legal, philosophical, political, commercial, interpersonal, and religious contexts. We might render it as something like "loyalty" or we might, depending on context, prefer the vocabulary of trust, confidence, duty, or another term that better captures its nuance.[29]

As classicist Teresa Morgan has argued, *pistis/fides* was not just about one person. It was inescapably relational. It required trust and reciprocity on both sides. It was a facet of many relationships but, as an attribute, it appeared more regularly in literary portrayals of "good slaves" and freedpeople than any other virtue except deference. This is not to say that *pistis* was only about enslavement—it was also a central virtue for wives, sons, and anyone who inhabited the underside of a hierarchical relationship—but rather that, when read in light of the many references to enslavement in the Pauline corpus, it often sounds like the loyalty expected of enslaved people.[30]

Enslaved fidelity in antiquity looks quite different from modern definitions of faith. Our modern understanding of the term is deeply conditioned by the fierce theological debates that pulled European Christianity apart during the Reformation. Martin Luther's famous dictum that salvation came *sola fide* (by faith alone) posited an influential distinction between what one believes and how one behaves. Though Luther thought (like most Protestants today) that good works would follow from faith, neither the distinction nor the modern secular definition of faith as a cognitive process or feeling would have made sense to a first-century resident of the Roman Empire, much less those who were enslaved. No "loyal slave" or freedperson was able to avoid their practical responsibilities. For enslaved people, faith involved both recognition of the relationship between enslaver and enslaved and a certain set of behaviors. The importance of this loyalty did not diminish with manumission. The exemplary freedman was the grateful, loyal freedman: Cicero identified *fidelitas* as his enslaved secretary Tiro's chief quality. Thus work and loyalty were inseparably linked. In this context, there was no loyalty dislocated from ethical obligations. As the once-enslaved philosopher Epictetus put it, people are most trustworthy when their actions and internal moral disposition cohere with one another.[31]

There is a heated theological conversation about whether God's free gift of salvation, as supplied through the self-effacing incarnation, death, and resurrection of Christ, demands any repayment. Are Christians obligated to repay God? The answer depends upon the contextual framework within which it is answered, but if we think about this question in terms of the historical relationship between enslavers and enslaved, then the answer is, quite obviously, yes. Even if Paul presents God as a different kind of enslaver, Roman patrons demanded active gratitude from those they manumitted. The freedperson was expected not only to provide their enslavers with services and work, but also to remain grateful to their former enslaver.[32]

Enslavers-turned-patrons felt the itch of ungrateful freedmen, and scratched their displeasure into monuments and, eventually, legal codes. Several historical sources suggest that there were proposals by the emperor and senate to reenslave freedmen who were considered ungrateful to their patron (usually by being disloyal, violent, or negligent). An inscription added to a Roman funerary altar in the first century CE condemned the deceased child's freedwoman mother, Acte, for behaving faithlessly, committing adultery, and "stealing" two enslaved children. The subtext for the inscription is that Acte had been manumitted only to marry her former enslaver turned husband. It was thus a conditional freedom. When she disobeyed, she was cursed not only for adultery but for being a "bad slave." There was nothing that she could have done to repay the debt of gratitude and obedience that her former enslaver felt she owed him. Even philosophers like Seneca weighed in on the legal debate, labeling ingratitude a heinous vice that would be judged by the gods. The unrepayable gift was a yawning chasm of obligation: if it did not necessitate repayment, that was only because there was no way to repay it. The "debt" would never be cleared.[33]

This complicated web of emotional, practical, and legal obligations was apparent to enslaved readers of Paul. Many think that Paul's congregations, and the nascent groups of Christ followers founded by others, were drawn largely from artisanal classes. These were people who, regardless of whether they were or had ever been enslaved, depended upon patrons (who may once have been their enslavers) for their livelihoods. The risks of appearing ungrateful to the deity who had freed them from bondage would have been obvious. *Pistis* was always reciprocal, but as in all hierarchies, these duties and obligations weighed more heavily on the side of the enslaved.

When thinking about what it means to be a loyal disciple, later readers of Paul, including some of the evangelists, drew upon the experiences of migrants, enslaved people, and outsiders. Discipleship began with familial alienation and financial precarity: the original disciples left their homes, families, and businesses to follow Jesus. The "eye of the needle" saying that we examined earlier was just the beginning. With his audience still reeling from his instructions to the rich young man in Mark 10, Jesus told his followers that they must abandon material possessions and also family, inheritance, and property. In speaking to his disciples—which in this scene is not only the Twelve but includes a larger group of men and women—he promised that those who give up everything would receive it back in the future. "There is no one who has left house or brothers or sisters or mother or father or children or fields, for my sake and for the sake of the good news, who will not receive a hundredfold now in this age—houses, brothers and sisters, mothers and children, and fields, with persecutions—and in the age to come eternal life" (Mark 10:28–30).

This is a difficult instruction for anyone to keep, which is precisely why few people today, even ordained clergy, take vows of poverty. Even Roman soldiers, who left everything familiar when they joined the military, received decent pay and a dependable pension if they survived to retirement. The harshness of Jesus' injunction is hardly balanced by the promise of family, property, and eternal life in the future. It is unclear that the putative disciple, here undeniably male, will receive the same family in the age to come.

The demand parallels the familial situation of Jesus himself. In the Gospels, after he was recognized as God's son, Jesus was expelled into the wilderness by the Spirit, acquired a new family of followers, and disavowed his biological kin. The yoke of discipleship also resembles the brutal constraints of enslavement and the violence of forced migration. Bills of sale from ancient Egypt dispassionately relate the trade in enslaved "homebred" children who learned the hard way that they had no home. Those who were trafficked left their names, languages, and identities behind. Such experiences of forced migration, renaming, and cultural alienation left marks in the consciousness of enslaved people, but these are experiences that the Jesus of the Gospels expected his followers to embrace.

We do not know the circumstances under which Blandina, Paul's secretaries, or any others first met their "mistresses" or "masters" in the flesh. It is possible that they too had been separated from family members and trafficked, and now recognized the conditions of discipleship in their own lives. The situation created a paradox in which the predicament of those who had been enslaved and trafficked more closely resembled the model of discipleship than those of the freeborn. This was a subversive move: migrants and enslaved people already had the inside track on discipleship. They already had given up everything, had left their homes, and were separated from family members. It was wealthy enslavers who had work to do and were imperiled.

For Blandina—like other enslaved hearers of gospel writings—it may have been reassuring that Jesus did not offer the promise of a new father, only a mother and siblings. This is, as others have argued, because God will be our father in the coming age. But perhaps there is a thread of resistance here too. For the enslaved, the *paterfamilias* (head of household) was a tyrannical and exploitative figure. That Mark's Jesus does not talk about a father figure in the family-to-come not only connects the disciple directly to God, but also eliminates one of the sources of oppression encountered by them in their daily lives. Having embraced social death and marginalization—what Paul would call "dying daily" and what political theorist Achille Mbembe calls necropolitics—the Christian anticipates adoption as a legal heir at the resurrection.[34]

In the interim, however, the Jesus follower experienced alienation and estrangement. Building on Mark, the Gospel of Matthew strengthens the connection between discipleship and slavery by likening Jesus' disciples to enslaved workers and Jesus himself to an enslaver (Matt. 10:24–25). The Christ follower should both labor under promises of future reward and lean into the paradoxical freedom that being abused, tortured, and killed for Christ presents. Jesus instructs the crowd of followers, "If anyone would come after me, let them deny themselves and take up their cross and follow me.... Whoever loses their life for my sake and the gospel will save it" (Mark 8:34–36). To soften the condition of death, the authors of Luke add "daily" after "take up your cross"; they thus transfigure the instruction into a metaphor for general, nonfatal modes of discipleship, or, to think in terms of enslavement, for the social dying of enslaved life. The authors of John were comfortable with the possibility of martyrdom but diffuse the specter of "slavishness" by shifting to a more congenial model of "lay[ing] down one's life for one's friends" (John 15:13). In one way or another, the New Testament evangelists agree that the power of discipleship lies in voluntarily accepting mistreatment, violence, and even death.[35]

The claim that discipleship demanded martyrdom is shocking and few are eager to embrace it, but it is less extraordinary if we think of disciples as enslaved to God. Valerius Maximus, the first-century CE freedman who compiled the compendium *Memorable Words and Deeds*, included a section on enslaved people who demonstrated exceptional loyalty (*fides*) to their enslavers. Given that enslaved workers were compelled through force to be obedient, it was difficult for enslavers to know if they were "trustworthy." They might "do good works," to use contemporary language, but be internally rebellious. Enslavers were thus deluding themselves to think that the loyalty of their workers was predicated only on a love or respect unrelated to their enslaved condition. The idea of being able to see into the hearts of their workers, as God does in the Sermon on the Mount, was something of an enslaver's fantasy. The authors of Blandina's story spoke to exactly this concern when they described the martyr as acting out of a sincere love for Christ. Blandina was, in other words, the ideal "loyal slave": she gave up her life for her Lord out of a genuine sense of affection. So, too, in Valerius Maximus's examples, enslaved workers prove themselves to be truly faithful by risking torture and death for their enslavers. Fidelity was expected in all kinds of ancient Greek and Roman relationships. That Jesus would describe it as requiring suffering and death, however, gave discipleship a distinctively "slavish" patina.[36]

This interpretation resonates in the writings of the first-century bishop Ignatius of Antioch. His letter to Christians in Rome asked that the recipients restrain themselves from preventing his death. "Now," he wrote, "I begin to become a disciple." And later, "once I have suffered, I shall become a freedman of Jesus Christ, and, united with him, I shall rise a free man. In the meantime, I am learning to desire nothing while in chains." A faithful death, Ignatius wrote, would manumit him from slavery. Resurrection, he thought, would transform him into a freeborn man. Until then he is in the "slavish" position of putting aside his own desires.[37]

Despite Paul's efforts to talk about Christ followers as enslaved to God, he did not encounter the logic and language of slavery in the same way as Blandina. As womanist New Testament scholar Angela Parker reminds us, "Paul did not share habitus or similar decreased body capital as the slaves in the Roman Empire or the slaves in the American colonial system." In other words, Paul was indulging in hyperbolic dress-up. That said, criminal bodies were permanently marked by practices of flogging and chaining that could leave distinctive physical and psychic scars. As someone who had been incarcerated and beaten, Paul might easily have been mistaken for an enslaved person. Nearly fifteen hundred years later, another famous traveler, the colonizer Christopher Columbus, would embrace the poetic nature of human bondage and request to be interred with his own chains. But in Paul's own day shackles were not mistaken for relics.[38]

As near to enslavement as captivity brought him, we should note that Paul was never himself enslaved and indeed he constructed a set of behavioral norms that excluded many enslaved people. His requirement that people abstain from fornication (*porneia*) by eschewing sex workers, for example, assumed that all members of his audience had sovereignty over their own bodies. Many did not, and a pattern of bodily violation may well have accompanied Paul's newly restrictive sexual ethic. Enslavers may have turned to enslaved people as acceptable outlets for their desires. This regime would have been doubly violent, terrorizing enslaved workers and barring them from full participation in the community.[39]

Moreover, it is not clear that enslaved people ever truly felt safe around—much less equal to—their enslavers, even in the idealistic assembly of believers in which there was "neither slave nor free." It was easier for Paul to say that enslaved status was irrelevant than it would have been for enslaved people to believe it. Later Christian writers openly acknowledged the coercive power with which enslavers dominated their enslaved Christian workers. Paul never denounced the evils of slavery, and enslavers have seen him as supportive of their project ever since.

For the enslaved collaborators who worked on these texts, the use of enslavement as an explanatory device for thinking about the relationship between human beings and gods may have been democratizing. It offered opportunities to push back and to insert moments where traditional "master-slave" hierarchies were inverted and subverted. This does not, of course, forgive the horrifying violence that New Testament texts have subsequently been used to support, but rather it suggests that at the time of their composition, these passages may have operated differently. Working within structures of confinement, some could use the idea of an enslaving relationship between God and Christians to craft spaces for themselves.

My goal here is certainly not to put slavery—a fundamentally unjust practice—back into Christianity or to suggest that anyone should think of God as an enslaver today. The language is irredeemable and has consistently been used to harm and oppress. My aim, rather, is to highlight both the vast chasm between definitions of what it meant to be a good Christ follower in the first and second centuries and what it means to be a good Christian now, and consider the iniquity of the ways in which the language of slavery has been abstracted and extracted from the Christian message. In the past two millennia, enslavement-based models of Christian identity have been metabolized beyond recognition. Some changes are subtle: An almost indiscernible prepositional shift has moved our understanding away from one biblical and traditional notion that we are possessed *by* the Spirit and towards a more autonomous model that we ourselves have—that is, we possess—the Spirit. If, originally, we had the Spirit and the Spirit had us, there has been a rebellion of sorts. Powerful Christians have moved from possessed to possessors, from enslaved to enslavers.

Similarly, modern readers have distanced what it means to be "faithful" from its original grounding in notions of enslaved obedience. The issue is not so much the abandonment of the idea that loyalty to God necessitates a certain kind of behavior, but that the powerful Christian majority have separated themselves from obligations that they find unpalatable. European Christianity has not severed itself from scriptural notions of filial piety or marital fidelity, but it has pried slavery out of the equation such that "faithfulness" now floats separately from slavery. We now describe things—most commonly translations—as "faithful but not slavish." This redefinition of "slavishness" as antithetical to or extractable from fidelity has only amplified the violence applied to enslaved people throughout history.

Most important of all is that when Christian households, institutions, businesses, and nations used the language of enslavement to organize themselves, they did so *selectively.* Pauline texts about the unilateral enslavement of Christians to God have been abstracted into metaphorical garb about intense devotion. Meanwhile the household codes—passages in letters attributed to Peter and Paul that outline a social structure predicated on obedience and submission—were used to structure Christian families and institutions, with devastating consequences for the victims of (among other things) Atlantic slavery. These texts exhorted real enslaved people to accept unjust beatings at the hands of their "masters," to remain enslaved, and to be, above all, obedient. In the long history of interpretation, it has seemed to many readers that Paul stood with the enslavers.[40]

To give but one example of the despotic use of the New Testament, Benjamin Palmer's *Plain and Easy Catechism, Designed Chiefly for the Benefit of Coloured Persons* (1828) provided a model prayer, drenched in biblical idiom, in which the enslaved person asks God to "help me to be faithful to my owner's interest....

May I never disappoint the trust that is placed in me, nor like the unjust steward, waste my master's goods." The unjust steward here is an enslaved character in a Gospel parable who manipulated his enslaver's books, erasing a portion of the debts that were owed to the enslaver (Luke 16:1–13). Ironically, Jesus' interpretation of the steward's behavior is quite different than Benjamin Palmer's. The prayer, and its crooked interpretation of scripture, reveals the ease with which early Christian fidelity was placed in the service of later enslaving tyrannies, and the eagerness with which powerful Christians cast themselves in the role of God as the divine head. (It is a parenthetical point here, but casting oneself in the role of God has been, in later Christian tradition, the central crime of the Devil.)[41]

This history of selective distancing is most profoundly felt in the bloody legacy of Atlantic slavery, but it can also be detected in the mistreatment of all marginalized people and in the exploitation of workers. The dehumanizing language of body parts continues to thrive in articulations of credit that treat exploited workers as automata, invisible, or will-less. The selective nature of these interpretative shifts reveals the interests at their center. Easy metaphorical moves benefit the powerful and dismiss the coercive force of ideas and language. To say that the language of enslavement in the New Testament is "just a metaphor" is to casually dismiss both the brutality of enslavement and the ways in which the Christian Bible was used to support the actual enslavement of millions of people ever since. This kind of willful forgetting threatens the moral integrity of any institution, church, or nation that undertakes it. It ignores the ways in which scripture has been used to cause harm. As distinguished American critic Hortense Spillers put it, "Sticks and stones *might* break our bones, but words will most certainly *kill* us."[42]

Paul is scriptural, but he has not had the final say. Even

within the canonical New Testament, we see resistance and pushback. Paul's language about sexual continence may have excluded sex workers and enslaved people—or at least those who were sexually exploited—from full participation in the body of Christ, but if that was his intention, then the evangelists and their enslaved collaborators undercut it. Each of the canonical Gospels narrates a story in which a woman approaches Jesus and anoints him. In Matthew and Mark, the woman is unnamed and anoints his head with expensive aromatic oil. In Luke, the woman is explicitly identified as a "sinner," an allusive way of referring to sexual misconduct, but even in Matthew and Mark the fact that the woman has access to perfume hints that she was a sex worker. (Perfume was unaffordable for most people. The exception was sex workers, who were sometimes gifted scented oils by wealthy patrons.) Though Luke's Jesus explicitly forgives the woman, in none of the versions of the story does he condemn her profession or behavior. Even if the roots of the story are traced back to Jesus himself, Mark's version sets an exceptional narrative spotlight on the woman. Jesus proclaims that she will be remembered wherever the gospel is preached.[43]

This story offers an important caveat to Paul's teaching. If Paul established regulations that implicitly excluded enslaved sex workers, the evangelists gently rejected them. Perhaps an enslaved scribe familiar with the dilemma highlighted the woman's behavior to offer a corrective to Paul. Modern readers, too, might feel empowered to make similar kinds of revisions, to push back against despotism, to read against the grain, and to craft new worlds of meaning. Such work, of course, has been in progress for centuries among communities of Black lay interpreters, as well as in the writings of prominent ministers and scholars representing an array of marginalized communities. To this I can only add a small footnote: the process of pushing back started early and is embedded in the interpretative practices of enslaved Christ followers as well. For those Christians worried about the legitimacy of this kind of rereading, it might be meaningful to know that it is not newfangled; it is authentically early Christian and began before the ink had dried on our first copies of the Gospels and the Pauline epistles.[44]

Paul noted that some people might be enslaved to sin, dark forces, or the law (Rom. 6:16, 7:25; Gal. 4:3, 9). The authors of 2 Peter wrote that false teachers who denied "the Divine Enslaver who purchased them" would bring swift destruction upon themselves (2 Pet. 2:1, Shively Smith's translation). These authors thus make visible the other side of an ancient binary that is most viscerally felt in the parables of Jesus: good followers are "faithful slaves," whereas disobedient ones are "bad slaves." Bad workers, to use the words of the social critic Sara Ahmed, were sinful only inasmuch as they were never "empty enough to be filled by human will." The mistreatment of "disobedient" slaves, those people who refused to become vessels for the will of an enslaver, divine or otherwise, has echoed through history.[45]

CHAPTER EIGHT

PUNISHING THE DISOBEDIENT

Sometime in the middle of the first century, we are told, an enslaved woman named Euclia lived in Patras, in the northern Peloponnese, in the home of the proconsul Aegeates and his wife, Maximilla. Patras was a cosmopolitan city on the rise, and Euclia's enslavers were its first citizens. She cloaked herself in the aura of prosperity and optimism that filled the port. Euclia was the sort of young woman who was not good at being invisible: her eyes twinkled a bit too brightly and she didn't seem to be trying to make herself small. To some, it seemed as if she had desires and a will of her own, which, of course, she did. This was a dangerous trait for an enslaved person.[1]

We meet Euclia as a minor character in a second-century story about the apostle Andrew. Maximilla, like the many wealthy wives who fluttered around the apostles, was drawn to this particular apostle's teachings and charisma. The fire of the convert burned in her, but her husband, Aegeates, remained coolly unaware. Increasingly, he seemed to her to be a brutish man. His savage temperament and rough hands, she thought, had no business on her body: she was now a bride of Christ. She could have asked for a divorce, a much more cursory affair for ancient Romans than it is today, but she did not. Perhaps she feared his rage, or perhaps she did not want to lose position, comfort, or face. Whatever her reasoning, she concocted a plan.

Maximilla approached Euclia and offered to become her benefactor. There were strings attached: the girl had to serve as her sexual surrogate. Maximilla's selection of Euclia was carefully made: Euclia was young, shapely, and insubordinate. Presumably she was also, in the most intimate of ways, a passable substitute for Maximilla. Maximilla played the madam. This newly pure soul dressed her "erotic body double" in jewels and expensive clothes, schooled her in the ruse, and turned her out to her husband. Euclia assented to the ruse but she had no real choice.[2]

While Euclia labored in the bedroom, Maximilla and her attendant Iphidamia would sneak out to hear Andrew preach. For eight months, this ritual of deception and abuse continued, but then Euclia began to flex her muscles. She may have been pregnant, or perhaps she sensed an opportunity, but in any case she decided to exert what power she had. Euclia asked for her freedom, which Maximilla apparently granted her.

Yet like so many freedwomen—if, in fact, Maximilla legally freed her—Euclia did not leave. She was in a middle place, straddling the division between enslaved and freed, working in the same spaces, vulnerable to the same bodily violations. She next requested a sizable sum of money and some jewelry, which, again, Maximilla provided. This might have been a nest egg, but her coworkers, who resented her bragging, saw her as a brazen and greedy sex worker. She was getting above her station and had forgotten her place. After Maximilla unsuccessfully attempted to buy their silence, they went to Aegeates, as their position dictated.

Euclia may have thought that Aegeates would understand

that she had no choice. She had done only what she was told. But he did not. Even after he tortured her to learn the truth, she remained his target. In his anger, he did not see her innocence, because, she realized, he had never seen her at all. To him she was just a fraud, an enslaved body that had dared to think it was really a freed woman. Maybe she begged for her child—for *his* child—but to no avail. Maybe Maximilla mumbled something about Euclia's wantonness, or perhaps she saw this as an opportunity to silence her increasingly difficult worker.

Then the cutting began. Aegeates began with her tongue, her impulsive tongue that had spoken out of turn. Of course, he did not do the cutting himself. Neither Aegeates nor Maximilla wanted to be sullied by sticky, staining liquids. Euclia's fellow workers, her former friends, maybe even a sibling, held her down. Perhaps she tried to make eye contact; perhaps they regretted having reported her. Did Aegeates call for a professional torturer, or did the doorman, who had failed to notice Maximilla's evening sojourns, efficiently pry open her mouth? The pain was shocking, but they were not done. Aegeates directed the workers to start on her hands and feet. The metal blade pressed its dirty face against other parts. The ligatures that stemmed the hemorrhage were bonds that kept her in her place. They had cut her down to size. Euclia did not remember much of it—the pain was too great and she was in and out of consciousness—but she did recall the final cut, when they threw her out of the villa, into the dirt and the darkness.[3]

"Bad slaves" were often chained outside at night, but Euclia was never to return so they did not bother. As she bled in a side street, the rare passerby might have gasped and averted their eyes, but no one brought her sustenance or attended to her wounds. Andrew, who had rescued others from the clutches of death, did not come to play the Good Samaritan. Though likely only a teenager, Euclia was her own woman. She was possessed by neither the Devil nor Christ, but rather of her own illicitly held will. She struggled for life and lived for days until, at last, the dogs came and portioned her still further. It is a truly horrifying story.

The apocryphal *Acts of Andrew*, which tells us Euclia's story, does so cruelly. It wants us to see her role as a bit part in the celibate love affair between Andrew and Maximilla. It wants us to condemn her as deceitful and greedy. It wants us to view her as deserving of "punishment," rather than as a victim of abuse. We will not. Instead, we observe how the Christian narrator colludes with Aegeates to blame Euclia for her own abuse. Having introduced Euclia as a narrative device to explain how the authorities decided to target Andrew and set the wheels of the apostle's martyrdom in motion, he leaves her in bits and pieces, out of sight. The violence of what was done to her is not redeemable. Nor is she forgettable. We will admire her willfulness and her refusal to play her part.[4]

The dismemberment vividly evoked in Euclia's story was the product of a sadistic imagination fed by real-world practices. When enslaved workers were called to testify in a trial, it was standard practice to torture them to "ascertain the truth." Only the pain of this "testing," the erroneous logic went, could penetrate the enslaved person's "natural" tendency to deceive. Even after the violence, the enslaved worker was not safe. One unnamed man who provided unexpected evidence under examination had his tongue cut out to ensure that he could not repeat the trick. Punitive amputation was rare, it was dangerous, and it impaired a person's ability to work, but in the Roman period, as during other periods of history, the feet or hands of enslaved people who attempted to run away or rebel were sometimes maimed or amputated.[5]

Euclia, like the rest of the apocryphal story, is fictional. But her tale is emblematic of the violence and mistreatment suffered by enslaved workers at the hands of their enslavers, Christian and pagan alike. It is about what happens to enslaved people who will not obey. It sums up two recurrent themes that are interwoven in Christian history and in histories animated by Christian values: that willfulness is disobedience and that disobedience will be (must be) violently punished. Just as Euclia symbolizes the "bad slave," her mistreatment—which is not at all condemned—narrativizes the torture that awaits all who are disobedient to God.

When later generations thought about eternal punishment, they took their inspiration from the violence visited upon enslaved workers and criminals. Though the incarcerated and the enslaved were not identical, both were often on the receiving end of the same abusive forms of confinement. When Christians, including the servile collaborators who produced early Christian literature, came to think about the consequences of disobedience to God, they used the violent mistreatment of prisoners and enslaved people as their guide. For enslaved collaborators, stories of eternal damnation may have offered the opportunity to push back against the injustices of their own time. Roman justice was never equitably administered; in their experience, it was usually only the impoverished, debtors, and other low-status people who found themselves imprisoned and tortured. There may have been something cathartic about a hell that visited judgment on the powerful and the affluent too.

For Christian readers, Euclia's fate sounds a familiar chord. The biblical Queen Jezebel and the unnamed cupbearer who slapped Thomas in the *Acts of Thomas* were also ripped apart by dogs. Animal consumption of disobedient bodies struck at the heart of the human social contract. Like us, ancient people were uncomfortable with corpse abuse. It was a fate reserved for the most despised. Plato refused burial only to those who were deemed "incurable" and cut off from society entirely. Roman executioners seem to have routinely left the bodies of crucifixion victims for the vultures and dogs. The more ambitious scavengers might have nibbled at the condemned while they still breathed. For Christians, this kind of dehumanizing punishment carried a more lasting threat: perhaps those who were ripped into pieces and eaten by animals would be cut off from the hope of resurrection and eternal reward.[6]

The denial of salvation leads readers to hell, Christianity's eternal torture chamber. If the faithful Christian anticipated a life of comfort and fine dining in the heavenly hereafter, the disobedient would instead be consigned to a subterranean prison. While Paul spoke only of God's imminent wrath, others envisioned the spaces and protocols for more systematic judgment. In the Gospel of Luke, Jesus rounds off one violent parable by explaining that the enslaved worker "who knew his master's will and did not get ready or act in accord with his will, shall receive many lashes" (Luke 12:47). We recall that Jesus told his followers that if their hand or foot caused them to stumble, it should, like Euclia's appendages, be cut off. In one Matthean tale, a wicked overseer is cut in pieces and thrown into a hellish place because he failed to manage the enslaved people in his care, beat them, and drank in taverns instead of working (Matt. 24:45–51).[7]

Throughout the parables we hear of agricultural workers, domestic workers, and messengers who are mistreated, tortured, abused, and killed. This mistreatment is sometimes incidental and barely rises to the level of a plot device. Ancient audiences who frequented the theater were used to encountering the "bad slave" (*servus callidus*) onstage. Alongside snacks of figs and walnuts, they imbibed caricatures of malicious tricksters who were deceitful, criminal, greedy, immoral, and self-serving. Over time, these performances deadened the empathetic responses of the audience; for most it might have seemed as if the unjust stewards of the parables surely received their just deserts.[8]

There may be hints that enslaved coauthors modified the general principle of punishment as a way to speak to their own circumstances. In some cases, the harshest punishments are meted out to enslaved overseers who mistreated their coworkers. One enslaved man, who racked up an astronomical debt, found himself punished for the lean mercy he showed to another worker (Matt. 18:23–35). Having been forgiven by his "master," he threw another unfree person in prison simply because they could not repay the equivalent of about four months' salary. Their colleagues, who were revolted by the injustice, reported the overseer to the king, who condemned the spendthrift's cruelty and instructed that he be tortured until his debt was repaid. Given that the debt was the rough equivalent of 160,000 years' worth of pay for a day laborer, the penalty fell somewhere between an epoch and an eternity. Just as Euclia's downfall was precipitated by her need to brag to her peers, so too was the unmerciful steward undone by his coworkers. Parables, like fables, were less about justice than about survival. But by reading with enslaved authors in mind, we might arrive at a lesson: survival requires (enslaved) solidarity. In some sense, the anonymous enslaved people are the invisible power.

Literary violence has a certain fecundity. Watered by the prurient interests of readers, its details mushroom in the darkness between the pages. The impression of hell that we only faintly sense in the Gospels—whiffs of sulfur, flashes of flames, the hair-raising wriggle of worms—flourishes in late antique Christian exposition. Tours of hell, allegedly given to religious heroes in visions, reveal the ever-grander scale of the underworld. The visions of Mary, Peter, Paul, and others flesh out the details of the subterranean torture chamber. Disobedient Christians, unlucky pagans, and merciless persecutors find themselves shackled and buried in a world of grime and pain. They are tortured with the same instruments, and according to the same logic, that the wealthy freeborn used to bring enslaved and impoverished people to heel. The degrading humiliation of public execution—through exposure to wild animals, hanging, burning, and other forms of cruelty—all feature in the infernal realm. In the egalitarian dystopia of Christian hell, punishments that under Roman law were only applied to the bodies of the disenfranchised, enslaved, and impoverished were now visited upon everyone, regardless of status. We might imagine that for mistreated enslaved coauthors and readers, these were stories about justice or revenge.[9]

These stories might be nightmarish, but they worked precisely because they drew from the conditions of real-world captivity. Architecturally we can map hell's floor plan onto the various spaces used for legal proceedings, incarceration, and punishment: Revelation's heavenly tax office, complete with a shuffle of angelic bureaucrats; the law courts of the martyrdom stories, equipped with attentive clerks; and, finally, hell itself, a prison carved not out of the imagination, but out of the rocks of underground prisons, "slave quarters," and mines. Even seemingly abstract statements had real-world referents. The hapless worker who received a single talent as a gift and buried the coin for safekeeping is banished to "outer darkness." Infernal overtones aside, the phrase gestures to the ordinary spaces of domestic and agrarian punishment. While some enslaved people were shackled in underground prisons or damp cisterns, many were chained to walls at night. A victim of the eruption of Mount Vesuvius in 79 CE was found by archaeologists still shackled to a wall in a storage room off an underground kitchen in Pompeii. Although Pompeii conjures images of fire, most of those restrained there were exposed to low nighttime temperatures. Those who were incarcerated in the windowless prison chambers farthest (that is, outermost) from light sources in Roman prisons were also confined in darkness. Like the frigid prisoners of hell, or Euclia alone in the side street, their chattering teeth gnashed from cold dark nights spent outside.[10]

The cutting-edge exploration of Roman carceral spaces by archaeologists Matthew Larsen and Mark Letteney helps explain the peculiar and at times scatological interests of Christian speculation. Although no two prisons were exactly alike, and caves and cisterns were sometimes repurposed to constrain people, prisons were generally subterranean spaces accessorized with stockades. For all prisoners, conditions were bleak and sometimes fatal: a number of those who were shut up alongside Blandina died there. They found themselves in cramped dark spaces.

Early modern engraving of male prisoners bound, shackled, and hanging. These real-world punishments also appear in contemporary Christian depictions of hell. Ancient prisons would have had much smaller windows and been subterranean.

Fetters would cut into the legs and birth sores that quickly grew angry and unguent. The food rations were barely enough to sustain life. Lethargic prisoners, weak from lack of nourishment and cramping with hunger, struggled to sleep amid the hubbub and crush. The air was filled with the sound of whistling, weeping, singing, and inarticulate cursing. You could not close your ears to the din. If you were lucky, as the apostle Paul may have been and some later generations of Christians were, friends would bribe the guards and smuggle you supplies. If you weren't, then you had only the desperate babel of fellow prisoners and the slow work of graffiti-making to entertain you.[11]

The liveliest place was the toilet. The foul-smelling cesspits that served as makeshift latrines teemed with intestinal parasites, but cesspits were a rare luxury for the incarcerated. Fecal matter was usually the sphere of low-status workers, who collected, removed, and recycled it for use in construction and farming, but in prisons—and in the visions of hell that they inspired—bodily waste was inescapable. For most prisoners it was everywhere, coating the floors and contaminating food. The stench of human excrement filled the space and, in imagined hell, people from every rank were consumed by parasitic worms or buried up to their waists or necks in excrement. In hell, as in bondage, you cannot escape your shit.[12]

Not every civic or imperial prisoner was in a state of forced lethargy. Some were compelled to work in mills or the mines. In the latter, the condemned would find themselves shoulder to shoulder with enslaved workers, suffocating from noxious gases, trapped under falling rocks and debris, physically exhausted, and thirsty. Some spaces, like the copper mine at Phaino (modern-day Umm al-Amad, in Amman, Jordan), were accessible only by crawling. In other mines it was possible, with various amounts of difficulty, to walk upright. But the experience was devastating to physical health, and the working conditions were dire. Beyond the tattooing, branding, head-shaving, beating, and shackling that took place there, the work hurt. The mines could leave prisoners with permanent health problems and deformities.[13]

The lower the prisoner descended in a mine, the more claustrophobic the space became. The air was deadly and difficult to endure, and the prisoner had to choose between light and oxygen. These working conditions explain why, from antiquity to Dante, the lower spaces of hell were reserved for the most sinful, why sinners found themselves trapped under rocks, and why sulfur perfumed the air of hell. Stories about the conditions quarried fear alongside copper and marble. The celebrated preacher John Chrysostom, the fourth-century bishop of Constantinople, traded on this anxiety when he told his parishioners that hell was like the mines, only worse.[14]

Roman copper mine at Phaino, Jordan. The average ceiling height here is 1.6 meters (5 feet 3 inches), meaning that many would have been unable to stand.

Though descriptions of hell also drew upon stories of the underworld from Greek mythology and from contemporary Judaism, the realities of lives of confinement (whether from incarceration or enslavement) can help explain the peculiarities of these Christian images of hell. Hell runs hot and cold. The damned are forced to serve as wet nurses to demonic beasts. Hell's inhabitants are stripped naked, exposed, suspended, emasculated, fettered, immobilized, blinded, branded, and pulled apart. The permanent effects of disobedience to God paralleled the strictures of ancient law. Under a Roman law passed in the early first century CE, anyone who had been branded, shackled, tortured and found guilty of a crime, imprisoned, or sent to a gladiatorial school was ineligible for citizenship. They lived in a kind of limbo as members of a perpetual legal underclass. So, too, the Christian who apostatized or blasphemed against the Spirit after baptism lost all hope of future redemption. Figurative flight from the

The tortures of hell according to fifteenth-century artist Jan van Eyck and an unnamed assistant

Spirit made one a "runaway slave"; unless, like Valerius Maximus's "loyal slaves," they gave their lives for God as martyrs, bad Christians would be shackled in hell.[15]

Interpreters of Jesus' parables often dismiss the violence, choosing instead to emphasize positive aspects of these stories. Some have argued, for example, that parables about enslaved workers dignify them by portraying them as moral agents capable of making ethical decisions. Others engage in philological and cultural gymnastics, pretending that the overseers are freeborn servants and insisting that the parables nestle in the quotidian hierarchical arrangements between wealthy employers and those who depended on them. Others still have argued that these stories are mere metaphors, the most capaciously allegorical part of Jesus' teaching.

What these interpretations overlook is the consistent rooting of early Christian identity in the structures of slavery. To put this in the language of the third-century Christian lawyer Tertullian, "We are slaves of the living God, whose judgment over his slaves consists not of fetters or the cap of freedom, but of eternal punishment or salvation."[16]

Early Christian sarcophagus in which Christ (center) separates the sheep (good Christians) from the goats (bad people) at the Last Judgment. In Christian theology of the period, the good would be rewarded and the bad would be punished.

The typical argument against taking the language of enslavement to God seriously is that there are no practical consequences for shirking one's responsibilities; if Christians are enslaved to God, then surely those bonds are loosely held and voluntarily undertaken. But this arrangement is only temporary, and terrible punishments await anyone who defies God. In the New Testament, God is the absentee landlord of the parables. The parables and tours of hell instruct that on Judgment Day, the remote deity will return to visit violent judgment on his human possessions. On this day, and for the aching eternity that follows, disobedient Christians and pagans will all be treated as "bad slaves." In this way, in some early Christian discourse, divine justice is structured by the grammar of enslavement. It is not that God does not treat humans as enslaved, it is simply that God does not treat humans as enslaved *just yet*.

Prisoners housed in the seventeenth-century Palazzo Chariamonte-Steri, in Palermo, Sicily, found their days and stomachs empty. Instead of writing letters like Paul or Thomas More, they inscribed the prison walls with images and words in Italian, Arabic, English, and Sicilian. The artists were resourceful; they used coal, linseed oil from lamps, shoe polish, urine, saliva, metal shavings (possibly from their chains), and tomato sauce borrowed from evening meals to create the colored paint that brought their impressions to life. Tucked among the trompe l'oeil in cell number three is a hellmouth summoned from Dante's *Inferno*. The gaping jaws of the monstrous mouth open like a crescent moon as a procession of biblical patriarchs spills out into the world. Inside the monster, we read Dante's words, "Abandon all hope, ye who enter." The call to "those who enter" echoes in graffiti throughout the prison complex. One incarcerated writer urged those entering the "horrendous abyss" to read the verses that the prisoners "wrote in blood." It was not only the prisoners who saw their confinement this way. Luca Pinelli, the supervisor of a local house for Jesuits, wrote in his *Meditationi* that "since Christ descended in the infernal regions to console and free the Holy Patriarchs, . . . so you should try to visit prisons and hospitals to bring help and comfort to the afflicted."[17]

The mouths on the walls of Palermo cells—for this is not the only one—offer an apt image for hell, one that predated the graffiti in Palermo by centuries and persists in first-person accounts of incarceration to this day. The prison consumes other things and parts of things, subsuming them into the body of the host, transforming them into parts of another, and expelling the rebellious bits in an excretive crush. While enslavement and incarceration are not identical, they are structurally similar, and they elicit similar fears of annihilation. In this way, we might see slavery as a system of cannibalization. Those who were trafficked on the ships that sailed the Middle Passage feared that they would be eaten by white men. Unfreedom consumes, digests, reshapes, and expels those who, like Euclia, resist incorporation.[18]

Alongside these threats of annihilation, there were splinters of resistance in the form of alternative readings predicated on enslaved authorship and interpretation. In early Christian discussions of resurrection, the good Christian who had been fed to wild beasts in the arena would be reassembled as themselves in the world to come. Even if they had been eaten by fish and subsequently consumed in a tavern or at a dinner table, they would never be destroyed; God would raise them up one day. Christian ideas about resurrection thus rejected the consumptive and cannibalistic impulses of captivity and enslavement.[19]

Similarly, it is significant that enslaved workers do not receive much treatment in tours of hell. To be sure, they are punished, but less frequently than children, women, and other generic groups. In one medieval text that otherwise rehearsed imperial power, we even find a reference to the punishment of cruel enslavers. These might be read as moments of enslaved protest. By broadening the violence of the judicial system to include everyone, the coauthors and coproducers of these texts created a parallel system of justice that is more equitable even if it is equally vile. We might see analogues in *defixiones*—inscribed lead curse tablets that petitioned deities to punish wrongdoers in the most violent of ways. The sentiment lingers on the walls of a late-antique prison in Corinth, where Christian prisoners scratched calls for vengeance. They asked the Lord "not [to] have mercy towards those who put us here" and to punish their enemies with "a bad death." In this sense, the punishments of hell might be a form of outlaw justice that pushed back against the loaded dice of imperial and enslaving power.[20]

Yet, like any other kind of justice, parallel systems of justice need constant revision. The problem is not necessarily with the revenge fantasies of disenfranchised people that use violence to metabolize mistreatment in their own day, but with what happens when the winds change and power dynamics are altered. The figments of eternal torment that had democratized punishment in the hereafter became blueprints for real-world carceral practices that, historically speaking, have targeted the most marginal members of society. In practice, justice is never equitably administered. Christian visions of the inferno smuggled the merciless logic of Roman enslavement into the present. Hell, incarceration, and slavery have remained intertwined. Hell's prisoner has become racialized in ways that have lived consequences for those who are incarcerated in the present. Although this might seem like a distinctly American problem, carceral violence is a global phenomenon. In many countries, for example, prisoners and those suffering from mental illness continue to be shackled and confined in cages.[21]

Christian hell is a merciless place but not a godless one. There, for many people, is the rub; originally it was angels, not demons, who administered God's justice. How and when Satan moved from inmate to warden is its own much longer story, but for the first four centuries of the Common Era the horrors of hell were intimately tied to divine actors. This was divine justice.

Christian hell is animated by the logic of Roman slavery. Eternal punishment is a facet of many religious traditions, and Christianity drew from some of the most ancient sources, but hell's physical and ideological architecture was shaped by the experience of real-world confinement. Its torments—the cold, the dark, the foul stench, and the hunger—were furnished by the conditions of civic prisons and imperial mines. They say people write what they know. The relentless violence of hell is utterly comprehensible in the context of the social order of late Roman antiquity, whose system of justice was fiercely punitive toward the socially disenfranchised. If early Christians were "enslaved to God," the punishments of hell were a logical consequence of their disobedience. For those engaged in the project of Christian education, the prospect of future damnation was a powerful weapon for the shaping of Christian novices and initiates. After learning about hell, the story of Jesus, forgiveness, and the salvation it afforded was a merciful relief. Ordinary human enslavers were not in the habit of providing people with second chances.[22]

It is only by focusing on the lived experiences of enslaved and incarcerated people that the intertwined histories of enslavement, Roman incarceration, and Christian hell come into view. Without that focus, hell is an oddly scatological warren of confined spaces and torture chambers. The realization that the experiences of enslaved people shaped not only the writing of the New Testament, but also ideas about Christian identity and expectations about postmortem punishment, raises thorny questions for those invested in these texts in the present. What other elements of Christian tradition require closer scrutiny? What other scriptural and theological ideas are informed by the logic of enslavement?[23]

Whether or not they are themselves religious, those who are concerned about the power of Christian scripture, biblical perspectives on enslavement, and their historical afterlives should reconsider their broader and long-lasting effects. Enslaving ideologies, which have been partly supported and transmitted by Christianity, have provided the foundations for cultural attitudes towards justice, punishment, racism, and poverty. Not all history sits tidily on a shelf. Some of it, once learned, demands change in our language, in our beliefs about the world, in our legislation, and in our actions.

EPILOGUE

It is often said that history is written by the victors. No one knew this better than Petilianus. A bishop of Cirta in fifth-century Algeria, Petilianus was what his religious contemporaries called a Donatist, though he would not have approved of that name. Following the arguments of the fourth-century bishop Donatus of Carthage, Petilianus thought that Christian leaders who had handed over religious books to secular authorities during the Great Persecution had forfeited the Holy Spirit. Handing over books was, to him, the equivalent of betraying Christ, and thus these bishops had polluted the church and left their successors and congregations spiritually bereft. Although Petilianus arguably held the moral high ground, he lacked political clout. By 411, when he attended the Council of Carthage, which was supposed to settle the Donatist dispute, the battle for wider and, more importantly, imperial support was already lost.[1]

And yet Petilianus fought for his words to be preserved. When proceedings were read aloud from shorthand notes, he protested that he had no way of knowing if what was being read aloud was what had actually been said. When church records were introduced into evidence, Petilianus demanded to know where and with whom they had been stored. Again and again, he worried about the details of record-keeping: about the words of Donatists not being entered into the official records, and about the textual corruption of the records.

Though his main critic, the considerably better-known Catholic bishop Augustine of Hippo, accused him of being a pedant who harped on technical matters, Petilianus's concerns may feel familiar to those who have been reading this book. The knowledge that the books of the New Testament were coauthored, copied, moved, curated, and interpreted by anonymous enslaved people might worry some. The fact that these collaborators may not even have been Christian only exacerbates the problem. It creates the opportunity for slippage, corruption, and alteration. When the touchstone for human conduct and the primary resource for personal salvation are on the line, surely the spirit resides in the details? If the New Testament is not the work of Jesus' disciples, can it be trusted?

The answer will depend on what you think the Bible is, and what you want to do with it. If you hold that the Bible is the infallible and inerrant Word of God, merely transcribed by the named authors, and divinely protected from alteration and correction, then yes, the prospect of coauthorship by enslaved collaborators who may or may not have been Jesus followers will present an insurmountable problem. Continuing to erase invisible workers, however, will not solve the problem. Even without enslaved collaborators, many of these issues remain. Christians have known about the variants in their manuscripts since the second century; theologians have doubted that Paul wrote the Letter to the Hebrews since the third century; and for hundreds of years, scholars — many of whom were ordained clergy — have debated the authorship of the books of the Bible and the accuracy of its claims. Ignoring servile workers does not solve these larger textual and historical problems. It merely reproduces the ancient enslaving logic of erasure that sought to oppress and dehumanize the most vulnerable.

The fact of enslaved collaborators' contributions to the New Testament does not bankrupt the Bible, even for those who think that it is divinely inspired scripture that speaks across time. Human beings have always been involved in the production of these texts. Their fingerprints are there even if they are invisible to the naked eye. That some of these fingerprints belong to enslaved workers may complicate our account of how the Bible came to be, but it does not divest it of meaning. On the contrary, if authors are important for our interpretation of the New Testament, then accepting the role of servile workers can broaden our ability to speak about what the Bible meant in the past and, for those who hold it as sacred, what it means in the present. This is true for those who are not Christian as well as for those who are. Whatever our relationship to the Christian Bible, centering enslavement in the story of the creation of the New Testament challenges us to rethink our ideas of how our own world is organized: whom we see and whom we do not, whom we credit and whom we overlook.

✝

In June 2022, I was walking on New York's Upper East Side when I committed an unequivocal violation of pedestrian etiquette: I stopped suddenly on the sidewalk. The murmurs of discontent I could hear from those behind me were muffled by the sight ahead. The Park Avenue Armory—a gorgeous Gothic redbrick that stands out among the pale wash of neutral-toned buildings—was advertising an upcoming performance of the ancient Greek dramatic trilogy the *Oresteia*. What struck me was not the performance itself, but the billing. Above the title were three names sharing equal weight and, seemingly, credit: the ancient playwright (and "father of tragedy," Aeschylus), the director, and the actor who played the leading role of the tragic heroine, Clytaemnestra.

The theatrical world is one of hierarchies—we speak of "A-list stars" and "top billing"—but this billboard suggested that the play was the production of three figures whose roles bled into one another. The *Oresteia* was no longer Aeschylus's alone. It was a shared creation.

This was a striking claim in an incongruous location. The Upper East Side is an area of Manhattan known for old money and fossilized social norms. The prewar apartment buildings that line Park Avenue contain "servants' quarters" the size of suburban pantries. Though most have been converted, they are an architectural holdover from an era when staff were kept ready to hand and out of sight. Traditionally, this is a place where people claim ownership of the labor of others; meals prepared by house-keepers and caterers, companies and wealth built by hundreds, and well-behaved children co-raised with the assistance of a fleet of drivers, nannies, and tutors. In a community that thrives on the principle that "if you pay for it, it's yours," a billboard that recognized the authorial roles of a director and actor felt out of place.

I was in Manhattan because for the previous two years the coronavirus had prevented me from conducting research in Europe (or seeing anyone but immediate family). If I seemed overly cautious, or even paranoid, it was with good reason. As an immunocompromised kidney transplant recipient, I was one of the "vulnerable population" who lived in the asterisk next to the health guidelines for "normal people." Like many others, I spent multiple years in self-imposed isolation, distanced from everyone but my closest relatives.

The isolation was made easy because New York has, for decades, been the poster child for convenience culture. Whether I needed groceries, medication, or a gym mat, everything could be delivered, usually within a few days, if not hours. (The linguistic conventions of delivery culture, like those of the Roman Empire, tend to erase the people who do the delivering. We speak of Amazon "delivering things," as if an abstract multinational company brought purchases to our home.) But privileged people like me were able to take the moral high ground associated with social distancing only because we had the means to do so. We had jobs that could be performed remotely and the resources to pay a premium in delivery fees. Many others did not. As someone who was high-risk, I could justify such extravagant expenditures as necessities, but I had no reason to think that those who delivered my food were any less vulnerable than I was. To face the bald truth: I survived the nadir of the pandemic because others were put in harm's way on my behalf.[2]

It is not only people who are obscured by our socially revealing linguistic conventions. Our social discourse also minimizes the character of their work. Delivery work is considered low-status labor, but in this historical moment those who performed it played life-saving roles, as did the workers in meat-processing facilities, and the janitorial staff who sanitized schools, hospitals, and grocery stores, and all the other essential personnel, alongside the brave doctors, nurses, radiological technicians, and laboratory workers for whom people applauded. These are just a few examples and yet, most of the time, this kind of work is invisible. Just as Romans only noticed enslaved workers when they did not accomplish their tasks perfectly, we only see invisible labor when things go wrong: when supply chains break down or packages fail to magically appear.

In antiquity, enslaved workers were rendered invisible in order to preserve a fiction of control, superiority, and independence among the elite. The erasure of low-status people from the world of literature in particular allowed elites to maintain a monopoly on the kinds of activities that they deemed worthy and noble.

Authorship—of books or ideas—was one such realm. It is because authorship was seen as an intellectual function, associated with desirable and masculine virtues like good judgment, that it was restricted to high-status individuals: those who were freeborn, well-educated, male citizens. When non-elites played authorial roles, they were either erased or their literary projects were described as authorless. It is no accident that the writings of enslaved and formerly enslaved authors were open to constant revision by others.

The idea of the author as a figure who was male, self-sufficient, sui generis, and solitary arose in antiquity, but a great deal has happened between the first century and the twenty-first. A succession of technological, theological, and social revolutions has transformed the world and its writing in interrelated ways. It was in eighteenth-century Romantic circles that the term *author* began to be associated with individualism and "genius." The roots of this idea, however, are found earlier and in a variety of intellectual circles. As Joseph Addison noted in 1711, "There is no Character more frequently given to a Writer, than that of being a Genius." Generally speaking, the authorial genius was seen to work without assistance or learning: his skills were the gifts of either God or Nature.[3]

Wherever the work of the genius is discussed, its foil is pictured as servile—as if servility and brilliant creativity are antithetical. The spirit of imitation, wrote philosopher John Stuart Mill, could productively be engaged without devolving into "slavish" copying, but others argued that anything that "falls short" of innovation and invention "is servile imitation." Philosopher Immanuel Kant, like Mill, could create space for emulation, but only in the context of freedom: "The product of genius is an example, not for imitation... but for emulation by another genius, who is thereby awakened to the feeling of his own originality, to exercise freedom from coercion in his art." In this way and in more recent periods as well, the author-genius has come to be defined against and in opposition to writing practices that are constructed as servile, mediated, constrained, and low-status.[4]

Accompanying these theories of literature and aesthetics were socioeconomic and technological innovations, such as the printing press, state censorship, and, most important, the birth of copyright law, that solidified the author as a person who not only created but, more importantly, also owned their work. Nascent notions of intellectual property echo through history, but with the birth of the printing press and the ensuing litigation between authors and publishers, the concept of copyright as ownership of an author's "original expression" came to have legal weight. Copyright normalized and naturalized the power dynamics and hierarchical structures between different kinds of writers and textual producers. As a consequence, *auctoritas* and "authorship" were squarely located, both conceptually and legally, in a singular person who now had moral rights. Other figures — secretaries, editors, publishers, pressmen, and proofreaders — were necessary, but their agency was relevant only inasmuch as it might threaten the autonomy and vision of the author.[5]

Alongside the imposing history of the "author," we find a complex history of scribal work. Beginning with Martin Luther, in the Reformation, the category of the "scribe" began to include two groups: the Jewish scribes who schemed against Jesus during his lifetime and the monastic "papist" scribes who had corrupted and imprisoned the Bible. That both these groups were allegedly motivated by sinister monopolizing agendas only served to tarnish the character of the scribe. It was the apostles themselves who served as amanuenses to the Holy Spirit. They received credit as authors because their *dictator*, though presumably omnipresent, was invisible. Scribal labor is a persistent theme in Reformation constructions of scripture, but the potency of the image required that the apostles themselves serve as assistants to the divine author. Others were obscured. Ironically, even as the printing press radically expanded the number of people involved in the production of written material, there was a dramatic reduction in the number of people acknowledged to be a part of this process.[6]

We are heirs to this hierarchical system that recognizes some actors while eliminating others. Our hierarchies are not always overtly religious or concerned with authorship, but they are concerned with their conceptual synonyms, power and authority. In the late nineteenth century, and as a direct consequence of the influx of "lady typists" into the workforce, stenography and typing were recategorized. In the British census of 1851, stenographers were classed alongside journalists, authors, lawyers, and doctors, but by the time of the 1901 census, shorthand writing and typing had been recategorized as a form of mercantile labor. The threat to masculine autonomy presented by female typists forced a gendered reconceptualization of secretarial labor that insisted upon its mindlessness. Women and metal mechanical devices were both referred to as "typewriters," much as catapult engineers and catapults could be confused centuries earlier. Thus the role of the amanuensis, or secretary—which enjoyed some visibility and recognition when performed by men in the medieval and early modern periods—slipped further down the authorial hierarchy and vanished into the mechanical world. From the second half of the nineteenth century, therefore, there was a gendered reconceptualization of certain kinds of secretarial work as mindless. In the field of New Testament scholarship, these depictions of the secretary were coupled with racially coded theories of enslavement. These social shifts and historical developments calcified an ancient understanding of literary assistants as agentless conduits for the wills of others.[7]

At the foundation of this commitment to the author is the idea that intellectual work is rarer, more valuable, and of higher status than other kinds of social contributions. We do not only prize authorship because of historical movements that have centered property rights and the ownership of ideas; we also prize authorship because we see cognitive labor (thinking, writing, planning, and managing) as more dignified than manual labor. It is a principle of any organization that its figurative minds—the managers, administrators, CEOs, named founders of artistic schools, and, indeed, professors—are better credited and better compensated than its other members. Just as ancient elites erased the contributions of lower-status collaborators to preserve their own fictions of superiority, people today do it to protect their own sense of importance. We writers do not like to be told that our books are not our own.

If only select individuals can be identified as the mind of any enterprise, others are just body parts. The traditional theory (often ascribed to Descartes but debatably older) that the mind is separate from and superior to the body looms large here. The distinction not only mislabels the contributions made by people figured as unthinking body parts, it also ignores the fact that expertise and knowledge do not reside just in the mind. They live in dexterous fingers and in many other forms of embodied, kinesthetic experience. This multisensory embodied expertise is as integral to the elite work of brain surgeons as it is to woodworkers and electricians. This is not to say that everyone deserves equal credit and compensation, but rather that all deserve acknowledgment. Knowledge—genius, even—dwells in all our parts, both individual and societal.[8]

The ancient and contemporary worlds are not identical, of course. Major shifts in the technologies of manufacturing and the organization of labor have radically changed how companies and organizations run. In antiquity, an enslaved manager was often empowered to make large investments, manage personnel, oversee the running of a company, and so on. So, too, an ancient secretary, copyist, or reader performed work worthy of a coauthor. In all of these cases, great power was entrusted to people who in many other senses had much less of it.

Similar dynamics are at play today. Even though modern systems of labor do not necessarily expect lower-status workers to do creative or interventionist work, people are still agentive beings. To ignore people's capacity for creativity and innovation seems to me to be bad business—now, as it was then.

The imagined authorial mind that prevents us from seeing enslaved coworkers is grounded in a knotty set of hierarchies that erroneously privileges minds over bodies. It is worth asking, therefore, what might be gained by decentering authorship and foregrounding collaboration instead?

We can start with the many interpretive problems that enslaved collaborators and their perspectives can fix for those invested in the significance of the New Testament. These range from the historical to the theological: Why is Mark named Mark? (Because associating copies of texts with a trusted servile worker was a way to guarantee a text's accuracy.) Why do some Pauline texts sound different from others? (Because they were collaborations produced with different servile coauthors, often when Paul was incarcerated and unable to "oversee" their production and editing.) Why doesn't Jesus know the timing of Judgment Day? (Because he is figured as an enslaved overseer who was not supposed to know this.) Why do the women at the tomb in Mark not pass on the good news? (Because engaging in this kind of supernatural gossip was dangerous for them.) Why are hellish spaces filled with worms? (Because hell is an ancient prison and ancient prisons lacked basic sanitation.) The perspectives of enslaved collaborators can explain plot details and narrative elements that trouble Christian readers and lay historians alike.

Focusing on the social status of the writers who created the New Testament also diffuses the inflammatory conversation that currently surrounds disagreement about "forgery" and writing in the names of others in antiquity. When enslaved people wrote in the names of authors as a part of their servile work, their "forgery" was less about deceit and more about status, or a lack thereof. Enslavement reframes the phenomenon. Just as theft is sometimes about hunger and desperation rather than greed, forgery is sometimes about a lack of access to power. Similarly, acknowledging servile copyists can contribute to the sometimes sticky conversations about diverging Christian manuscripts. Differences between manuscripts are not necessarily evidence of efforts to pervert Christian literature; instead, they shine a light on the many venues in which enslaved collaborators—readers, secretaries, and copyists—made decisions about their work.[9]

Though these are meaningful interventions, the point of centering enslavement and enslaved workers should not be to fix the problems that interpreters currently have when they read the Bible, nor should it be about the explanatory power that enslavement has when it comes to narrating the history of Christianity. Centering enslavement is about doing justice, sharing credit, and recognizing harms. As the idea of Christ followers as part of the body of Christ reveals, the same passage can be used either to foster equality or to enforce hierarchy and oppression. Even benign metaphors can be harmful if we are not attentive to how they work and how they have been used. Reparative work in this case involves excising the explicit violence from, and acknowledging the power embedded in, cherished concepts and ideas about Christianity. It may not be Paul's fault that subsequent generations of others have used his work to enslave and oppress, but it is ours if we do not notice the opportunities for abuse that his words have afforded them.

Acknowledging servile workers might seem burdensome. It is simpler and easier to refer to a single person as an author than to recognize the wider array of ancient meaning-makers involved in the creation of a text or a religion. In a modern world that drowns us in information, storytelling almost always entails the stripping back of characters and detail. Some facts and some people always end up on the cutting-room floor. But even when those fictions have laudatory goals, they are still acts of erasure. Minimizing intermediaries draws us closer to others—to friends as well as the human and divine "authors" of our texts—but this is not justice. Ultimately, erasure always harms.

Attentiveness to those obscured by this process of simplification makes us aware of other ways of reading that can be cathartic. The fates of the disobedient in hell are horrifying, but they are, in our Christian sources, sometimes also democratizing. The undercurrent of enslaved solidarity that runs through the parables resists efforts to divide enslaved workers from one another. It sounds a note of caution about the perils of abusing power. Similarly, in Paul's model of the indwelling of the Spirit, volition never quite recedes from view. It is a tear in the patchwork fantasy of control: the Christ follower must choose to align themselves. The Holy Spirit is not a despot because the faithful do not allow it to be.

Once we accept biblical collaboration as fact and recognize its participants as oppressed human beings who nevertheless had agency, we are forced to confront a truth that can be unsettling to some readers of scripture: that the meaning of the Bible is fluid. Not only is it constantly in motion, but it is also constantly being produced—now, as then. Just as every homily offers a fresh expression of the gospel message tailored to the needs of the day, so too did every ancient scriptural performance give enslaved readers the opportunity to present scripture anew. Novel technologies of reading developed by anonymous workers—the indices, verse divisions, concordances, and tables of contents still found in modern Bibles—create alternate pathways through texts. Following alternate pathways has always been an enslaved mode of resisting power and it offers modern readers too the opportunity to read otherwise; to read against the grain.

Seeing the involvement and participation of enslaved workers in the writing of the Bible is not about change so much as it is about expansion: we still have authors and apostles; we just have many more, and with them a broader range of intentions, experiences, and interpretive modes with which to think. These alternate pathways offer modern readers, and Christian readers in particular, opportunities to broaden their horizons. To do the kind of ethical reading that is reparative as it listens to neglected voices, past and present. To read with erased collaborators and to attend to invisible actors—in the past and, just as importantly, in the present.

ACKNOWLEDGMENTS

This book, like all books, is not mine alone. Though my name is on the cover, it is a group project and I cannot fully represent the debt that I owe to others. I am tremendously grateful to my editor, Alex Littlefield, for believing in this book from the beginning and to the end. The copious feedback he gave me on the manuscript surely made this a better book. I know how fortunate I am to have worked with him through this process. I am grateful to my agent, Roger Freet, for over ten years of friendship, advice, and support. Thank you for sticking with me. Zach Philips and Morgan Wu, thank you for your work and belief in the manuscript. To everyone at Little, Brown, and Company from the editorial team, typesetters, copyeditors, publicists, warehouse staff, janitors, and production team, thank you for the care you have lavished on my book.

My research for this project was enriched by conversations that took place after presentations I delivered at the annual meetings of the Society of Biblical Literature, the Society for Classical Studies, and the European Association of Biblical Studies; at seminars at the University of Cambridge, Columbia University, the Institute for the Study of the Ancient World at New York University, Australian Catholic University, and the University of Leuven; and at the "Divided Worlds," "Wakeful Night," and "Writing, Enslavement, and Power" workshops. Thank you to all who attended.

ACKNOWLEDGMENTS

I thank my colleagues at the University of Birmingham and the Institute for the Study of the Ancient World at New York University for their support throughout this project. Without the remarkable work of their collective library staff, it would have been impossible to write this book during the height of the pandemic.

I am grateful to the many colleagues and friends who shared work with me prior to publication, read portions of the book in earlier drafts, and shared flashes of their genius with me in conversations: Chance Bonar, Claire Bubb, Mike Chin, Joel Christensen, Christy Cobb, Javal Coleman, Jeremiah Coogan, Nick Elder, Tom Geue, Joseph Howley, John Izzo, Cat Lambert, Matthew Larsen, Mark Letteney, AnneMarie Luijendijk, Timothy Luckritz Marquis, Marcia Moss, Ellen Muehlberger, Brent Nongbri, Matthew Novenson, Angela Parker, Kelsie Rodenbiker, Sarah Rollens, Katherine Shaner, Lily Reed, Laura Smith, Mitzi Smith, Shively Smith, Isaac Soon, Brett Stein, and Robyn Walsh. I must single out Matthew Larsen and Mark Letteney in particular, who not only read parts of my work but shared their own monumentally important study of ancient incarceration in advance of publication. I owe a particular debt to Jeremiah Coogan, Meghan Henning, Luis Menéndez-Antuña, and Tim Whitmarsh, who were somehow able to stomach reading and commenting on the whole thing. Finally, Nicolette D'Angelo performed invaluable editorial work on the first two sections of the book and saved me from many hideous mistakes.

As I was finishing up the manuscript, I learned of a new Italian regulation governing the use of images. As I did not have time to seek permission from the Italian Ministry of Culture, others shared images, gave me advice, and helped me secure permissions. My thanks to Sarah Bond, Sophie Hay, Robin Jensen, Lauren Larsen, Carole Raddato, and Arthur Urbano; to the omni-talented Dan McClellan for the line drawings; and to James Fenelon for the beautiful maps.

This book would never have happened were it not for Joseph Howley, whose work on enslavement and literate workers first sparked my interest in this topic. Thank you for sharing and for encouraging me to pursue this project. Similarly, I cannot have imagined writing this book were it not for my weekly conversations with my most brilliant friend, colleague, and collaborator Jeremiah Coogan. In many ways this is as much his book as mine. His friendship, genius, and kindness continue to inspire me as a scholar and a person.

I wrote this book during a pandemic that killed millions and greatly affected those who, like me, are immunocompromised. I am grateful to my medical teams at New-York Presbyterian Columbia and Cornell-Weill hospitals for their excellent care. So too I remain indebted to my uncle, James Fairbairn, for the kidney that keeps me alive.

Many friends have supported me through the somewhat rocky journey of writing this book: Jennifer Barry, Sarah Bond, Nyasha Junior, Jonathan Marks, Christine Luckritz Marquis, and Shannon Monaghan, thank you. Karina Hubbard, I could not have survived a year of remote school much less written this book without you. Liane Marquis Feldman, you are a daily inspiration. Robyn Walsh, you are a wonder, I am grateful to whatever unseen force brought you into my life.

My thanks to all the members of my many-pronged family: to my sisters, Pandora Moss, Serena Wise, and Sophie Moss, each of whom is wonderful in her own way. Serena and Roe, you are the daughters I never had. I would walk across burning coals for you. To my soul-sister Meghan Henning, whose love and support have sustained me through two decades of trials and joys. To my brothers (in-law) Barrett Foa and Tim Barnett, and

Tiffany McFerrin, my coparent. To my parents, by biology and by choice, Katrina Wise, Peter Wise, Marcia Moss, and Robert Moss, for all the individual ways you have shaped me and made me who I am. I will miss you always, Mama. I wish you hadn't missed all the good stuff.

Max and Luke, the children of my heart, you are the largest impediment to my writing and my greatest joy. I am so grateful to Mom and Dad for having you and sharing you with me.

This book is dedicated to my husband, Justin Foa. You turned my life upside down and made me speak in romantic clichés (which I did not want and for which I do not forgive you), and you gave me a whole family, a fairy-tale life, and a real sense of home (which, it turns out, I very much did want). Hopefully you read this far.

A NOTE ON ABBREVIATIONS
AND TRANSLATIONS

This book employs standard abbreviations for biblical and rabbinic texts. Except where otherwise noted, translations follow
or are emended from the New Revised Version of the Bible and
the Loeb Classical Library. Some references can be challenging
to locate as scholars utilize diverging number schemes. Further
information about identifying these references can be located
on the website associated with this book.

PRIMARY SOURCES

1 Apol. Justin Martyr, *First Apology*
1 Clem. *1 Clement*
2 Clem. *2 Clement*
Ac. Scil. *Acts of the Scillitan Martyrs*
AE *L'Année épigraphique* (Paris: Presses Universitaires de France, 1888–)
Aff. Dig. Galen, *Passions of the Soul*
Ann. Tacitus, *Annals*
Ant. Flavius Josephus, *Antiquities*
Att. Cicero, *Letters to Atticus*
Att. Cornelius Nepos, *Life of Atticus*
Aug. Suetonius, *Life of Augustus*
Ben. Seneca, *On Benefits*
Bryson Simon Swain, *Economy, Family, and Society from Rome to Islam: A Critical Edi-
    tion, English Translation, and Study of "Bryson's Management of the Estate"* (Cam-
    bridge: Cambridge University Press, 2016)
Cels. Origen, *Against Celsus*
CIL *Corpus Inscriptionum Latinarum I–XVI* (Berlin: Akademie der Wissenschaften,
    1863–)

A NOTE ON ABBREVIATIONS AND TRANSLATIONS

Comm. Matt. Origen, *Commentary on Matthew*
Dial. Tacitus, *Dialogue on Oratory*
Did. *Didache* or *Teaching of the Twelve Apostles*
Digest *Digest* of Justinian
Disc. Epictetus, *Discourses*
Dom. Suetonius, *Life of Domitian*
Ep. Cyprian of Carthage, *Letters*
Ep. Horace, *Epistles*
Ep. Libanius, *Letters*
Ep. Pliny the Younger, *Letters*
Ep. Seneca the Younger, *Letters*
Eth. Nic. Aristotle, *Nicomachean Ethics*
Eum. Cornelius Nepos, *Life of Eumenes*
Fab. Babrius, *Fables*
Fab. Phraedrus, *Fables*
Fam. Cicero, *Letters to Friends*
Fast. Ovid, *On the Roman Calendar*
Fin. Cicero, *On the Ends of Good and Evil*
Haer. Hippolytus of Rome, *Refutation of All Heresies*
Haer. Irenaeus of Lyon, *Against Heresies*
Herm. Man. Shepherd of Hermas, *Mandates*
Herm. Vis. Shepherd of Hermas, *Visions*
Hipp. 1 Epid. Galen, *On Hippocrates' "Epidemics," Book 1*
Hipp. 6 Epid. Galen, *On Hippocrates' "Epidemics," Book 6*
Hist. Cassius Dio, *History*
Hist. eccl. Eusebius of Caesarea, *Church History*
IEph. *Inscriptions from Ephesus*, H. Wankel, H. Engelmann, eds., *Die Inschriften von Ephesos* (8 vols., IGSK 11–17, Bonn: Rudolf Habelt, 1979–84)
Ign., Eph. Ignatius of Antioch, *Letter to the Ephesians*
Ign., Phld. Ignatius of Antioch, *Letter to the Philadelphians*
Ign., Smyr. Ignatius of Antioch, *Letter to the Smyrnaeans*
Ign., Trall. Ignatius of Antioch, *Letter to the Trallians*
ILS Hermann Dessau, *Inscriptiones Latinae Selectae* (Berlin, 1892–1916)
Ind. Lucian, *Ignorant Book Collector*
Inst. Quintilian, *Institutes of Oratory*
J.W. Josephus, *Jewish War*
Kühn C. G. Kühn, *Claudii Galeni Opera Omnia* (20 vols., Leipzig: Cnobloch, 1821–33; repr. in 22 vols., Hildesheim: Olms, 1964–65)
Lib. prop. Galen, *On My Own Books*
Marc. Tertullian of Carthage, *Against Marcion*
Martial Martial, *Epigrams*
Mart. Pol. *Martyrdom of Polycarp*
NA Aulus Gellius, *Attic Nights*
Nero Suetonius, *Life of Nero*
NH Pliny the Elder, *Natural History*

A NOTE ON ABBREVIATIONS AND TRANSLATIONS

Or. Dio Chrysostom, *Orations*

Chron. Jerome, *Interpretation of the Chronicle of Eusebius*

P. Ant. Papyri from Antinoopolis, Egypt

Paed. Clement of Alexandria, *Christ the Educator*

Pass. Perp. *Passion of Perpetua and Felicity*

P. Berol. Papyri originally owned by the Königlischen Museum, Berlin

P. Duk. Inv. Papyri formerly in the possession of Duke University

P. Lond. Litt. H. J. M. Milne, *Catalogue of the Literary Papyri in the British Museum* (London: British Museum, 1927)

P. Oxy. *The Oxyrhynchus Papyri* (London: The Egypt Exploration Society in Graeco-Roman Memoirs, 1898–)

Praesc. Tertullian, *Prescription against Heretics*

QFr Cicero, *Letters to His Four Brothers*

Rhet. Her. *Rhetoric for Herennius*

Rust. Varro, *On Agriculture*

Sat. Petronius, *Satyricon*

SBF. Preisigke et al., *Sammelbuch griechischen Urkunden aus Ägypten* (Berlin: de Gruyter, 1915–)

SEG *Supplementum epigraphicum graecum* (1923–)

Serm. Augustine of Hippo, *Sermons*

Strom. Clement of Alexandria, *Miscellanies*

TpSulp. Giuseppe Camodeca, *Tabulae Pompeianae Sulpiciorum* (*Edizione critica dell'archivio puteolano dei Sulpicii*, 2 vols., Rome: Quasar, 1999)

Trad. ap. *The Apostolic Tradition*

Tusc. Cicero, *Tusculan Disputations*

UPZ U. Wilcken, *Urkunden der Ptolemäerzeit (ältere Funde)* (2 vols., Leipzig: De Gruyter, 1927–34)

Val. Max. Valerius Maximus, *Memorable Sayings and Deeds*

Vir. ill. Jerome, *Lives of Illustrious Men*

JOURNAL EDITIONS, SERIES, CATALOGUES, AND REFERENCE WORKS

BibInt *Biblical Interpretation*

BZNW *Beihefte zur Zeitschrift für die neutestamentliche Wissenschaft*

CBQ *Catholic Biblical Quarterly*

CE *Chronique d'Egypte*

CQ *Classical Quarterly*

EC *Early Christianity*

FGH *Die Fragmente der griechischen Historiker* (ed. F. Jacoby, Leiden: Brill, 1954–)

GR *Greece and Rome*

GRBS *Greek, Roman, and Byzantine Studies*

HSCP *Harvard Studies in Classical Philology*

JBL *Journal of Biblical Literature*

JECH *Journal of Early Christian History*

A NOTE ON ABBREVIATIONS AND TRANSLATIONS

JECS *Journal of Early Christian Studies*
JFSR *Journal of Feminist Studies in Religion*
JRS *Journal of Roman Studies*
JTS *Journal of Theological Studies*
LCL Loeb Classical Library (Cambridge, MA: Harvard University Press, 1913–)
NovT *Novum Testamentum*
NPNF *Nicene and Post-Nicene Fathers*
NTS *New Testament Studies*
P&P *Past and Present*
PG Patrologia Graeca [= *Patrologiae Cursus Completus: Series Graeca*] (ed. J.-P. Migne, 162 vols., Paris, 1857–1886)
PL Patrologia Latina [= *Patrologiae Cursus Completus: Series Latina*] (ed. J.-P. Migne, 217 vols., Paris, 1844–1864)
VC *Vigiliae Christianae*

NOTES

The parameters of this book do not allow me to supply as much supporting detail as I would like. A more detailed set of notes, additional maps, study guides, and complete bibliography can be found on the website associated with this book. See www .candidamoss.com/gods-ghostwriters.

Author's Note

1   Saidiya V. Hartman, "Venus in Two Acts," *Small Axe: A Caribbean Journal of Criticism* 12 (2008): 1–14; Saidiya Hartman, *Lose Your Mother: A Journey Along the Atlantic Slave Route* (New York: Farrar, Straus & Giroux, 2008), 16; Saidiya Hartman, *Scenes of Subjection: Terror, Slavery, and Self-Making in Nineteenth-Century America* (Oxford: Oxford University Press, 1997). On agency: There is a thoughtful debate among scholars of Atlantic slavery about social death and agency. The important and influential work of Orlando Patterson, *Slavery and Social Death* (Cambridge, MA: Harvard University Press, 1982), looms large here.

2   Imagination is not only a necessity for historical work, it is equally important when it comes to engaging with one's contemporaries. In the early twentieth century, sociologist Amy Tanner and a friend took jobs working as waitresses in a café connected to a military apartment house. She found herself working long, aching hours for an employer who was oblivious to the burden they forced upon her staff. Later, when she published her findings, Tanner wrote, "This mistress, then, sinned chiefly in her inability to imagine." Even up close, Tanner reveals, powerful people in asymmetrical relationships fail to imagine the lives of others well. Her point is that imagination is the foundation of empathy and human connection. If all history writing is an exercise in measured imagination, and if imagination is grounded in human experience, then the goal of telling the story of Christianity necessarily shifts. The questions are now: With whom do we choose to imagine and live? Do we challenge ourselves to move beyond the stubborn limits of our own experiences and closely held assumptions? See Amy E. Tanner, "Glimpses at the Mind of a Waitress," *American Journal of Sociology* 13 (1907): 48–55 [54].

NOTES

3 For the website, see www.candidamoss.com/gods-ghostwriters. Spectral listening: Avery F. Gordon, *Ghostly Matters: Haunting and the Sociological Imagination* (Minneapolis: University of Minnesota Press, 1997), 23.

4 Abstractions can be useful: See Frederick Cooper, *Colonialism in Question: Theory, Knowledge, History* (Berkeley: University of California Press, 2005), 17. But, as Cooper notes, abstractions do not shed light on the social or political experience of enslavement.

5 Vincent Brown and Walter Johnson argue convincingly that we should more carefully theorize questions of agency, resistance, and humanity. Social death was a compelling metaphysical threat in the lives of enslaved people, but agency is an aspect of existence that should be assumed. See Walter Johnson, "On Agency," *Journal of Social History* 37 (2003): 113–24; Vincent Brown, "Social Death and Political Life in the Study of Slavery," *American Historical Review* 114 (2009): 1231–49 [1246–48].

6 P. Gabrielle Foreman et al., "Writing about Slavery / Teaching About Slavery: This Might Help," community-sourced document, accessed November 20, 2020, https://naacpculpeper.org/resources/writing-about-slavery-this-might-help/.

7 On presentism in its various forms, see Laurent Loison, "Forms of Presentism in the History of Science: Rethinking the Project of Historical Epistemology," *Studies in History and Philosophy of Science* 60 (2016): 29–37. I am grateful to historian of science Daryn Lehoux for leading me to these terms.

Introduction

1 I do not mean to suggest that those in the Roman provinces were not also powerful and wealthy, or that Paul could have expected to have mingled with the upper echelons of society. On wealth in the provinces, see John Weisweiler, "Capital Accumulation, Supply Networks, and the Composition of the Roman Senate, 14–235 CE," *P&P* 253 (2021): 3–44.

2 The phrase "brothers and sisters," which in Greek just reads "brothers," is used as shorthand for the community in Rome in Rom. 1:13, 7:1, 8:12, 10:1, 11:25, 12:1, 15:14, 30, and 16:14. The social connections are mentioned in Rom. 16.

3 Tertius: Heikki Solin, *Die stadtrömischen Sklavennamen: ein Namenbuch* (Stuttgart: Steiner, 1996), 1.152–53.

4 On the baptism of enslaved workers, see Jennifer A. Glancy, *Slavery in Early Christianity* (Oxford: Oxford University Press, 2002), 47. On the circumcision of enslaved workers by Jewish enslavers, see the directive in Gen. 17:12–13, and Catherine Hezser, *Jewish Slavery in Antiquity* (Oxford: Oxford University Press, 2005), 30–31.

5 "Neither slave nor free": Gal. 3:28. See Angela N. Parker, "One Womanist's View of Racial Reconciliation in Galatians," *JFSR* 34.2 (2018): 23–40. The task here is to excavate both culpability (that is, of Jesus followers who willfully participated in slavocracy) and responsibility (what it would mean to admit this past and deal responsibly and reparatively with it in the future).

6 Jamaica Kincaid, "In History," *Callaloo* 20 (1997): 1–7.

NOTES

Chapter One

1 For the graffito, see Heikki Solin and Marja Itkonen-Kaila, *Graffiti del Palatino*, vol. 1, *Paedagogium* (Helsinki: Acta Instituti Romani Finlandiae, 1966), 210–12, 246, and discussion in Peter Keegan, "Reading the 'Pages' of the *Domus Caesaris*: *Pueri Delicati*, Slave Education, and the Graffiti of the Palatine Paedagogium," in *Roman Slavery and Roman Material Culture*, ed. Michelle George (Toronto: University of Toronto Press, 2013): 69–98; Felicity Harley-McGowan, "The Alexamenos Graffito," in *The Reception of Jesus in the First Three Centuries*, ed. Chris Keith (London: T & T Clark, 2019): 105–140; and Tyler Schwaller, "Picturing the Enslaved Christ: Philippians 2:6–8, Alexamenos, and a Mockery of Masculinity," *JECH* 11 (2021): 38–65.

2 For the use of the name Alexander among Jews in Rome, see David Noy, *Jewish Inscriptions of Western Europe*, vol. 2, *The City of Rome* (Cambridge: Cambridge University Press, 1995), 514. For those enslaved in 70 CE, see Josephus, *J.W.* 6.9.3. On the price of enslaved workers after the Bar Kokhba revolt, see Catherine Hezser, *Jewish Slavery in Antiquity* (Oxford: Oxford University Press, 2005), 253.

3 Ibn Butlan, *General Treatise*, likely adapted from Rufus of Ephesus's *On the Purchase of Slaves*, in Swain, *Bryson*, 271.

4 On the development of the category of race, see Henry Louis Gates Jr. and Andrew S. Curran, eds., *Who's Black and Why? A Hidden Chapter from the Eighteenth-Century Invention of Race* (Cambridge, MA: Harvard University Press, 2022). Walter Scheidel estimates that at least 100 million people were trafficked in the Roman Empire. See Walter Scheidel, "The Roman Slave Supply," in *The Cambridge World History of Slavery*, vol. 1, *The Ancient Mediterranean World*, eds. Keith Bradley and Paul Cartledge (Cambridge: Cambridge University Press, 2011): 287–310 [309].

5 Hippocratic *Airs, Waters, Places* 23; Greekness and *paideia*: Isocrates, *Panegyricus* 50; toga-wearing race: Suetonius, *Aug.* 40.5. Jews worshipping donkeys: Josephus, *Against Apion* 2.79; Jews "born to be slaves": Cicero, *On the Consular Provinces* 5.10.

6 Emma Dench, "Race," in *A Cultural History of Western Empires in Antiquity*, ed. Carlos Noreña (London: Bloomsbury, 2019), 201–22.

7 Benjamin Isaac, *The Invention of Racism in Classical Antiquity* (Princeton, NJ: Princeton University Press, 2009); Rebecca Futo Kennedy and Molly Jones-Lewis, eds., *The Routledge Handbook of Identity and the Environment in the Classical and Medieval Worlds* (New York: Routledge, 2020).

8 On hostages: Theophrastus, *Economics* 1.5.6 (note that this text circulates under Aristotle's name as Aristotle, *Economics* 1.1244b); compare Varro, *Rust.* 1.17.5. On the demand for "home-born" enslaved children, see Harriet Flower, "The Most Expensive Slave in Rome: Quintus Lutatius Daphnis," *Classical Philology* 117 (2022): 99–119.

9 On the sources of enslaved people, see Walter Scheidel, "Quantifying the Sources of Slaves in the Early Roman Empire," *JRS* 87 (1997): 156–69; and Scheidel, "The Roman Slave Supply."

NOTES

10   On Melior, see *CIL* 14.472 and Hella Eckardt, *Writing and Power in the Roman World: Literacies and Material Culture* (Cambridge: Cambridge University Press, 2017), 130.

11   Donkey and mill inscription: Solin and Itkonen-Kaila, *Graffiti*, 1.289.

12   Uniforms: Seneca, *On Mercy* 1.24.1. Ointment: This is alluded to in Petronius, *Sat*. 75.8.

13   On the jobs for enslaved children, see Christian Laes, "Child Slaves at Work in Roman Antiquity," *Ancient Society* 38 (2008): 235–83.

14   Hadrian: Galen, *De propriorum animi cuiuslibet affectuum dignotione et curatione* 4. "Crippled Slave": Hieronymus of Rhodes, fr. 19.

15   Libanius, *Ep*. 131. Carolyn Marvin, "The Body of the Text: Literacy's Corporeal Constant," *The Quarterly Journal of Speech* 80.2 (1994): 129–49 [132].

16   Pliny, *Ep*. 8.1.

17   Galen, *Hipp. 1 Epid*. I. 102.29.

18   Fear: John Chrysostom, *Homily on Acts* 12.4 (PG 60.104); *Homily on 1 Timothy* 16.2 (PG 62.590); Chris de Wet, *Preaching Bondage: John Chrysostom and the Discourse of Slavery in Early Christianity* (Berkeley: University of California Press, 2015), 170–219; Blake Leyerle, *The Narrative Shape of Emotion in the Preaching of John Chrysostom* (Berkeley: University of California Press, 2020), 112–49.

19   On carceral mechanics, see Sandra R. Joshel, "Geographies of Slave Containment and Movement," in *Roman Slavery and Roman Material Culture*, ed. Michele George, 99–128.

20   W. Martin Bloomer, "Schooling in Persona: Imagination and Subordination in Roman Education," *Classical Antiquity* 16 (1997): 57–78.

21   Pliny, *NH* 35.58.201; Tacitus, *Ann*. 12.53.4, and discussion in Rose MacLean, *Freed Slaves and Roman Imperial Culture: Social Integration and the Transformation of Values* (Cambridge: Cambridge University Press, 2018), 107–11.

22   Scent of enslavement: Valerius Maximus 6.2.8. Epaphroditus: Tacitus, *Ann*. 15.55; Suetonius, *Nero* 49; Suetonius, *Dom*. 14. Reenslavement: Suetonius, *Claudius* 25.1; Cassius Dio, *Hist*. 60.13.2; Tacitus, *Ann*. 13.26–7; *Dig*. 25.3.6.1. Henrik Mouritsen, *The Freedman in the Roman World* (Cambridge: Cambridge University Press, 2011).

23   Pliny, *Ep*. 7.29; 8.6.2.

24   Manumission at the age of thirty was a result of the *lex Aelia Sentia* of 4 CE. This applied predominantly to men. Women were not typically manumitted until they were in their forties and their childbearing years were over. On gender and manumission, see Matthew J. Perry, *Gender, Manumission, and the Roman Freedwoman* (Cambridge: Cambridge University Press, 2013). Expelled to freedom: Lucian, *The Dependent Scholar*, 40–42.

25   On self-enslavement, see Monika Trümper, *Graeco-Roman Slave Markets: Fact or Fiction?* (Oxford: Oxbow, 2009). On the demographics of slavery in general, see Scheidel, "Quantifying the Sources of Slaves."

26   Pliny, *Ep*. 6.16.

27   On gender and comportment: Maud W. Gleason, *Making Men: Sophists and Self-Presentation in Ancient Rome* (Princeton, NJ: Princeton University Press, 1995).

NOTES

On foreign language and identity: Olivia Elder, "Citizens of the Wor(l)d? Metaphor and the Politics of Roman Language," *JRS* 112 (2022): 79–104.

28 Palatine children: see discussion in Keegan, "Reading," 79–80; Cornelius Nepos, *Att.* 13. Atticus's footmen are called *pedisequi*, and in the imperial family (*familia Caesaris*) may have shared the same status as *nomenclatores* (people who remembered names) and *tabellarii* (messengers).

29 P. Oxy. IV 724. On shorthand: Hans C. Teitler, *Notarii and Exceptores: An Inquiry into Role and Significance of Shorthand Writers in the Imperial and Ecclesiastical Bureaucracy of the Roman Empire (from the Early Principate to c. 450 AD)* (Leiden: Brill, 1985); Candida R. Moss, "The Secretary: Enslaved Workers, Stenography, and the Production of Early Christian Literature," *JTS* 74 (2023): 20–56. On secretaries in general, see E. Randolph Richards, *The Secretary in the Letters of Paul* (Tübingen: Mohr Siebeck, 1991).

30 On Caesar: John Robert Gregg, "Julius Caesar's Stenographer," *Century Magazine* (May 1921), 80–88. Bar Kokhba shorthand: *Mur.* 164; Pierre Benoit, Józef T. Milik, and Roland de Vaux, eds., *Discoveries in the Judaean Desert*, vol. 2: *Les grottes de Murabba'ât* (Oxford: Clarendon, 1961), 1.275–277 and plates CIII–CV.

31 For Tiro, see Jerome, *Chron.* 1.194. For a freedman of Maecenas, see Cassius Dio, *Hist.* 55.7.6. H. J. Milne, *Greek Shorthand Manuals* (London: Egypt Exploration Society, 1934), to be read with Sofía Torallas Tovar and Klaas A. Worp, *To the Origins of Greek Stenography (P. Monts. Roca I)*, Orientalia Montserratensia 1 (Barcelona: Publicacions de l'Abadia de Montserrat, 2006).

32 For voluntary associations paying copyists fees and leasing space for documents, see *IEph* 1687 (31 BCE); *IErythrai* 122 (100 BCE), *IPriene* 111 (100 BCE); *SEG* 32:1149. For archives: *IKyme* 13.79 (130 BCE); *IPriene* 108.222 (129 BCE); and discussion in Richard Last and Philip A. Harland, *Group Survival in the Ancient Mediterranean: Rethinking Material Conditions in the Landscape of Jews and Christians* (London: T & T Clark, 2020), 89–91.

33 On writing technologies, see Georgios Boudalis, *The Codex and Crafts in Late Antiquity* (Chicago: University of Chicago Press, 2018); and Bruce Holsinger, *On Parchment: Animals, Archives, and the Making of Culture from Herodotus to the Digital Age* (New Haven, CT: Yale University Press, 2023).

34 Houseguest: P. Oxy. LVI 2860.

35 For a full treatment of the intersection of enslavement, disability, and writing, see Nicholas Horsfall, "Rome without Spectacles," *GR* 42 (1995): 49–56; Candida R. Moss, "Disability," in Jeremiah Coogan, Joseph A. Howley, and Candida Moss, eds., *Writing, Enslavement, and Power in the Roman Mediterranean, 100 BCE–300 CE* (Oxford: Oxford University Press, forthcoming); Jane Draycott, *Prosthetics and Assistive Technology in Ancient Greece and Rome* (Cambridge: Cambridge University Press, 2022), 154–68.

36 Vision was superior: Quintilian, *Inst.* 1.12.8. Child *lectores* in Christianity: Cyprian *Ep.* 38.1.2; Augustine, *Serm.* 352; Cicero, *Tusc.* 5.112–13. On gestures, see more in chapter six. On unconscious lipreading, see John Plass et al., "Lip Reading without Awareness," *Psychological Science* 25 (2014): 1835–37.

37 Suetonius, *Galba* 21; Fronto, *Ep.* 2.3.

38 On the effects of bookwork on the person: Seneca, *Ep.* 15.6; Celsus, *On Medicine* Pr. 6 and 1.2.
39 Seneca, *Ep.* 27.

Chapter Two

1 On Jews as enslavers, see Catherine Hezser, "Slavery and the Jews," in *The Cambridge World History of Slavery*, vol. 1, *The Ancient Mediterranean World*, eds. Keith Bradley and Paul Cartledge, 438–55; and Catherine Hezser, *Jewish Slavery in Antiquity* (Oxford: Oxford University Press, 2002).
2 Sarah E. Rollens, "Rethinking the Early Christian Mission," in *The Gospels and Their Receptions: Festschrift Joseph Verheyden*, eds. Henk Jan de Jonge, Mark Grundeken, John Kloppenborg, and Christopher Tuckett (Leuven: Peeters, 2022), 557–78.
3 On associations of Roman citizens, see Sailakshmi Ramgopal, "Mobility," in *A Cultural History of Western Empires in Antiquity*, ed. Carlos F. Noreña (New York: Bloomsbury, 2018), 131–52.
4 Ulrike Roth, "Paul and Slavery: Economic Perspectives," in *Paul and Economics: A Handbook*, eds. Thomas R. Blanton IV and Raymond Pickett (Minneapolis: Fortress, 2017), 155–82.
5 Ephesus fishermen: *IEph* 20; four freedwomen: *AE* 1975.179.
6 Luke 8:3.
7 On Paul and citizenship: Calvin J. Roetzel, *Paul: The Man and the Myth* (Minneapolis: Fortress, 1999), 19–22.
8 Paul and work: Todd D. Still, "Did Paul Loathe Manual Labor? Revisiting the Work of Ronald F. Hock on the Apostle's Tentmaking and Social Class," *JBL* 125 (2006): 781–95. Greco-Roman voluntary associations and early Christianity: see John S. Kloppenborg, *Christ's Associations: Connecting and Belonging in the Ancient City* (New Haven, CT: Yale University Press, 2019).
9 Emerson B. Powery, "Reading with the Enslaved: Placing Human Bondage at the Center of the Early Christian Story," in *Bitter the Chastening Rod: Africana Biblical Interpretation after "Stony the Road We Trod" in the Age of BLM, SayHerName, and MeToo*, eds. Mitzi J. Smith, Angela N. Parker, and Ericka S. Dunbar Hill (Minneapolis: Fortress, 2022), 71–90.
10 Quinquatrus: Ovid, *Fast.* 3.809–21.
11 Celsus: Origen, *Cels.* 3.55. Laundering clothes: Revelation 7:14; Mark 9:3; Pliny, *Ep.* 10.96; Justin Martyr: *Acts of Justin* A.3.
12 Warehouse manager: *TPSulp.* 46 and 44. On co-ownership, see Cleon, a trilingual worker enslaved to salt farmers near Cagliari in Sardinia (*CIL* I² 2226); and see a legal ruling in *Dig.* 2.4.10.4 that presumes that corporate entities could "own" enslaved people. See also *CIG* 3071, in which a wealthy man bequeathed enslaved people to assist with the dedication of a sanctuary gifted by him to his associates in Pergamum. On early Christians pooling resources, see Acts 4:32. See also Ulrike Roth, "Paul, Philemon, and Onesimus," *ZNW* 105 (2014): 102–30.

NOTES

13 Quote from Roth, "Paul and Slavery," 164.

14 Later Christian writers: Eusebius, *Hist. eccl.* 3.5.3; Epiphanius, *Panarion* 29.7.7–8; Epiphanius, *On Weights and Measures* 15.

15 Pompey (63 BCE) and Cassius (52–51 BCE) enslaved thirty thousand Jews at Tarichea (Josephus, *J.W.* 1.8.9) and later enslaved four cities (Josephus, *J.W.* 1.11.2; Josephus, *Ant.* 14.11.2); Gaius (4 BCE) enslaved those who resisted in the Galilee (*J.W.* 2.5.1). Claudia Aster: *CIL* X 1971. On Paul as a religious expert akin to those enslaved and trafficked, see Heidi Wendt, *At the Temple Gates: The Religion of Freelance Experts in the Roman Empire* (Oxford: Oxford University Press, 2016).

16 On the titles of the Gospels: Annette Yoshiko Reed, "ΕΥΑΓΓΕΛΙΟΝ: Orality, Textuality, and the Christian Truth in Irenaeus' *Adversus Haereses*," *VC* 56 (2002): 11–46. On anonymity and its power: Tom Geue, *Author Unknown: The Power of Anonymity in Ancient Rome* (Cambridge, MA: Harvard University Press, 2019).

17 Papias is cited in Eusebius, *Hist. eccl.* 3.39.15 (in *Apostolic Fathers*, vol. 2, LCL, trans. Bart D. Ehrman).

18 Mark's knowledge of Aramaic: Mark 5:41; 7:11, 34; 14:36; 15:22, 34. Latinisms in Mark include 4:21 (*modius*); 12:14 (*census*); 12:42 (*quadrans*); 15:15 (*flagellare*); and 15:16 (*praetorium*).

19 For a more detailed exposition of my argument here, see my "Fashioning Mark: Early Christian Discussions About the Scribe and Status of the Second Gospel," *NTS* 67.2 (2021): 181–204.

20 Aulus Gellius, *NA* 1.7.1, 13.21.16–17; James E. G. Zetzel, "Emendavi ad Tironem: Some Notes on Scholarship in the Second Century AD," *HSCP* 77 (1973): 225–43.

21 Porphyry, *On the Life of Plotinus*, 8.

22 On outdoor education, see Raffaella Cribiore, *Writing, Teachers, and Students in Graeco-Roman Egypt* (Atlanta: Scholars Press, 1996), 18, 25.

23 Market-square vendors: P. Oxy. VI 932; Roger S. Bagnall and Raffaella Cribiore, *Women's Letters from Ancient Egypt, 300 BC–AD 800* (Ann Arbor: University of Michigan Press, 2006), 62.

24 Origen: see Eusebius, *Hist. eccl.* 6.8.2 (self-castration) and 6.23.1–2 (Ambrose's gift). To be read with discussion in Kim Haines-Eitzen, *Guardians of Letters: Literacy, Power, and the Transmitters of Early Christian Literature* (Oxford: Oxford University Press, 2000), 42–43.

25 *Hexapla*: Anthony Grafton and Megan Williams, *Christianity and the Transformation of the Book: Origen, Eusebius, and the Library of Caesarea* (Cambridge, MA: Harvard University Press, 2006).

26 Origen's hypothesis is reported in Eusebius, *Hist. eccl.* 6.12–14.

27 Tools: Aristotle, *Eth. Nic.* 1161a30–b6; Varro, *Rust.* 1.17.1. Body Parts: Cicero, *Fam.* 16.10.2; Martial, *Ep.* 1.10, 14.208. Enslaved worker as body part: Sarah Blake, "Now You See Them: Slaves and Other Objects as Elements of the Roman Master," *Helios* 39.2 (2012): 193–211; Sarah Blake, "*In Manus*: Pliny's Letters and the Arts of Mastery," in *Roman Literary Cultures: Domestic Politics, Revolutionary Poetics, Civic Spectacle*, eds. Alison Keith and Jonathan Edmondson

(Toronto: University of Toronto Press, 2016), 89–107. Jewish authors: Hezser, *Jewish Slavery*, 277–299 (y. Peah 4:6, 18b and y. Qid. 1:3 60a).

28 Inscription: *ST* Sa 35 =*Ima. Ita. CIL* 12.3556a; Sandra R. Joshel and Lauren Hackworth Peterson, *The Material Life of Roman Slaves* (Cambridge: Cambridge University Press, 2014), 87–88.

29 James C. Scott, *Domination and the Arts of Resistance: Hidden Transcripts* (New Haven, CT: Yale University Press, 1990); Dan-el Padilla Peralta, "Epistemicide: The Roman Case," *Classica: Revista Brasileira de Estudos Clássicos* 33.2 (2020): 151–86 [167].

30 P. Mich. 223.2665. H. C. Youtie, "Callimachus in the Tax Rolls," in *Proceedings of the Twelfth International Congress of Papyrology*, ed. Deborah Samuel (Toronto: Hakkert, 1970): 545–51.

31 Candida R. Moss, "Between the Lines: Looking for the Contributions of Enslaved Literate Laborers in a Second-Century Text (*P. Berol.* 11632)," *SLA* 5 (2021): 432–52.

32 Exhortations to wakefulness in the New Testament are connected to the Parousia and eschatological expectations. Compare Rom. 13:11–14; Eph. 5:14; Mark 13:35; Luke 12:35–40; and Matt. 25:13. On enslaved people (as Christians) staying awake all night for the return of the enslaver, see Luke 12:35–40. On sleep deprivation and enslaved workers, see Mitzi Smith, *Insights from African American Interpretation* (Minneapolis: Fortress, 2017), 80–97.

33 *Styloi, stoicheia*: This language of bookwork was pointed out to me by Jeremiah Coogan. Paul himself seems to have embraced the language when, in the section written in his own hand, he refers to the *stigmata* on his own body. The marks are often seen as scars or brands, but they could also refer to written marks (Gal. 6:17).

34 Johan Huizinga, *Homo Ludens: A Study of the Play-Element in Culture*, trans. R. F. C. Hull (London: Routledge, 2002), 3.

Chapter Three

1 My rendition follows Mark 2:1–12, but versions of the story are also found in Matt. 9:2–8 and Luke 5:17–26. See Anna Rebecca Solevåg, *Negotiating the Disabled Body: Representations of Disability in Early Christian Texts* (Atlanta: SBL Press, 2018).

2 Academic translation and commentary: Joel Marcus, *Mark 1–8* (Anchor Yale Bible Commentaries series; New Haven, CT: Yale University Press, 2002), 215: "And a paralytic was brought to him, carried by four of his friends."

3 "See through": phrase adapted from Joseph A. Howley, *Aulus Gellius and Roman Reading Culture: Text, Presence, and Imperial Knowledge in the 'Noctes Atticae'* (Cambridge: Cambridge University Press, 2018), 175.

4 For an assessment of traditional narratives about the composition of the Gospel of John, see Hugo Méndez, "Did the Johannine Community Exist?," *JSNT* 42 (2020): 350–374.

5 Hagar: Nyasha Junior, *Reimagining Hagar: Blackness and the Bible* (Oxford: Oxford University Press, 2019).

6 Enslaved Mary: Winsome Munro, *Jesus, Born of a Slave: The Social and Economic Origins of Jesus' Message* (Lewiston, NY: Mellen, 1998); Mitzi J. Smith, "Abolitionist Messiah: A Man Jesus Named Born of a *Doulē*," in *Bitter the Chastening Rod*, eds. Mitzi J. Smith, Angela N. Parker, and Ericka S. Dunbar Hill (Minneapolis: Fortress, 2022), 53–70; Mitzi J. Smith, *Re-Reading the Lukan Jesus for Liberation: Anointed Abolitionist Born of a Doule Called Mary* (Eugene, OR: Cascade, forthcoming). Mistranslation of *doulos*: Smith, "Abolitionist Messiah"; Clarice J. Martin, "Womanist Interpretations of the New Testament: The Quest for the Holistic and Inclusive Translation and Interpretation," in *I Found God in Me: A Womanist Biblical Hermeneutics Reader*, ed. Mitzi J. Smith (Eugene, OR: Cascade, 2015), 19–41.

7 Celsus: Origen, *Cels.* 1.28–32; Tertullian, *On the Shows*, 30. The Talmudic traditions relay a number of different spellings for Panthera's name.

8 On natal alienation, see Patterson, *Slavery and Social Death*, 13.

9 On the relationship between the death of Jesus and biographies of Aesop, see Adela Yarbro Collins, "Finding Meaning in the Death of Jesus," *JR* 78 (1998): 175–96.

10 Phaedrus, *Fab.* 3, prologue 43–47, where Phaedrus writes that where Aesop had built a footpath, he had constructed a highway. On the importance of Aesop, see Leslie Kurke, *Aesopic Conversations: Popular Tradition, Cultural Dialogue, and the Invention of Greek Prose* (Princeton, NJ: Princeton University Press, 2011). On the fables and their relationship to the parables of Luke, see Justin David Strong, *The Fables of Jesus in the Gospel of Luke: A New Foundation for the Study of Parables* (Leiden: Brill Schöningh, 2021).

11 Quote is from Babrius, *Fab.* 47. On parables and fables, see Mary Ann Beavis, "Parable and Fable," *CBQ* 52 (1990): 473–98.

12 On popular morality, and the social origins of fables, see Teresa Morgan, *Popular Morality in the Early Roman Empire* (Cambridge: Cambridge University Press, 2007).

13 On the selection of overseers, see Columella, *De re rustica* 1.2–9. I am grateful to Joseph Howley's work on despotics for this argument.

14 Hilary of Poitiers: Kevin Madigan, *The Passions of Christ in High-Medieval Thought: An Essay on Christological Development* (Oxford: Oxford University Press, 2007).

15 On the problem of managing estates from a distance, see Columella, *De re rustica* 1.2.1–2.

16 Courageous interpreters: Munro, *Jesus, Born of a Slave*; Smith, *Re-Reading the Lukan Jesus*.

17 Ancient funerary inscription: *ILS* 7479, discussed in Jane Gardner, "Slavery and Roman Law," in *The Cambridge World History of Slavery*, vol. 1, *The Ancient Mediterranean World*, eds. Keith Bradley and Paul Cartledge (Cambridge: Cambridge University Press, 2011), 420; and Laura Nasrallah, *Archaeology and the Letters of Paul* (Oxford: Oxford University Press, 2019), 44n14.

18 On meandering, see Stephanie M. H. Camp, *Closer to Freedom: Enslaved Women and Everyday Resistance in the Plantation South* (Chapel Hill: University of North Carolina Press, 2004).

NOTES

19 In this case, crucifixion turned victims into the letter *tau* or *T*. The association between *tau* and crucifixion is ancient; see the conclusion to Lucian, *The Consonants at Law*.

20 For crucifixion and humor, see Amy Richlin, *Slave Theater in the Roman Republic: Plautus and Popular Comedy* (Cambridge: Cambridge University Press, 2017), 83.

21 Pagan critics on the death of Jesus: Origen, *Cels.* 7.53–55.

22 Jon Sobrino, *Jesus in Latin America* (Eugene, OR: Wipf & Stock, 2004); James H. Cone, *The Cross and the Lynching Tree* (Maryknoll, NY: Orbis, 2011); M. Shawn Copeland, *Knowing Christ Crucified: The Witness of African American Religious Experience* (Maryknoll, NY: Orbis, 2018).

23 Susan Sontag, *Regarding the Pain of Others* (New York: Farrar, Straus & Giroux, 2003), 108.

24 See Maureen Carroll, "'The Mourning Was Very Good': Liberation and Liberality in Roman Funerary Commemoration," in *Memory and Mourning: Studies on Roman Death*, eds. Valerie M. Hope and Janet Huskinson (Oxford: Oxbow Books, 2011), 126–49.

25 Wil Gafney, "Of Gods, Men, and Kings," a sermon published on February 6, 2018, https://www.wilgafney.com/2018/02/06/of-god-men-and-kings/.

26 Katherine Shaner, "Enslavement in Early Christianity," in a special panel at the New England / Eastern Canada regional meeting of the Society of Biblical Literature, March 19, 2022.

Chapter Four

1 The *Acts of Thomas* is one of a cluster of second-century apostolic acts that circulated among early Christians. Translations adapted from Han J. W. Drijvers, "Acts of Thomas—Introduction and Translation," in *New Testament Apocrypha: Writings Related to the Apostles, Apocalypses and Related Subjects*, ed. Wilhelm Schneemelcher, trans. Robert McLean Wilson (Louisville: Westminster John Knox, 1992), 322–411.

2 Jennifer Glancy, "Slavery in *Acts of Thomas*," *JECH* 2 (2012): 3–21.

3 Multiple messengers: Cicero, *Att.* 2.19.5. Greek translator: Plutarch, *Themistocles* 6.2. Alexander: Pseudo-Callisthenes, *The Alexander Romance* 1.37. Puteoli: Cicero, *Against Verres* 5.154.

4 Ovid, *Met.* 9.568–81; divorce certificate: M. Git 2.3 and T. Git. 2.4.

5 Enslaved messengers: P. Duk. Inv. 609 and *TPSulp.* 48. On travel and Christianity, see Timothy Luckritz Marquis, *Transient Apostle: Paul, Travel, and the Rhetoric of Empire* (New Haven, CT: Yale University Press, 2013). Fifty miles a day: John H. Nicholson, "The Delivery and Confidentiality of Cicero's Letters," *Classical Journal* 90 (1994): 33–63 [34].

6 *Did.* 11.3–12; 12:1–5.

7 Ignatius's journey: Yonatan Moss, "'From Syria All the Way to Rome': Ignatius of Antioch's Pauline Journey to Christianity," in *Journeys in the Roman East: Imagined and Real*, ed. Maren R. Niehoff (Tübingen: Mohr Siebeck, 2017),

NOTES

409–21. Memory of messengers: Jürgen Blänsdorf, *Das Thema der Sklaverei in den Werken Ciceros* (Stuttgart: Steiner, 2016), 91, 97.

8 "Runaway": The language of running away presupposes that slavery is a legitimate social structure. On the use of children as a kind of "hostage" that kept enslaved workers docile, see chapter 1. For a servile worker who wanted to return "home" after serving Paul, see Phil. 2:25–26. The request to stay: Ign., *Eph.* 2.1. Burrhus as a servile name: William R. Schoedel, *Ignatius of Antioch: A Commentary on the Letters of St. Ignatius of Antioch* (Minneapolis: Fortress, 1985), 46. "Word of honor": Ign., *Phld.* 11.2. "Copy": Ign., *Eph.* 2.1; 11.2. When Ignatius speaks of Burrhus and Crocus, he consistently refers to the honor that they bring to the Ephesians and Smyrnaeans. He describes them as literate objects, calling them "living cop[ies]" of the love of the Ephesians. The word for "copy" here is *exemplarium*, a Latin loanword used to describe copies of legal documents (*Dig.* 31.47). Other servile messengers (Onesimus, Fronto, and Euplus) are also named in the account (Ign., *Eph.* 2.1).

9 Ign., *Eph.* 2.1; Ign., *Smyr.* 12.1. Timing of approach: Cicero, *Fam.* 9.16.1 and Head, "Onesimus," 643.

10 Heroic work: Blänsdorf, *Das Thema der Sklaverei*, 91.

11 Children: See Benjamin Hinson, "Send Them to Me by This Little One: Child Letter-carriers in Coptic Texts from Late Antique and Early Islamic Egypt," *Journal of Near Eastern Studies* 80 (2021): 275–89; Christian Laes, "Child Slaves at Work in Roman Antiquity," *Ancient Society* 38 (2008): 235–83. Letter from Hermopolis: *SB* XII.11084.

12 Catullus 50 and Duncan F. Kennedy, "Crossing the Threshold: Genette, Catullus, and the Psychodynamics of Paratextuality," in *The Roman Paratext: Frame, Text, Readers*, ed. Laura Jansen (Cambridge: Cambridge University Press, 2014), 19–32.

13 Cicero, *Fam.* 12.30.3 LCL.

14 "Copy": Ign., *Eph.* 2.1; 11.2. Role of letter carriers: Peter M. Head, "Named Letter-Carriers Among the Oxyrhynchus Papyri," *JSNT* 31 (2009): 279–99 [294, 298]; Pieter J. J. Botha, "Letter Writing and Oral Communication in Antiquity: Suggested Implications for the Interpretation of Paul's Letter to the Galatians," *Scriptura* 42 (1992): 17–34.

15 Pieter J. J. Botha, *Orality and Literacy in Early Christianity* (Eugene, OR: Wipf & Stock, 2012), 243.

16 Pseudepigraphic life: Chris Londa, "Letters," in Coogan, Howley, and Moss, *Writing, Enslavement, and Power*. Paul's messengers: Timothy (1 Cor. 16: 10–11), Onesimus (Philemon 17), Tychicus (Eph. 6:21; Col. 4:7), Epaphroditus (Phil. 2:29), Titus (2 Cor. 7:15), and Phoebe (Rom. 16:1-2). Medieval tradition maintains that Phoebe was the enslaver of Tertius, the secretary to whom Paul dictated the text. The ninth-century Mount Athos, Monastery of the Lavra A.88, fol. 99 verso (GA 049) titles Romans "Letter to (the) Romans Written from Corinth Through (*dia*) Phoebe the Deacon." The fourteenth-century Paris, Bibliothèque Nationale de France, grec 47, fol. 244 recto (GA 18) has: "The Letter to (the) Romans Written Through (*dia*) Tertius and Sent Through (*dia*) Phoebe from Corinth."

NOTES

17 Botha, *Orality and Literacy*, 243. The estimate of this reading time is based on a presumed vocalized reading speed of 150 words per minute.

18 The following section is influenced by Gianni Guastella, *Word of Mouth: Fama and Its Personifications in Art and Literature from Ancient Rome to the Middle Ages* (Oxford: Oxford University Press, 2017); and Marianne Bjelland Kartzow, *Gossip and Gender: Othering of Speech in the Pastoral Epistles* (BZNW 164; Berlin: De Gruyter, 2009).

19 Plutarch, *On Being a Busybody* 9 (519F). Some early Christians shared this view: Kartzow, *Gossip and Gender*, 208. In the minds of elites, authorless rumors accrued layers of editorializing and embellishment. They were untrustworthy. In many examples of military hearsay, the essential message about the outcome of the conflict is correct but, away from the scrutinizing glare of verification, the details had mushroomed in the dark.

20 Martial, *Ep.* 8.75. On funerary workers, see Sarah E. Bond, *Trade and Taboo: Disreputable Professions in the Roman Mediterranean* (Ann Arbor: University of Michigan Press, 2016), 59–96.

21 Origen, *Cels.* 3.44, trans. Chadwick.

22 Sleeping: Tacitus, *Histories* 1.43; Pliny, *Ep.* 7.27.13; Franco Luciani, "Public Slaves in Rome: 'Privileged' or Not?," *CQ* 70.1 (2020): 368–84. Romantic relationships: *CIL* 5.3707 and Rose MacLean, *Freed Slaves and Roman Imperial Culture: Social Integration and the Transformation of Values* (Cambridge: Cambridge University Press, 2018), 24.

23 Women: Margaret Y. MacDonald, "Was Celsus Right? The Role of Women in the Expansion of Early Christianity," in David L. Balch and Carolyn Osiek, eds., *Early Christian Families in Context* (Grand Rapids, MI: Eerdmans, 2003), 157–84; Kartzow, *Gossip and Gender*, 208. Quote from Dionysius of Halicarnassus, *On Literary Composition* 25.193. This construction of authorship emerged over time. On the emergence of singular elite authorship and elite status, see Joseph Howley, "Visible Erasure: Writing Personnel and Equipment in Latin Verse" (forthcoming).

24 Matt. 26:51, 69.

25 Lucius Domitius: Suetonius, *Nero* 1.1. Barber: Plutarch, *On Talkativeness* 13 (509B). On the safety of anonymity in Roman literary culture, see Geue, *Author Unknown*.

26 Plutarch, *On Talkativeness* 13 (503D); Hesiod, *Works and Days*, 760–64.

27 On the windlike qualities of rumor, see Guastella, *Word of Mouth*, 26–33. Peter's speech is clearly an important factor: Acts wants us to imagine that bold public speech and subversive speech operate together. On Christian condemnation of gossip and slander, see 1 Tim. 4:7; 2 Tim. 4:3; Tit. 1:10–11; Kartzow, *Gossip and Gender*, 195–201.

Chapter Five

1 Codex Bobiensis (sometimes spelled Bobbiensis): An extraordinary history of the text is provided in Matthew D. C. Larsen, "The Real-and-Imagined Biography of a Gospel Manuscript," *EC* 12.1 (2021): 103–131.

NOTES

2 *Gospel of Peter* 39.

3 Pliny, *Ep.* 6.16; Lucian, *Ind.* 6.

4 Larsen, "Real-and-Imagined Biography."

5 Those who specialize in ancient manuscripts tend to distinguish between the figures of the scribe and the copyist, reserving the latter term for those whose intention was to produce a precise copy. A copyist may also have done editorial and secretarial work. That secretarial labor may well have involved composing sentences, phrases, paragraphs, and even whole letters in the names of others (on this, see Moss, "The Secretary"). So, too, someone whose status was identified as a secretary (e.g., Tiro) would also have copied. For the purposes of this chapter, I will try to highlight activities performed by copyists (*scribae*). On the disrepute of copying, see *Rhet. Her.* 4.6. Cornelius Nepos, *Eum.* 1.5. On bureaucratic *scribae*, see Benjamin Hartmann, *The Scribes of Rome: A Cultural and Social History of the Scribae* (Cambridge: Cambridge University Press, 2020), 13–60.

6 For an example of attempts to persuade monks to continue as copyists, see the abbot of Sponheim, Johannes Trithemius, *In Praise of Scribes* (1492); *Martyrdom of Polycarp* 22.3.

7 On Christian manuscripts and copying, see Harry Y. Gamble, *Books and Readers in the Early Church: A History of Early Christian Texts* (New Haven, CT: Yale University Press, 1995); David C. Parker, *The Living Text of the Gospels* (Cambridge: Cambridge University Press, 1997); Kim Haines Eitzen, *Guardians of Letters: Literacy, Power, and the Transmitters of Early Christian Literature* (Oxford: Oxford University Press, 2000); Larry W. Hurtado, *The Earliest Christian Artifacts: Manuscripts and Christian Origins* (Grand Rapids, MI: Eerdmans, 2006); and AnneMarie Luijendijk, *Greetings in the Lord: Early Christians and the Oxyrhynchus Papyri* (Cambridge, MA: Harvard University Press, 2008). On copyists in the Roman world: T. Keith Dix, "'Beware of Promising Your Library to Anyone': Assembling a Private Library at Rome," in *Ancient Libraries*, eds. Jason König, Katerina Oikonomopoulou, and Greg Woolf (Cambridge: Cambridge University Press, 2013), 209–36; Raymond J. Starr, "The Circulation of Literary Texts in the Roman World," *CQ* 37.1 (1987): 213–23; for books as gifts, see Cicero, *Fam.* 16.20. Acquiring books in the homes of others: Cicero, *Fin.* 3.2.7.

8 Horace, *Ep.* 1.20. Freedman bookshop owners included Secundus, the freedman of Lucensis (Martial 1.2.7). Of the seven identifiable booksellers in the city of Rome, four have Greek names (Atrectus [Martial 1.117.13], Sextus Peducaeus Dionysius [*CIL* 6.9218], Dorus [Seneca, *Ben.* 7.6.1], and Trypho [Martial 4.72.2, 13.3.4]), a detail that has led several readers to conclude that they were formerly enslaved.

9 For more information about bookshops, see Peter White, "Bookshops in the Literary Culture of Rome," in *Ancient Literacies: The Culture of Reading in Greece and Rome*, eds. William A. Johnson and Holt N. Parker (Oxford: Oxford University Press, 2009), 268–86.

10 We should note that it is difficult to know to what extent the price edict was reliable. See Jan Heilmann, "The Relevance of Ancient Book Prices and the Book Market for Ancient Reading Culture," in *Economic Aspects of Reading in*

NOTES

Antiquity, eds. Jan Heilmann and Robyn F. Walsh (Cambridge: Cambridge University Press, forthcoming). On false advertising: Strabo, *Geography* 13.1.54; Cicero *QFr.* 3.4.5, 3.5.6; Martial 2.8. Diocletian's price edict: 7.39–41.

11 On documentary/literary hands, a nuanced discussion is in William A. Johnson, *Bookrolls and Scribes in Oxyrhynchus* (Toronto: University of Toronto Press, 2004), 161; Brent Nongbri, *God's Library: The Archaeology of the Earliest Christian Manuscripts* (New Haven, CT: Yale University Press, 2018). For discussions of early Christian manuscripts, see Luijendijk, *Greetings in the Lord*, and Luijendijk, "A New Testament Papyrus and Its Owner: P. Oxy. II 209/P10, an Early Christian School Exercise from the Archive of Leonides," *JBL* 129.3 (2010): 575–96. Deluxe copy of Virgil: P. Ant. I 29; Haines-Eitzen, *Guardians of Letters*, 68–75.

12 F. C. Burkitt, "Further Notes on Codex *k*," *JTS* 5 (1903): 100–107 [107]; non-Christian readers: Nongbri, *God's Library*, 23; Robyn F. Walsh, *The Origins of Early Christian Literature Contextualizing the New Testament within Greco-Roman Literary Culture* (Cambridge: Cambridge University Press, 2021), 134–69.

13 On paratexts, see Gérard Genette, *Paratexts: Thresholds of Interpretation* (Cambridge: Cambridge University Press, 1997); and Laura Jansen, ed., *The Roman Paratext: Frame, Text, Readers* (Cambridge: Cambridge University Press, 2014).

14 The list of paratexts is inexhaustive and the literature is too extensive to discuss here. See Martin Wallraff and Patrick Andrist, "Paratexts of the Bible: A New Research Project on Greek Textual Transmission," *Early Christianity* 6 (2015): 237–43. For a full treatment of the history of this manuscript and the *Pericopae adulterae*, see Jennifer Knust and Tommy Wasserman, *To Cast the First Stone: The Transmission of a Gospel Story* (Princeton, NJ: Princeton University Press, 2018). Knust and Wasserman's work underpins my reading of this passage.

15 On bookmaking, see Georgios Boudalis, *The Codex and Crafts in Late Antiquity* (Chicago: University of Chicago Press, 2018). Eye of the needle: Matt. 19:24; Mark 10:25; Luke 18:25. The origins of the myth of a pedestrian gate have been traced to Anselm by Agnieszka Ziemińska, in "The Origin of the 'Needle's Eye Gate' Myth: Theophylact or Anselm?," *NTS* 68.3 (2022): 358–61. On Family 13, see Didier Lafleur, *La famille 13 dans l'évangile de Marc* (Leiden: Brill, 2013). Although the idea of a "Caesarean text type" has fallen out of vogue, Family 13 reflects a relatively controlled cluster of texts associated with the city.

16 On the cognitive skills involved in work, Mike Rose, *The Mind at Work: Valuing the Intelligence of the American Worker* (New York: Viking, 2004). On attention, see David LaBerge, *Attentional Processing: The Brain's Art of Mindfulness* (Cambridge, MA: Harvard University Press, 1995). Bookmaking required steady hands and fresh eyes. The worker relied upon the tactile feedback supplied by the cord and needle. Rulers are visible in our sources as trusted implements, but the smell of leather and glue, the feel of the grain of the leather or the roughness of the cord, the sound that the connection of writing material and writing implement made, even the viscosity of different kind of inks: all provided sensory feedback. Reed pens had to be sharpened and papyrus was sometimes too thin. A medley of sensory, kinesthetic, and cognitive abilities that contributed to the biomechanical skills of bookwork are a neurological marvel in themselves, but

they were maximized in the constrained environments in which the copyists and bookmakers worked alongside one another. Cognitive science and studies of modern labor practices reveal that this kind of tactile work is always intimately connected to the use of tools. Technologies of bookmaking: John L. Sharpe, "Wooden Books and the History of the Codex: Isocrates and the Farm Account, Evidence from the Egyptian Desert," in *Roger Powell: The Compleat Binder, Liber Amicorum*, ed. John L. Sharpe (Turnhout: Brepols, 1996), 107–29; Boudalis, *Codex and Crafts*.

17 A clerical worker named Elayne, who was tasked with data entry at Banker's Trust in the 1970s, relayed how she played games with herself to pass the time. "Sometimes," she said, "I spell out 'Pool Number,' other times I write 'pl#.' Interest rate I might go '9.50 percent' or '9.5%.'" Such "inconsistencies" in her digital footprint are owing not to varying sources, but to the copyist herself. Elayne was not incompetent, she was bored. "I guess you do anything for a little change," she said; "something to *do* inside your head." Elayne is cited in Barbara Garson, *All the Livelong Day: The Meaning and Demeaning of Routine Work*, rev. ed. (New York: Penguin, 1994), 243. See also Jesper Isaksen, "Constructing Meaning Despite the Drudgery of Repetitive Work," *Journal of Humanistic Psychology* 40.3 (2000): 84–107. Other dehumanized clerical workers who were routinely told that their jobs were mindless played different kinds of games. Ellen (not her real name), a young woman who proofread documents at Fair Plan Insurance Company around the same time as Elayne, noticed that one client had insured his store for $165,000 against vandalism and $5,000 against fire. It was surely a mistake, but after some mental back-and-forth, she decided to do nothing. "I'm not supposed to understand it," Ellen said. "If they're gonna give me a robot's job to do, I'm gonna do it like a robot." Ellen is cited in Garson, *All the Livelong Day*, x.

18 Aesop: *Life of Aesop* G 38 (oil), G 41 (lentil pot); David Graeber, *Bullshit Jobs: A Theory* (New York: Simon & Schuster, 2018).

19 Heilmann, *Lesen*; Luijendijk, *Greetings in the Lord*.

20 Cicero, *Att.* 4.4a. On libraries, see Jason König, Katerina Oikonomopoulou, and Greg Woolf, eds., *Ancient Libraries* (Cambridge: Cambridge University Press, 2013). This section on organization owes a great deal to Alexandra Leewon Schultz, "Collection," in Coogan, Howley, and Moss, *Writing, Enslavement, and Power*.

21 Galen, *Lib. prop.* 1. Extant book tags reveal that whoever made them was clearly literate (P. Lond. Litt. 27). See discussion in Brent Nongbri, "Maintenance," in Coogan, Howley, and Moss, *Writing, Enslavement, and Power*. For enslaved workers in libraries in general, see George W. Houston, "The Slave and Freedman Personnel of Public Libraries in Ancient Rome," *Transactions of the American Philological Association* 132 (2002): 139–76. Female librarians: Susan Treggiari, "Jobs for Women," *American Journal of Ancient History* 1 (1976), 76–104 [78, 90]; and Haines-Eitzen, "'Girls Trained in Beautiful Writing': Female Scribes in Roman Antiquity and Early Christianity," *JECS* 6 (1998), 629–46 [634–40].

22 Codex Fuldensis (F), produced between 541 and 546 CE.

NOTES

23 On Marcion's collection, see Ulrich Schmid, *Marcion und sein Apostolos: Rekonstruktion und historische Einordnung der marcionitischen Paulusbriefausgabe* (Berlin: de Gruyter, 1995).

24 Pasted rolls: Cicero, *Att.* 9.10. On 2 Cor., I follow Brent Nongbri, "2 Corinthians and Possible Material Evidence for Composite Letters in Antiquity," in *Collecting Early Christian Letters: From the Apostle Paul to Late Antiquity*, eds. Bronwen Neil and Pauline Allen (Cambridge: Cambridge University Press, 2015), 54–67.

25 Mary Beard, "Ciceronian Correspondences: Making a Book out of Letters," in *Classics in Progress: Essays on Ancient Greece and Rome*, ed. T. P. Wiseman (Oxford: Oxford University Press, 2002), 103–144.

26 On indices and tables of contents: Andrew M. Riggsby, *Mosaics of Knowledge: Representing Information in the Roman World* (Oxford: Oxford University Press, 2019). On subversive alternate reading schemes: Roy Gibson, "Starting with the Index in Pliny," in Jansen, *The Roman Paratext*, 33–55.

27 Jeremiah Coogan, *Eusebius the Evangelist: Rewriting the Fourfold Gospel in Late Antiquity* (Oxford: Oxford University Press, 2022).

28 Coogan, *Eusebius the Evangelist*, 46–54 (enslaved workers) and 123–71 (influence).

29 Strabo, *Geography* 13.1.54.

30 Dampness: Vitruvius, *On Architecture* 6.4.1; Aulus Gellius, *NA* 9.4. Military doctor: P. Ross. Georg. 3.1. On parasites, see Cat Lambert, "The Ancient Entomological Bookworm," *Arethusa* 53 (2020): 1–24.

31 Alexandra Leewon Schultz, "Imagined Histories: Hellenistic Libraries and the Idea of Greece," PhD diss., Harvard University, 2021; Lambert, "Bookworm."

32 Enslaved curators: Cicero, *Att.* 4.4a, 4.8.2; Cornelius Nepos, *Att.* 13.3–4. Enslaved curators of clothes: Petronius, *Sat.* 78. On care for rolls: Lucian, *Ind.* 17. See also P. Fam. Tebt. 15, ll. 35–37, in which an inspector complains that documents are damaged and moth-eaten. On cedar oil as a depilatory: Pliny, *NH* 32.47. For books: Pliny, *NH* 24.11; Ausonius, *Epigrams* 19.1.

33 Horace, *Ep.* 1.20; Martial 1.117.15. On bookshops and publication as sex work, see Ellen Oliensis, "Life After Publication: Horace, *Epistles* 1.20," *Arethusa* 28 (1995): 209–24. Rabbinic texts: m. B. Meṣ 2.8–9; b. B. Meṣ. 29b.; frayed beards: Martial, *Ep.* 14.84.

34 Lucian, *Ind.* 22; rabbinic text: m. Git. 2:4.

35 Knust and Wasserman supply a pithy history of some of these issues in *To Cast the First Stone*, 18–46. Perhaps the most famous recent example of scholarship focused on the theological ramifications of manuscript evidence is Bart Ehrman, *Misquoting Jesus: The Story Behind Who Changed the Bible and Why* (San Francisco: HarperOne, 2005). For a response to Ehrman's work, see H. A. G. Houghton and D. C. Parker, eds., *Textual Variation: Theological and Social Tendencies? Papers from the Fifth Birmingham Colloquium on the Textual Criticism of the New Testament* (Piscataway, NJ: Gorgias, 2008).

36 Aulus Gellius, *NA* 9.4. For overviews of early Christian textual criticism and literary theory, see Jennifer Wright Knust, "Early Christian Re-Writing and the History of the *Pericope adulterae*," *JECS* 14.4 (2006): 485–536. Origen specifies

NOTES

four reasons for textual difference: well-intentioned mistakes, indolent alterations, audacious and rash emendations, and mistaken correction (*Comm. Matt.* 15.14).

37 For a similar challenge, the famous mathematician Archimedes published a fake set of mathematical theorems as a trap to ensnare those who would steal his ideas. The inadequacy of the plagiarists would be unveiled by their inability to identify and produce proofs. See Reviel Netz, *The Works of Archimedes*, vol. 2: *On Spirals* (Cambridge: Cambridge University Press, 2017), 12, 19, 28–30.

38 Galen, *Hipp. 6 Epid.*

39 Theodotus's origins: Eusebius, *Hist. eccl.* 5.28; H. Gregory Snyder, "Shoemakers and Syllogisms: Theodotus 'the Cobbler' and His School," in *Christian Teachers in Second-Century Rome: Schools and Students in the Ancient City*, ed. H. Gregory Snyder (Leiden: Brill, 2020), 183–204. On the alleged textual meddling and servile quality of unorthodox Christians see Jeremiah Coogan and Candida Moss, "The Textual Demiurge: Social Status and the Academic Discourse of Early Christian Forgery," *NTS* (forthcoming).

40 Bookstores: Galen, *Lib. prop.* 1 (K 19.8–9); Martial 2.17; Cicero, *Fam.* 16.17.1. Theodotians: see Lampe, *From Paul to Valentinus*, 344–48.

41 Eusebius, *Hist. eccl.* 5.23.13–19 (modified translation).

42 Marcion's origins: Justin, *1 Apol.* 26.5; 58.1; Irenaeus, *Haer.* 1.27.2; Eusebius, *Hist. eccl.* 5.13.3; Tertullian, *Marc.* 1.1.3. Marcion's wealth: Tertullian, *Praesc.* 30.2; Tertullian, *Marc.* 4.4.3. See discussion in Lampe, *From Paul to Valentinus*, 241–57.

43 Marcion: Tertullian, *Marc.* 1.1.5, 4.2.3–4; Irenaeus, *Haer.* 1.27.2, 3.11.7, 3.12.12, 3.14.4.

44 Corrected and recovered: Tertullian, *Marc.* 4.4.4; 4.4.5; Pontic mouse: Tertullian, *Marc.* 1.15; dismembering Paul: Irenaeus, *Haer.* 1.27; theological commitments: Tertullian, *Marc.* 4.6.2; dowry for Marcion's work: Tertullian, *Marc.* 1.19.4; 4.1.1. Tertullian described the *Antitheses* as the "dowry" for Marcion's gospel, claiming that, to Marcion's followers, the *Antitheses* was the more important work.

45 Mistakes and errors: Tertullian, *Marc.* 1.20; 2.8.4; 2.24.1–2; 3.8.1; 4.12.9; 4.29.6. Circumcised the Gospel: Tertullian, *Praescr.* 38.9. Tertullian was troublingly anti-Semitic, although it is doubtful how many Jews he had actually met. I use the language of anti-Semitism here deliberately; Tertullian's prejudice was more likely directed against the Punic locals that he identified as Semitic, non-Roman, and barbarian.

46 Celsus had accused Jesus of being a mere construction worker who "fabricated" the miraculous story of his birth, implying that people who fabricate buildings and furniture might also fabricate texts; Origen, *Cels.* 1.28, 2.27. See J. Coogan, "Meddling with the Gospel: Celsus, Early Christian Textuality, and the Politics of Reading," *NovT* 65 (2023, forthcoming); and Coogan and Moss, "Textual Demiurge."

Chapter Six

1 My construction of this reading scene relies on Robyn F. Walsh, *The Origins of Early Christian Literature Contextualizing the New Testament within Greco-Roman*

NOTES

Literary Culture (Cambridge: Cambridge University Press, 2021). This chapter has benefited enormously from the work of classicist Cat Lambert, who kindly shared her dissertation with me prepublication. See Cat Lambert, "Bad Readers in Ancient Rome," PhD diss., Columbia University, 2022. For a detailed discussion of early Christian reading practices, see Chris Keith, *The Gospel as Manuscript: An Early History of the Jesus Tradition as Material Artifact* (Oxford: Oxford University Press, 2020), 163–200; and see Christoph Markschies, "Liturgisches Lesen und die Hermeneutik der Schrift," in Peter Gemeinhardt and Uwe Kühneweg, eds., *Patristica et Oecumenica* (Marburg: N. G. Elwert, 2004), 77–88.

2 For textual criticism, see Parker, *Living Text*, 124–47; Claire Clivaz, "Looking at Scribal Practices in the Endings of Mark 16," *Henoch* 42 (2020): 373–87.

3 William A. Johnson, *Bookrolls and Scribes in Oxyrhynchus* (Toronto: University of Toronto Press, 2004), 160. On reading in antiquity, see Jan Heilmann, "Ancient Literary Culture and Meals in the Greco-Roman World: The Role of Reading During Ancient Symposia and Its Relevance for the New Testament," *JTS* 73.1 (2022): 104–25; and *Lesen in Antike und frühem Christentum: Kulturgeschichtliche, philologische sowie kognitionswissenschaftliche Perspektiven und deren Bedeutung für die neutestamentliche Exegese* (Tübingen: Narr Francke Attempto, 2021). On the *lector*, see Christian Laes, "Lectors in the Latin West: The Epigraphical Evidence (c. 300–800)," *Arctos* 53 (2019): 83–127.

4 On learning to read, see William A. Johnson, *Readers and Reading Culture in the High Roman Empire: A Study of Elite Communities* (Oxford: Oxford University Press, 2010), 3–16. Some scrolls from Qumran have word divisions and practical Latin texts, and some inscriptions had interpuncts for word division. Decipherment is a feature of all reading, regardless of what language a text is written in, and my intention here is only to flag the differing junctures at which interpretation took place in the ancient languages under study.

5 Ancient Jewish reading: Rebecca Scharbach Wollenberg, "The Dangers of Reading As We Know It: Sight Reading as a Source of Heresy in Early Rabbinic Traditions," *JAAR* 85 (2017): 709–45; rabbinic experts: b. Shabbat 152b; b. Ketubot 106b. Aulus Gellius, *NA* 13.31; Dio Chrysostom, *Or.* 18.6–7.

6 On silent reading, see William A. Johnson, "Towards a Sociology of Reading in Classical Antiquity," *American Journal of Philology* 121 (2000): 593–627; Quintilian, *Inst.* 10.3.22–26; Dio Chrysostom, *Or.* 18.6–7 LCL.

7 Speaking and acting: Pliny, *Ep.* 3.18, 5.56.17, 7.17.1; Tacitus, *Dial.* 13; Suet. *Nero* 10. See Dan Nässelqvist, *Public Reading in Early Christianity: Lectors, Manuscripts, and Sound in the Oral Delivery of John 1–4* (Leiden: Brill, 2016), 100–103.

8 Christian texts that assume public reading: 1 Thess. 5:27; Col. 4:16; Rev. 1:3. Justin Martyr: *1 Apol.* 67.2. On benefits for the reader: Rev. 1:3 (compare 1 Tim. 4:13); *2 Clem.* 19.1. On reading practices and the use of readers, see William David Shiell, *Reading Acts: The Lector and the Early Christian Audience* (Leiden: Brill, 2004); Laes, "Lectors"; Heilmann, *Lesen*; and Nicholas A. Elder, *Gospel Media: Reading, Writing, and Circulating Jesus Traditions* (Grand Rapids, MI: Eerdmans, 2023).

9 Child readers: Quintilian, *Inst.* 1.12.8; Victor of Vita, *History of the Vandal Persecution* 3.34; Cyprian, *Ep.* 38.1.2; *Ac. Scil.* 12. See Laes, "Lectors," 88–90, 92–94.

On Speratus as a name for enslaved workers, see Ronald Syme, " 'Donatus' and the Like," *Historia* 27 (1978): 588–603.

10 Dio, *Or.* 20.10.

11 Sulpicia Petale: *AE* 1928, 73. Butcher's wife: Trastevere, second century, Staatliche Kunstsammlungen, Dresden, inv. ZV 44. Natalie Kampen argues that the woman is a scribe, in *Image and Status: Roman Working Women in Ostia* (Berlin: Mann, 1981), 81. On the *lectrix*, see Susan Treggiari, "Jobs in the Household of Livia," *Papers of the British School at Rome* 43 (1975): 48–77. Grapte: Herm. *Vis.* 2.4. Grapte is identified as a teacher of women. Her name suggests that she was enslaved or formerly enslaved; see Solin, *Griechische Personennamen*, 3.1171–73. Perpetua: *Pass. Perp.*

12 Eckardt, *Writing and Power in the Roman World*, 154–74.

13 See b. Megillah 18b; m. Megillah 4.4; t. Megillah 3:39; Wollenberg, "The Dangers of Reading As We Know It." The dates of many of these rabbinic sources cited here are later than the period under discussion and we should be cautious about assuming that they supply equally firm evidence about an earlier period.

14 Mark 13:14 was first seen as an instruction for an enslaved *lector*, over a century ago, by Julius Wellhausen, in *Einleitung in die drei ersten Evangelien* (Berlin: Reimer, 1905), 103.

15 On gesture and communication, see Shiell, *Reading Acts*; and Erik Gunderson, *Staging Masculinity: The Rhetoric of Performance in the Roman World* (Ann Arbor: University of Michigan Press, 2000).

16 Quint., *Inst.* 10.1. On performance with a scroll, see Johnson, *Readers and Reading Culture*, 119–20.

17 Pliny, *NH* 35.9–10. Quote from David Petrain, "Visual Supplementation and Metonymy in the Roman Public Library," in König et al., *Ancient Libraries*, 332–46 [340n36].

18 Tertullian, *Praescr.* 36.1–2.

19 Clement, *Strom.* 1.1.13.1–4; on the ear: *Strom.* 1.1.15.2, ix.45.1; 2.5.23.3–vi.25.3; 7.14.88.4. On heretics: *Strom.* 3.4.29.1.

20 Irenaeus, *Haer.* 3.7.2; Augustine, *Serm.* 352.

Chapter Seven

1 For a historical analysis, see Candida R. Moss, *Ancient Christian Martyrdom: Diverse Practices, Theologies, and Traditions* (New Haven, CT: Yale University Press, 2012), 100–122. For a discussion of the historical incidence of persecution in the first three centuries, see *The Myth of Persecution: How Early Christians Invented a Story of Martyrdom* (San Francisco: HarperOne, 2013). While I am skeptical about the extent to which Roman authorities deliberately targeted Christians before the Diocletianic persecution, I maintain that some early Christians died as martyrs during this period.

2 The story of Blandina is part of the *Letter of the Churches of Lyon and Vienne*, which is preserved by the fourth-century historian Eusebius of Caesarea (*Hist. eccl.* 5.1–2). My reading of the story of Blandina draws heavily on my earlier

work on martyrdom, and on Ronald Charles, *The Silencing of Slaves in Early Jewish and Christian Texts* (London: Routledge, 2019), 166–70.

3 Charles, *Silencing of Slaves*, 180. Insensibility to pain is a recurring theme in accounts of martyrdom. See L. Stephanie Cobb, *Divine Deliverance: Pain and Painlessness in Early Christian Martyr Texts* (Berkeley: University of California Press, 2016).

4 Blandina: Eusebius, *Hist. eccl.* 5.1.17; 5.1.41.

5 For the view of Blandina as active agent, see Elizabeth A. Goodine and Matthew W. Mitchell, "The Persuasiveness of a Woman: The Mistranslation and Misinterpretation of Eusebius' *Historia Ecclesiastica* 5.1.41," *JECS* 13 (2005): 1–19; Cobb, *Divine Deliverance*, 75–77. For the view that Blandina is eclipsed, see Charles, *Silencing Slaves*, 166–70. For Felicity, see *The Passion of Perpetua and Felicity*, 15.6, trans. Thomas Heffernan (Oxford: Oxford University Press, 2012), 132.

6 See Jennifer A. Glancy, *Slavery in Early Christianity* (Oxford: Oxford University Press, 2002), 102–29; Sheila Briggs, "Can an Enslaved God Liberate? Hermeneutical Reflections on Philippians 2:6–11," *Semeia* 47 (1989): 137–53. Metaphorical language of enslavement: Marianne Bjelland Kartzow, *The Slave Metaphor and Gendered Enslavement in Early Christian Discourse: Double Trouble Embodied* (London: Routledge, 2018), 21–46; Sam Tsang, *From Slaves to Sons: A New Rhetorical Analysis on Paul's Slave Metaphors in His Letter to the Galatians* (New York: Peter Lang, 2005). De Wet, *Unbound God*, 7.

7 Shively T. J. Smith, *Interpreting 2 Peter Through African American Women's Moral Writings* (Atlanta: SBL Press, 2023). Smith allows for the possibility that those involved in the composition of the Petrine epistles were not enslaved but were those who found the model useful for Christian identity and community imperatives.

8 On the ways in which redemptive suffering harms Black women, see Delores S. Williams, *Sisters in the Wilderness: The Challenge of Womanist God-Talk* (Maryknoll, NY: Orbis, 1993).

9 Marcus Aurelius, *Meditations* 8.48.

10 Blandina: Eusebius, *Hist. eccl.* 5.1.18.

11 New Testament exorcism: See Matt. 12:43; Mark 1:23–26, 3:30, 5:2–8, 7:25, 9:25; Luke 8:29, 11:24. Note that the language is also used in Zech. 13:2 and may reflect a first-century Jewish idiom. Pre-baptismal exorcism: Hippolytus, *Trad. ap.* 20.1–4. Kiss of the peace: Hippolytus, *Trad. ap.* 18.3.

12 The ensuing discussion of spiritual possession draws a great deal on recent scholarship by Giovanni B. Bazzana in *Having the Spirit of Christ: Spirit Possession and Exorcism in the Early Christ Groups* (New Haven, CT: Yale University Press, 2020).

13 *Herm. Man.* 5.1.2–4, trans. Chance Bonar, in "Enslaved to God: Slavery and Divine Despotics in the *Shepherd of Hermas*," PhD diss., Harvard University, 2023. Bonar's translation is slightly modified here. Conversations with Bonar inform not only my reading of the *Shepherd of Hermas* but also my thought about the Spirit as instrument of divine extensibility.

14 Medical writer: Celsus, *On Medicine* 4; *Herm. Man.* 5.1.2–4.

NOTES

15 Bazzana, *Having the Spirit of Christ*, 136.

16 Vettius Epagathus: Eusebius, *Hist. eccl.* 5.1.9–10. For Christians as temples of the Holy Spirit, see 1 Cor. 3:16, 6:19; 2 Cor. 6:16. For Paul's language of being "filled by the Spirit," see Eph. 3:19, 5:18; Col. 1:9. I have gendered God as male here because in formulations of masterly extensibility the body of the "master" is always male.

17 City as body: Margaret M. Mitchell, *Paul and the Rhetoric of Reconciliation: An Exegetical Investigation of the Language and Composition of 1 Corinthians* (Louisville: Westminster John Knox, 1993). On masterly extensibility, see Brendon Reay, "Agriculture, Writing, and Cato's Aristocratic Self-Fashioning," *Classical Antiquity* 24.2 (2005): 331–61. Palestinian Talmud: y. Peah 4:6, 18b and y. Qid. 1:3, 60a. The "faithful [enslaved worker]": Fabian Udoh, "The Tale of an Unrighteous Slave (Luke 16:1–8 [13])," *JBL* 128 (2009): 311–35 [330].

18 Bryson §61 (trans. 12). Bazzana sees the Spirit as connecting body parts (*Having the Spirit of Christ*, 136). Bonar sees an analogous process in the *Shepherd of Hermas*.

19 See Peter of Alexandria, Canons 5–7, and discussion in Daniel Vaucher, "Glaubensbekenntnis oder Sklavengehorsam? — Petrus von Alexandrien zu einem christlichen Dilemma," *VC* 72 (2018): 533–60. Peter of Alexandria condemned the practice, recognizing that the workers were coerced, and suggested a penalty of a year's penance (Canon 6).

20 Bryson §61 (trans. 12). On prosthetics, see Don Ihde, *Technology and the Lifeworld: From Garden to Earth* (Bloomington: Indiana University Press, 1990), 75; and David Wills, "Preambles: Disability as Prosthesis," in *Derrida Downunder*, eds. Laurence Simmons and Heather Worth (Palmerston North, New Zealand: Dunmore Press, 2001), 35–52.

21 See Sara Ahmed, *Willful Subjects* (Durham, NC: Duke University Press, 2014), 103.

22 Amy Richlin, "Cicero's Head," in *Constructions of the Classical Body*, ed. James I. Porter (Ann Arbor: University of Michigan Press, 1999), 190–211 [194]. Logic of slavery: Chris L. de Wet, *The Unbound God: Slavery and the Formation of Early Christian Thought* (London: Routledge, 2018), 8. See J. Achille Mbembe, "Necropolitics," *Public Culture* 15 (2003): 11–40 [22]; Mbembe draws on Susan Buck-Morss, "Hegel and Haiti," *Critical Inquiry* 26 (2000): 821–65.

23 Blandina, it is important to note, only works as a Christian exemplar because her obedience and will align so precisely with that of God. In narratives of loyal enslaved people, it is not accidental that the will of "good slaves" is recognized only in and after their self-sacrificial deaths. These stories repeat the fiction of the "happy slave" who obeys, places themselves in harm's way, and is warmly remembered by others. Richard Hofstadter, "U. B. Phillips and the Plantation Legend," *Journal of Negro History* 29 (1944): 109–24.

24 Nicolas Malebranche, *The Search After Truth*, eds. Thomas M. Lennon and Paul Olscamp (Cambridge: Cambridge University Press, 1997), 333.

25 The language of the "slave market" and the importance of sale in 1 Corinthians come from Laura Salah Nasrallah, *Archaeology and the Letters of Paul* (Oxford: Oxford University Press, 2019), 40–75.

26 Manumission to deities: Theophrastus, *Economics* 1344b15–22; Keith Hopkins, *Conquerors and Slaves* (Cambridge: Cambridge University Press, 1978), 118; de Wet, *Preaching Bondage*, 21. Gods as theo-economic agents: See Jennifer A. Quigley, *Divine Accounting: Theo-Economics in Early Christianity* (New Haven, CT: Yale University Press, 2021). Chance Bonar discusses this kind of enslavement in his forthcoming work, and I am grateful for conversations with him on this.

27 Rose MacLean, *Freed Slaves and Roman Imperial Culture: Social Integration and the Transformation of Values* (Cambridge: Cambridge University Press, 2018), 162. Inscription: *ILS* 7479, discussed in Jane Gardner, "Slavery and Roman Law," in *The Cambridge World History of Slavery*, vol. 1: *The Ancient Mediterranean World*, eds. Keith Bradley and Paul Cartledge (Cambridge: Cambridge University Press, 2011), 414–37 [420]; and Nasrallah, *Archaeology*, 44n14. On the adoption of freed-persons, see Jane F. Gardner, "The Adoption of Roman Freedmen," *Phoenix* 43 (1989): 236–57; and Jane F. Gardner, *Family and Familia in Roman Law and Life* (Oxford: Clarendon Press, 1998), 179–90. Vineyard parable: Herm. *Man.* 5.

28 Terence, *The Brothers* 455–6, trans. Henrik Mouritsen, in *The Freedman in the Roman World* (Cambridge: Cambridge University Press, 2011). 37. Cicero, *For Rabirius* 15, trans. Mouritsen, *Freedman in the Roman World*, 144; Ulrike Roth, "Men Without Hope," *Papers of the British School at Rome* 79 (2011): 71–94.

29 The theological conversation about faith is nuanced and vast. I cannot possibly hope to do justice to it here. On *pistis*, see Teresa Morgan, *Roman Faith and Christian Faith: Pistis and Fides in the Early Roman Empire and Early Churches* (Oxford: Oxford University Press, 2015). On *pistis* in Paul, see Jennifer Eyl, *Signs, Wonders, and Gifts: Divination in the Letters of Paul* (Oxford: Oxford University Press, 2019), 170–212. This is striking precisely because Christianity, following a particular line of Protestant interpretation, has so effectively reified the notion of faith. Today, many people see faith as an exclusively cognitive process: we have faith, we believe. The most influential instantiation of this definition is that of Martin Luther, whose notion of justification by faith alone is a sturdy foundation stone in the many declensions of Protestantism generated by his writings. The whispered alternative to salvation by faith alone is salvation through works or actions. In simplistic caricatures of Protestant and Catholic theology, this binary is the distinction between the faith-focused descendants of Luther and the works-righteousness children of Saint Peter. Our understanding of what faith is has been shaped both by fierce post-Reformation intra-Christian debates about salvation, and by the ubiquitous way in which faith has become a synonym for religion and religiosity. In predominantly Christian countries, "faith" is now the default intellectual and affective state in which people "do religion."

30 Reciprocity: Morgan, *Roman Faith*, 4. Wives, sons: Eyl, "Soldiers, Slaves, Sons, and Brides."

31 *Pistis/fides* and freedmen: Mouritsen, *Freedman in the Roman World*, 61. For Cicero on Tiro, see *Fam.* 16.16.2; *Att.* 9.17.2. It is significant that Tiro's work was literary. Epictetus, *Disc.* 2.22 (26–30).

32 Repayment: Quigley, *Divine Accounting;* and Devin Singh, *Divine Currency: The Theological Power of Money in the West* (Stanford, CA: Stanford University Press, 2018).

33 Reenslavement: Suetonius, *Claudius* 25.1; Cassius Dio, *Hist.* 60.28.1, 68.13; Mouritsen, *Freedman*, 55–118. Acte inscription: *CIL* 6.20905 and Javal Coleman and Dan-el Padilla Peralta, "Rhetoric," in Coogan, Howley, and Moss, *Writing, Enslavement, and Power;* Seneca, *Ben.* 3.

34 On God as father, see Michael Peppard, *The Son of God in the Roman World: Divine Sonship in Its Social and Political Context* (Oxford: Oxford University Press, 2011), 147ff. Dying daily: 1 Cor. 15:31. Mbembe, "Necropolitics."

35 For the view that Matthew presents followers of Jesus as "volunteer slaves," see Edmund Neufeld, "Vulnerable Bodies and Volunteer Slaves: Slave Parable Violence in the Rest of Matthew," *Bulletin for Biblical Research* 30.1 (2020): 41–63. For this view with respect to Luke, see Kyoung-Jin Kim, *Stewardship and Almsgiving in Luke's Theology* (Sheffield: Sheffield Academic, 1998), 128.

36 Valerius Maximus, *Memorable Works and Deeds*, 6.8. Deluded: Sandra R. Joshel and Sheila Murnaghan, eds., *Women and Slaves in Greco-Roman Culture: Differential Equations* (New York: Routledge, 1998), 14–15; Blandina: Eusebius, *Hist. eccl.* 5.1.17.

37 Ign., *Rom.* 4.3, modified from Ehrman, *Apostolic Fathers* 1.275.

38 Angela N. Parker, "One Womanist's View of Racial Reconciliation in Galatians," *Journal of Feminist Studies in Religion* 34 (2018): 23–40 [37].

39 Glancy, *Slavery*, 71–101. The Pauline texts that feature in academic conversation about this question are 1 Cor. 5:1–13 (instructions against sexual immorality), 1 Cor. 7 (instructions about marriage and social status), and 1 Thess. 4:3–8 (where Paul instructs each person to "obtain his own vessel"). On these, see S. Scott Bartchy, *First-Century Slavery and the Interpretation of 1 Corinthians 7:21* (Atlanta: Scholars Press, 1973); J. Albert Harrill, "Revisiting the Problem of 1 Corinthians 7:21," *Biblical Research* 65 (2020): 77–94; and Briggs, "Can an Enslaved God Liberate?"

40 For the influence of the household codes: Clarice J. Martin, "The *Haustafeln* (Household Codes) in African-American Biblical Interpretation: 'Free Slaves' and 'Subordinate Women,'" in *Stony the Road We Trod: African American Biblical Interpretation*, ed. Cain Hope Felder (Minneapolis: Fortress, 1991), 206–31. For liberative reinterpretations of Paul in the context of antebellum slavery, see Allen Callahan, *The Talking Book: African Americans and the Bible* (New Haven, CT: Yale University Press, 2006); Brian K. Blount, *Then the Whisper Put on Flesh: New Testament Ethics in an African American Context* (Nashville: Abingdon, 2001); and Emerson B. Powery and Rodney S. Sadler Jr., *The Genesis of Liberation: Biblical Interpretation in the Antebellum Narratives of the Enslaved* (Louisville: Westminster John Knox, 2016). Paul and enslavers: Clarice J. Martin, "'Somebody Done Hoodoo'd the Hoodoo Man': Language, Power, Resistance, and the Effective History of Pauline Texts in American Slavery," *Semeia* 83/84 (1998): 203–33; Vincent Wimbush, "The Bible and African Americans: An Outline of an Interpretive History," in Felder, *Stony the Road We Trod*, 89–93; Harrill, *Slaves in the New Testament*, 165–92. For a recent overview, which includes examples of

subversive readings, see Lisa M. Bowens, *African American Readings of Paul: Reception, Resistance, and Transformation* (Grand Rapids, MI: Eerdmans, 2020).

41 Benjamin M. Palmer, *A Plain and Easy Catechism, Designed Chiefly for the Benefit of Coloured Persons, to Which Are Annexed Suitable Prayers and Hymns* (Charleston, SC: Observer Office Press, 1828), 32.

42 The importance of remembering and not forgetting is emphasized by womanist scholar and Roman Catholic theologian M. Shawn Copeland in her classic book, *Knowing Christ Crucified: The Witness of African American Religious Experience* (Maryknoll, NY: Orbis, 2018). Hortense J. Spillers, "Mama's Baby, Papa's Maybe: An American Grammar Book," *Diacritics* 17.2 (1987): 64–81 [68].

43 Mark 14:3–9; Matt. 26:6–13. Compare Luke 7:36–50 and a parallel story in John 12:1–8, in which the woman who anoints Jesus is Mary, the sister of Lazarus. On the woman who anoints Jesus as a sex worker see Lily Reed, "The 'Sinful' Woman of Luke 7:36–50: An Exploration of Her Actions in Light of Ancient Bathing Practices," MA diss., University of Birmingham, 2023.

44 This line of argument is inspired by Angela N. Parker, *If God Still Breathes, Why Can't I? Black Lives Matter and Biblical Authority* (Grand Rapids, MI: Eerdmans, 2021). For African American women involved in the interpretation of scripture, see Shively T. J. Smith, "Witnessing Jesus Hang: A Womanist Reading of Mary Magdalene's View of Crucifixion through Ida B. Wells' Chronicles of Lynching," in Felder, *Stony the Road We Trod*, thirtieth anniversary edition (Minneapolis: Fortress, 2021), and reprinted in *Wisdom Commentary: 1–2 Peter and Jude*, ed. Pheme Perkins (Collegeville, MN: Liturgical Press, 2022). Key figures in this interpretive project include Gay Byron, Renita Weems, Vanessa Lovelace, Vincent Wimbush, Mitzi Smith, Fernando Segovia, and Elizabeth Schüssler Fiorenza; for a fuller list of scholars involved in this work, and additional resources for locating their scholarship, see the online notes.

45 Translation of 2 Peter 2:1 is from Smith, *Interpreting*, 133. Ahmed, *Willful Subjects*, 200.

Chapter Eight

1 My reading of Euclia draws heavily on the work of Ronald Charles, *The Silencing of Slaves in Early Jewish and Christian Texts* (New York: Routledge, 2019), 194–200; and Christy Cobb, "Hidden Truth in the Body of Euclia: Page duBois' *Torture and Truth* and *Acts of Andrew*," *BibInt* 25.1 (2017): 19–38. My discussions of body parts, wholes, and willfulness is shaped by Sara Ahmed, *Willful Subjects* (Durham, NC: Duke University Press, 2014). The story of Euclia appears in the final part of the *Acts of Andrew*, also known as the *Passion of Andrew*. Translations are adapted from Dennis Ronald MacDonald, *The Acts of Andrew* (Santa Rosa, CA: Polebridge Press, 2005), 12–13. References to the Greek text follow Jean-Marc Prieur, ed., *Acta Andreae* (Turnhout: Brepols, 1989).

2 "Erotic body double": Jennifer A. Glancy, *Slavery in Early Christianity* (Oxford: Oxford University Press, 2002), 22, 155. On Euclia's lack of choice, compare Ahmed, *Willful Subjects*, 55; Charles, *Silencing of Slaves*, 197; and Cobb, "Euclia's Story," 42.

3 For a professional enslaved torturer in Puteoli, see *AE* 1971, 88, and discussion in Bond, *Trade and Taboo*, 238n43. See also Petronius, *Sat.* 49.

4 In the prefatory material that opens *In Search of Our Mothers' Gardens* (New York: Houghton Mifflin Jovanovich, 1983), Alice Walker defines a "womanist" as a "black feminist or feminist of color... usually referring to outrageous, audacious, or *willful* behavior," xi.

5 Page duBois, *Torture and Truth* (New York: Routledge, 1991). Unnamed man: *CJ* 6.1.3.

6 On Thomas and the cupbearer, see discussion in chapter 4. On the exposure of low-status bodies, see Julia Hillner, *Prison, Punishment, and Penance in Late Antiquity* (Cambridge: Cambridge University Press, 2015).

7 This section is greatly influenced by the work of and conversations with Meghan Henning, *Hell Hath No Fury: Gender, Disability, and the Invention of Damned Bodies in Early Christian Literature* (New Haven, CT: Yale University Press, 2021); and Larsen and Letteney, *Ancient Mediterranean Incarceration*.

8 Enslaved people are explicitly identified in six Matthean parables: the weeds and wheat (13:24–30), the "unmerciful slave" (18:23–25), the wicked tenants (21:33–41), the wedding banquet (22:1–10), the unjust steward (24:45–51), and the parable of the talents (25:14–30). On the importance of enslaved people in the parables, see Munro, *Jesus, Born of a Slave*, 327; Mary Ann Beavis, "Ancient Slavery as an Interpretive Context for the New Testament Servant Parables with Special Reference to the Unjust Steward (Luke 16:1–8)," *JBL* 111.1 (1992): 37–54; Jennifer A. Glancy, "Slaves and Slavery in the Matthean Parables," *JBL* 119.1 (2000): 67–90 [70–71]; and Llewellyn Howes, "Agricultural Slavery and the Parable of the Loyal and Wise Slave in Q 12:42–46," *Acta Classica* 58 (2015): 70–110. On the *servus callidus*, see Amy Richlin, *Slave Theater in the Roman Republic: Plautus and Popular Comedy* (Cambridge: Cambridge University Press, 2017).

9 Sulfur: Gen. 19:24; Rev. 9:17–18, 14:10. Flames of hell: Luke 16:24. Worms: Mark 9:48.

10 Parable of the talents: Matt. 25:30. Outer darkness: Matt. 8:12, 22:13, 25:14–30. On cisterns as carceral spaces, see examples in Letteney and Larsen, *Ancient Mediterranean Incarceration*. On chattering teeth in places of punishment, see Matt. 8:12; 13:42; 22:31; 24:51; 25:30; Luke 13:28; Henning, *Hell*, 99–100.

11 Noise: Lucian, *Menippus* and *Apocalypse of Paul* 43. Food: Diodorus Siculus, *Library of History* 31.9.2–3. Fetters: O. *Epiphanius* 176.

12 On worms: *Apocalypse of Peter* 7–9; *Apocalypse of Paul* 36–37; *Latin Vision of Ezra* 34–36; Henning, *Hell*, 96–99.

13 Mills: Bond, *Trade and Taboo*, 145–46. Mines: Letteney and Larsen, *Ancient Mediterranean Incarceration*.

14 Air: Strabo, *Geography* 12.3.40 (modified translation). Mines and hell: Letteney and Larsen, *Ancient Mediterranean Incarceration*; Henning, *Hell*, 42–44. John Chrysostom, *Homily on Matthew* 43.5.

15 For examples of collars for "runaways," see David L. Thurmond, "Some Roman Slave Collars in *CIL*," *Athenaeum* 82 (1994): 459–93. Branding: Rev. 13:16–17. On blasphemy against the Spirit, see Mark 3:28–29 and Rev. 13:6.

16 Tertullian, *Of Patience* 4.1–2 (translation modified from *ANF*).

17 On the Palermo graffiti, see Giuseppe Pitrè and Leonardo Sciascia, *Urla senza suono: Graffiti e disegni dei prigionieri dell'Inquisizione* (Palermo: Sellerio, 1999); Luca Pinelli, *Meditationi utilissime sopra I Quindici Misteri del Santissimo Rosario* (1591), trans. Andrea Celli, in *Dante and the Mediterranean Comedy: From Muslim Spain to Post-Colonial Italy* (Cham, Switzerland: Palgrave Macmillan, 2022), 133.

18 Consumption: Angela Y. Davis, "Racialized Punishment and Prison Abolition," in Joy James, ed., *The Angela Y. Davis Reader*, 96–107 [99]. Fears of consumption: Hartman, *Lose Your Mother*, 110–25. On the persistent association of hell and incarceration among prisoners, see Judith Vasquez, "On the Verge of Hell," in *Hell Is a Very Small Place: Voices from Solitary Confinement*, eds. Jean Casella, James Ridgeway, and Sarah Shourd (New York: The New Press, 2016), 55–60 [58]; and Galen Baughman, "The Freshman," in *Hell Is a Very Small Place*, 129–36 [131].

19 Cannibalism and resurrection: Athenagoras, *On the Resurrection*; Tertullian, *On the Resurrection of the Dead* 32; Methodius, *On the Resurrection* 1.20–24.

20 Medieval text: *Latin Vision of Ezra* 50. For *defixiones*: Laura Salah Nasrallah, "Judgment, Justice, and Destruction: *Defixiones* and 1 Corinthians," *JBL* 140 (2021): 347–67. For prison graffiti: C. Breytenbach, "Christian Prisoners: Fifth- and Sixth-Century Inscriptions from Corinth," *Acta Theologica* 36, Supplement 23 (2016): 302–9.

21 On modern incarceration and its connection to Atlantic slavery and subsequent emancipation, see W. E. B. Du Bois, "The Spawn of Slavery: The Convict-Lease System in the South," in *African American Classics in Criminology and Criminal Justice*, eds. Shaun L. Gabbidon, Helen Taylor Greene, and Vernetta D. Young (Thousand Oaks, CA: Sage Publishing, 2002), 81–88; Angela Davis, *Are Prisons Obsolete?* (New York: Seven Stories, 2003); David Oshinsky, *Worse Than Slavery: Parchman Farm and the Ordeal of Jim Crow Justice* (New York: Free Press, 1996); Dennis Childs, *Slaves of the State: Black Incarceration from the Chain Gang to the Penitentiary* (Minneapolis: University of Minnesota Press, 2015); and Michelle Alexander, *The New Jim Crow: Mass Incarceration in the Age of Colorblindness, rev. ed.* (New York: The New Press, 2012).

22 On hell in Christian education, see Henning, *Hell*.

23 To give but two small examples, the language of "punishing" enslaved people, as it reflects ancient slaveholding and biblical sources, suggests that enslaved people were in some way deserving of the unjust violence they experienced. So, too, as public theologian and scholar Esau McCaulley has argued, Christians (including New Testament scholars) continue to refer to Onesimus as a "runaway slave," as if a person who had been kidnapped and held against their will was in some way at fault for escaping. No one who uses such language supports enslavement, but it reveals that we have not thought deeply about rooting it out, either. These turns of phrase show how ideologies of enslavement are deeply embedded in the interpretation of scripture, and how much work still needs to be done. Esau McCaulley, *Reading While Black: African American Biblical Interpretation as an Exercise in Hope* (Westmont, IL: IVP Academic, 2020), 156: "We must stop

calling [Onesimus] a runaway slave. To call him a runaway centers the opinion of slave holders because when someone runs away, the logical thing is to return them. But Onesimus had no desire to be returned. Onesimus did not run away; *he escaped.*" On the problem of the language of "punishment," see Diana Paton, "Afterword: Punishment, Slavery and Legitimacy," *Journal of Global Slavery* 7 (2022): 203–209, which draws upon Vincent Brown, *Tacky's Revolt: The Story of an Atlantic Slave War* (Cambridge, MA: Belknap / Harvard University Press, 2020).

Epilogue

1 On Petilianus and Church councils, see Thomas Graumann, *The Acts of the Early Church Councils: Production and Character* (Oxford: Oxford University Press, 2021), 38–39.

2 Two weeks after my encounter with the billboard, I contracted the most docile variant of the virus; it was quite dramatic, and I should confess that, as of this moment, I have not yet recovered fully.

3 Joseph Addison, *The Spectator* 160 (3 September 1711), in *The Spectator*, ed. Donald F. Bond, 5 vols. (Oxford: Oxford University Press, 1965): 2.126–30.

4 John Stuart Mill [Antiquus, pseud.], "On Genius," *Monthly Repository* 6 (1832): 649–59; Immanuel Kant, *Critique of the Power of Judgment*, trans. Paul Guyer and Eric Matthews (Cambridge: Cambridge University Press, 2000), 195–96.

5 On copyright: Paul K. Saint-Amour, *The Copywrights: Intellectual Property and the Literary Imagination* (Ithaca, NY: Cornell University Press, 2003). I do not want to pretend that anonymity did not have a rich life in the eighteenth and nineteenth centuries. It had expedience for women, for those who did not wish to create a stir, those who wished to disrupt social norms, and so on. See, for example, Mark Vareschi, *Everywhere and Nowhere: Anonymity and Mediation in Eighteenth-Century Britain* (Minneapolis: University of Minnesota Press, 2018).

6 Martin Luther, *Address to the Christian Nobility of the German Nation*, in *Luther's Primary Works*, eds. Henry Wace and C. A. Buchheim (London: John Murray, 1883), 169–71.

7 Leah Price and Pamela Thurschwell, introduction to *Literary Secretaries / Secretarial Culture*, eds. Leah Price and Pamela Thurschwell (Aldershot: Ashgate, 2005), 3. See also Harriet Flower, "The Most Expensive Slave in Rome: Quintus Lutatius Daphnis," *Classical Philology* 117 (2022): 99–119 [119].

8 On kinesthetic expertise, see Roger Kneebone, *Expert: Understanding the Path to Mastery* (New York: Viking, 2020).

9 On power and forgery, see Jeremiah Coogan, Candida Moss, and Joseph Howley, "The Socioeconomics of Fabrication: Textuality, Authenticity, and Social Status in the Roman Mediterranean," *Arethusa* (forthcoming); and Coogan and Moss, "Textual Demiurge."

CREDITS LIST

Alicia Aldrete—Copyeditor, online notes
Linda Arends—Production Editor
Anna Brill—Marketer
Erin Cain—Digital Production Coordinator
Bryan Christian—Marketing Director
Laura Essex—Audio Producer
Elizabeth Garriga—Senior Director, Publicity
Ian Gibbs—first proofreader
Lauren Hesse—Social Media Director
Deborah P. Jacobs—second proofreader
Brandon Kelley—Marketing Operations
Lucy Kim—Art Director, Jacket Designer
Sheryl Kober—Interior Designer
Albert LaFarge—Copyeditor
Alex Littlefield—Editor
Dan Lynch—Senior Production Manager
Thomas Mis—Audio Production Manager
Bruce Nichols—Publisher
Elizabeth Shreve—Founder and Managing Partner, Shreve Williams Public
    Relations, LLC
Stacy Shuck—Manufacturing Coordinator
Mary Tondorf-Dick—Managing Editor
Morgan Wu—Editorial Assistant
Craig Young—Deputy Publisher
The staff of the Hachette Book Group Distribution Center in Lebanon,
    Indiana
The information technology and administrative teams at Hachette Book
    Group

LIST OF ILLUSTRATIONS

p. 73, Coptic ostracon with lines from Homer, probable writing exercise, Thebes, 580–640 CE. **The Metropolitan Museum of Art, New York, Rogers Fund, 1914.**

p. 80, Rendering of terra-cotta tile with footprints inscribed by Detfri and Amica, Pietrabbondante, Italy, 100 BCE. **Line drawing by Dan McClellan.**

p. 84, Papyrus fragment, Egypt, second century CE. **P. Berol 11632.** Berlin Papyrus Database, Ägyptisches Museum und Papyrussammlung, Staatliche Museum, Berlin.

p. 86, Marble statuette of an enslaved boy with a lantern, waiting for his enslaver, Egypt, first–second century CE. **The Metropolitan Museum of Art, New York, Rogers Fund, 1923.**

p. 90, *Healing of the Paralytic*, from the Dura-Europos Baptistery, Dura-Europos, third century CE. **Yale University Art Gallery, Yale-French Excavations at Dura-Europos.**

p. 95, *John the Baptist Baptizing Jesus*, from the so-called Anastasis Sarcophagus. **Musée départemental Arles antique, Arles. Photo © Arthur Urbano. Inv. FAN.92.00.2483/2484.**

p. 117, Sarcophagus with nautical scene, Ny Carlsberg Glyptotek, Copenhagen, third century CE. **Photo © Marie-Lan Nguyen / Wikimedia Commons.**

p. 126, Marble relief showing Roman soldiers colllaring prisoners, Smyrna, 200 CE. **Ashmolean Museum, Oxford. Photo courtesy of Jennifer Strawbridge.**

p. 142, Edouard Manet, *The Dead Christ with Angels*, French, Paris, 1864. Oil on canvas. **The Metropolitan Museum of Art, New York, H. O. Havemeyer Collection, Bequest of Mrs. H. O. Havemeyer, 1929.**

p. 150, Codex Regius (*L*), circa 700s CE. **© Bibliothèque Nationale de France, Folio 220r. Grec 62. Used with permission.**

p. 161, Eusebian Canon Tables, Carolingian Gospel book, circa 825–850 CE. **The Metropolitan Museum of Art, New York, H. O. Havemeyer Collection, The Cloisters Collection and Director's Fund, 2015.**

p. 187, Funerary relief for a butcher, 125–150 CE. **Ashmolean Museum, Oxford. Photo courtesy of Jennifer Strawbridge.**

p. 190, Unswept-floor mosaic of a Roman dining room, fifth century CE. **Mosaïque au sol non balayé, scène de symposium. Collection privée en dépôt au Musée de la vigne et du vin au château de Boudry (Suisse). © Musée de la vigne et du vin, Château de Boudry.**

p. 203, Jacques Callot, *Sainte Blandine et ses compagnes* (*St. Blandina and Her Companions*), etching of June 2, from *Les Images de tous les saincts et saintes de l'année* (*Images of All the Saints and Religious Events of the Year*), French, 1636. **The Metropolitan Museum of Art, New York, Purchase, Joseph Pulitzer Bequest, 1917.**

p. 211, Plaque with the Pentecost, South Netherlands, circa 1150–675. **The Metropolitan Museum of Art, New York, The Cloisters Collection, 1965.**

p. 244, The Prison; a group of men in a dungeon bound in chains and shackles, to the right a figure hanging from his arms, tied to a boulder. Formerly attributed to Giorio Ghisi. Engraving, Italian, 1499?–1546. **The Metropolitan Museum of Art, New York, Purchase, Joseph Pulitzer Bequest, 1917.**

p. 246, Roman mine at Phaino, Wadi Faynan, Jordan. **Photo © Lauren Larsen.**

p. 247, Jan van Eyck and workshop assistant, *The Crucifixion*; *The Last Judgment*, Netherlandish, circa 1440–41. **The Metropolitan Museum of Art, New York, Fletcher Fund, 1933.**

p. 248, Sarcophagus lid with Last Judgment, Roman, late third–early fourth century. **The Metropolitan Museum of Art, New York, Rogers Fund, 1924.**

INDEX

ABOUT THE AUTHOR

Candida Moss is Edward Cadbury Chair of Theology at the University of Birmingham, England, prior to which she taught for almost a decade at the University of Notre Dame. The award-winning author or co-author of seven books, she has also served as Papal News Commentator for CBS News and writes a column for *The Daily Beast*, in addition to contributing writing and commentary to many other media outlets. She lives in New York.